SINGLEWIDE

SINGLEWIDE

Chasing the American Dream
in a Rural Trailer Park

**Sonya Salamon and
Katherine MacTavish**

CORNELL UNIVERSITY PRESS **ITHACA AND LONDON**

First published 2017 by Cornell University Press

Printed in the United States of America

Library of Congress Cataloging-in-Publication Data

Names: Salamon, Sonya, author. | MacTavish, Katherine, date, author.
Title: Singlewide : chasing the American dream in a rural trailer park /Sonya
    Salamon and Katherine MacTavish.
Description: Ithaca : Cornell University Press, 2017. | Includes bibliographical
    references and index.
Identifiers: LCCN 2017007546 (print) | LCCN 2017008749 (ebook) |
    ISBN 9781501713217 (cloth : alk. paper) | ISBN 9781501713224 (pbk :
    alk. paper) | ISBN 9781501712326 (epub/mobi) | ISBN 9781501709685 (pdf)
Subjects: LCSH: Mobile home living—United States. | Mobile home parks—
    United States. | Rural poor—Housing—United States. | Housing, Rural—
    United States. | United States—Rural conditions.
Classification: LCC HD7289.62.U6 S36 2017 (print) | LCC HD7289.62.U6 (ebook) |
    DDC 333.33/8—dc23
LC record available at https://lccn.loc.gov/2017007546

Cornell University Press strives to use environmentally responsible suppliers
and materials to the fullest extent possible in the publishing of its books. Such
materials include vegetable-based, low-VOC inks and acid-free papers that are
recycled, totally chlorine-free, or partly composed of nonwood fibers. For further
information, visit our website at cornellpress.cornell.edu.

For my sons, David and Aaron,
and
For my sister, Carla Blank, my loyal cheerleader
—Sonya Salamon

For my father, Cameron J. Mactavish (1932–2016),
who got me in the starting gate.
Miles down the road, I am here.
—Katherine MacTavish

Contents

SINGLEWIDE

GALVANIZED GHETTOS?

Trailer home ownership is a hard-won status for rural families of modest means, pivotal to their expectations for stability, security, accomplishment, and respect. A manufactured home represents superior housing compared with the available alternatives of a drafty farmhouse or a rental apartment in rural America. Yet when a family sites their typically singlewide home in a rural trailer park, their lives become an ongoing struggle to realize their dreamed-for benefits of home-ownership because of the costs and burdens imposed by this type of housing.

> *Standing shoeless, her ankle-length skirt stretched tight across her hips, Amy surveys the living room of her twelve-by-forty-foot singlewide. Boxes holding the family's possessions line the walls. A big-screen TV her father gave her one year for Christmas and a dryer she's renting to own are among the few heavy items left to load in the minivan. "I've been remembering a lot of times in this place today." Her blond hair pulled up off her neck in the heat of an Illinois June afternoon, Amy leans back against the door jamb and lights a cigarette. Sunlight streams in through the sliding glass doors that look into her neighbor's house twenty feet to the east. "I was remembering the first time I brought Gabriella [her youngest child] home from the hospital. This was the room she came home to. And this is where Gabby took her first steps." Amy loses herself to the memory and takes another draw on her cigarette.*
>
> *Buying a home in Prairieview Manor Mobile Home Park was trans-formative for Amy and her family. As a twenty-year-old single mother*

with a seventh-grade education, she purchased the trailer new, paying for it with cash when her mother's death left her with a "large sum" of money. Owning a home has meant a kind of stability for her girls that Amy never experienced. The frequent moves, school changes, and even stretches of homelessness that defined Amy's early life have been unknown to her daughters. Instead they have shared a room at the hitch end of the trailer for as long as they can remember. With the home paid for, a monthly lot rent of $165 and utilities constitutes the bulk of Amy's housing costs. A three-bedroom apartment in the complex across the road from the park would have run $650 a month. And there she would share a wall or maybe two with other renters, not her preference here in rural Illinois.

But now Amy is looking to move on. Recently she met Jack after he became a regular at the breakfast place where she waits tables. He offered to have Amy and the girls move into his house in town. For Amy, it seemed a pathway to the fulfillment of her aspirations. "I've always had this dream to have a husband and a white picket fence and all that." And so her packing began.

Amy's story highlights the essential restlessness of trailer-park life among young families. Buying a trailer altered her life trajectory, shifting Amy and her daughters away from a risky pattern of residential instability.[1] Yet uniformly, Amy and the other young families we met yearned to soon move on from the trailer park where they lived. They all seemed convinced that life would be better in what they termed a "real" house or at least in a house on land they owned. It is their shared dream.

Uneasiness with a trailer park as a long-term housing solution is an enduring sentiment in the history of this housing form. Several rich accounts trace the history of trailer parks.[2] According to these accounts, land-lease parks like Prairieview Manor began showing up in post–World War II 1940s America. Returning veterans and urbanites wanting to trade a rental apartment in the city for the bucolic life in the suburbs created an ownership demand limited only by a scarcity of the housing supply. Trailer parks emerged as a stopgap solution providing a place to own a home and live until a real house became available.[3] Trailer homes became larger and more accommodating of family life, and park owners began developing communities that approximated all the trappings of a suburban development in the hopes of attracting long-term residents. The quality of life in these parks stood in stark contrast to the roadside trailer camps of the 1920s and 1930s that alternately housed "tin can tourists" and Depression-era transients, but the desire to move on remained among families who were homeowners but land tenants.

The burgeoning demand for homeownership spurred commercial responses. Mass-built, lower-cost housing by such developer icons as William Levitt, Joseph

Eichler, and Henry Kaiser and generous federal mortgage insurance supports paved the way to conventional home ownership.[4] By midcentury, two of every three American households owned their home, up from one in three in the 1930s.[5] As conventional homeownership grew, it produced a slow drain on trailer-park populations as those who could move did.[6] Left behind were working-class households for whom ownership of a single-family conventionally built home on owned land remained out of reach. By the end of the twentieth century, the main population of rural trailer parks consisted of a town's poorer residents, like those we focus on. That demographic became emblematic of this housing form.[7]

Today an estimated twenty million Americans live in mobile or manufactured housing.[8] For about half of them, that home is located in a mobile home park or—in the industry's preferred terminology—a "manufactured home community." Three out of four of those communities are found in rural areas outside of what is defined as urban America.[9] Some are designated adult-only or "fifty-five and over," but many, like those on which we concentrate, are home to families raising children. By our best estimate, close to five million rural children reside in some forty-five thousand mobile home or trailer parks that dot the US countryside.[10] As a nation, therefore, we cannot ignore the critical role trailer parks play in providing homeownership access to lower-income rural families in particular.

For the rural poor and working poor parents, the purchase of a mobile home in a park holds tantalizing appeal.

> For Gladys Turner, or Ms. T. as she is known, in the shabby, older River Breeze Trailer Park in the small eastern North Carolina city of Addington, buying a trailer in a park was as much about getting away from a bad situation as it was about moving toward some ideal. For fourteen years, since leaving her parents' home as a single mother with two small children, Ms. T. had moved from one to another in a series of subsidized apartments in a complex locals term "The Projects." "I hated it out there. I hate to say it, but it's too ghetto there. There was too much hanging out, smoking weed and drinking. I didn't like it." She began searching for options to take her family, and especially her teenaged son, away from all that. She heard about a trailer for rent from a friend living in River Breeze park. When she first looked at the fourteen-year-old singlewide, it needed too many repairs to make it work as a rental. "Initially he told me I could rent the home but then he changed his mind about renting it. He didn't want to mess with it by putting more money in it." What the owner did agree to was a contract sale. Ms. T. paid him half of the $6,000 asking price up front, and after just six payments of $500 each, she'll have the trailer paid off.
>
> Slowly she's getting the home organized, working extra shifts at her service job to keep on top of expenses. She replaced the living room carpeting

and has already picked out new tile for the kitchen. For now, she sleeps on a small twin bed. With no dining table, the family eats on the living room suite she purchased with cash from a birthday pool she organized at work. Without a working oven, her cooking options are limited. For Ms. T., a large African American woman and a self-described "feeder," that's a significant drawback. "That's my next step—to buy new appliances." Despite these shortcomings she boasts, "I do like the home. I think I like it because it's mine." But she's also quick to add, "This place is temporary and it is just a stepping-stone. I want to move back home where we have land."

Some two thousand miles to the south and west in Mesa Vista, New Mexico, buying a home in a trailer park was for Darlene and Ron Vega a step that logically followed marriage and a growing family. When the couple found the 1993 singlewide to buy, they were living in a rental house in town searching for a home that would fit their budget. "We saw an ad in the paper for a rent-to-own and we got this." After a casual handshake arrangement, they began making payments to the home's owner, who continued to carry the fifteen-year mortgage in his name. No mortgage qualification process or down payment meant the family could move in right away, just as Ms. T. did.

The home sits on the first lot to the left on entering Tumbleweed Mobile Home Park. Since it had been used for only two years, the trailer is much newer and bigger than most homes in this park. It completely covers the twenty-by-fifty-foot lot sized for 1970s-era homes. Still, the family finds space for outdoor activities. In the narrow alley between the home and the chain-link fence, seven-year-old Dylan gets in some target practice with his BB gun. His six-year-old sister, Dominique, helps their mother tend a small vegetable plot of tomatoes, squash, and a bit of lettuce near the trailer's hitch end. Metal steps lead up and into the home's living room, which is furnished with a matching couch and love seat in a pastel blue print, a coffee table, and a console housing a large-screen TV.

Darlene and Ron purchased this first home before either reached the age of twenty-five. After leading nomadic lives in their early adult years, including ten moves in eight years for Darlene, both were ready to settle down. The impending birth of a third child makes that a more pressing goal. Yet while they have no complaints about the home itself, it hasn't proved the stable housing solution they had hoped for. One day they came home after work to find a repossession notice glued to their front door. The seller had stopped making loan payments; the bank was taking the home back. Darlene scrambled to avoid this loss. They are working to change over the loan to their names to avoid future problems, yet the $450-a-month *house payment with lot rent included, plus the $250 for propane and elec-tricity, strains the family budget. As her due date nears, Darlene grows less clear about how they'll afford to stay in the home with the new baby and more clear about regretting this home deal: "I hope to be out of here in a year. I got a bad deal. I wish I could get out of it."*

Amy, Ms. T., the Vegas, and other young park families ardently believe in the possibilities of what James Truslow Adams first described in the early years of the Great Depression as "that American dream of a better, richer, happier life for all our citizens of every rank."[11] That dream motivated their purchase of a mobile home. A mobile home, in addition to being an ownership opportunity, is a chance to fulfill the promises attached to that status.[12] For Amy, it is a way to stabilize life for her young daughters and to give them access to a good educa-tion. For Ms. T., it means control over her home and limiting her son's exposure to a "too ghetto" way of life. For the Vegas, it was a way for the young couple to improve their family's life by taking the next step toward a more secure future than they believe renting provides.

Yet although the three families' hope for a better life motivated a move into a rural trailer park, it also underscored their desire to move on. A central belief among young families is that a trailer park is only a temporary address, occupied on the way to something better. While they are pragmatists who believe that buy-ing a trailer means their money is going toward something, park families yearn for more than what they view as "second best" housing. Uniformly, they plan to be out of the park in a year or two (perhaps five at the longest), anticipating that by then they will have purchased a conventionally built home on land they own. Coupled with an achievement ideology that promotes the notion that with hard work all things are possible, optimistic dreams have motivated gen-erations of Americans, like trailer-park families, to seek social mobility through their housing.[13]

While inspiring a sense of personal agency, the economic and social aspira-tions that drive the families we studied bring substantial, oft-overlooked harm to identity and optimism. Fundamentally, if one holds a deeply entrenched belief in universal possibilities, the tendency is to blame oneself for not achieving success; the steep barriers that exist in society are seldom subject to criticism.[14] Econo-mists and demographers tell us that fewer than one in three individuals born into the lower quintiles of American society, a position shared by park families, will move into the middle class in their lifetime.[15] More often, individuals go on to reproduce the class status of their parents by acquiring about the same outcomes in education, occupation, and income. This tendency toward social reproduction by families is tied to society's unequal distribution of resources important to social mobility: access to jobs that pay a decent wage and offer benefits, educational experiences that position one for better opportunities, social networks that link with wider opportunities, and some possibility for accumulation of wealth.[16]

Across rural America, resources critical to social mobility have, over recent decades, grown further out of reach for families like those we met in our study communities. The well-paid, traditionally male jobs (often in manufacturing or extractive industries) that existed a generation ago have dramatically declined and been replaced by service jobs that offer neither a wage that supports a family nor decent benefits.[17] While trailer-park adults, like their rural counterparts in general, have outpaced their parents in educational achievement, those gains are in higher rates of high school completion and some college rather than the four-year credential so vaunted in today's economy.[18] Studies have documented class difference in social network formation that contributes to an uneven distribution of opportunities critical to social advancement.[19] While homeownership, even after the 2008 housing crisis, continues to be seen as a major pathway to asset accumulation in the United States,[20] recent policy analysis has called into question whether low-income homeowners realize economic investment benefits in ways similar to those available to middle-class homeowners.[21] When that ownership is a mobile home in a trailer park, as is proportionally more likely in a rural area, for a myriad of reasons we illustrate, ownership does not seamlessly translate into a launching pad for socioeconomic mobility. The goal that rural trailer-park families seek of a better life beyond the park, then, appears not reliably within their reach.

The central aim of this book is to describe life in trailer parks from the perspective of young families who live there. The fundamental question this book addresses is whether trailer parks are a good, or at least neutral, place to raise a family. Whether owning a home in a rural trailer park allows families a pathway toward their aspirations is central to our assessment of what happens in their lives. With this leading question in mind, we explore the following:

> Question One: Are there lasting effects to family and child identity that come from living in a trailer park—a neighborhood form so widely mocked and assumed to be culturally uniform across the nation?

"Drag a hundred-dollar bill through a trailer park, you never know what you'll find," commented the Democratic strategist James Carville about Paula Jones, who in 1991 accused President Bill Clinton of sexual harassment. Such remarks express a national contempt for a particular housing form and those who call it home. Embodied in the familiar "trailer trash" slur are fundamental assumptions that people who live in trailer parks are simple-minded, drunken, promiscuous, lawless, casually spawning broods of similar offspring, and indifferent to the very behaviors that label them as trailer trash.[22] Anthropologists consider such a slur *toxic*—a harmful and pernicious brand that stigmatizes an entire category of people so as to marginalize them from mainstream society.[23] The trailer-trash stigma is thus capable of undermining a rural trailer-park family's identity or self-worth, which includes satisfaction with their hard-won life, their sense of accomplishment as homeowners, and their understanding of their place in the small-town environment where they live.[24]

> Question Two: Does owning a trailer home sited in a trailer park pay off as the first rung on a housing-tenure ladder for rural families?

Landlessness is chief among the factors that make owning a trailer home in a land-lease park an uncertain stage in a rural family's socioeconomic advancement. Without land ownership, any investment potential of mobile homeownership is dramatically diminished.[25] Further, trailer home buyers who do not own the land rely on a financial system well documented to involve high-interest loans and predatory lending practices.[26] Additional homeownership vulnerabilities associated with land-lease park life—such as the threat of eviction, annual lot rent increases, and the possibility of losing it all should a park be sold for what is called a higher and better real estate use—call into question whether the potential tradeoffs of trailer home ownership add up for a family.[27]

> Question Three: Does living in a rural trailer park affect a family's sense of belonging to their immediate neighborhood or the nearby community?

The sense of community or deep attachment to place so central to a rural identity seems particularly challenged by a housing form termed "mobile." Deep roots in a hometown where successive generations were born and raised produce a community culture in which life is not anonymous but rather takes places among people who know you, your family, and your family's reputation.[28] Although rural people complain about their nosy neighbors, they realize that when everyone knows everyone else, support can be depended on when needed. A temporary orientation where home is defined as "a roof over head and a place to live, that's all" may prevent park families from gaining a sense of permanence about their neighborhood and town.[29]

> Question Four: Does a rural trailer park have the power to define the life chances of the children and youth who grow up there?

Community sociologists have for decades been concerned with answering the essential question posed by Malcom Gladwell, "What effect does where you live have on how you turn out?"[30] That a trailer park concentrates a homogeneously young, poor, less well-educated population may mean isolation from mainstream behavior patterns and role models so important to positive development among young people—a process well documented in the community effects literature.[31] In contrast, the distinctive traits of small-town life combine to make for good environments for child development. Low population turnover, actively engaged parents, intergenerational connections, and the overlap of school, church, and civic organizations are all community traits important to children's well-being.[32] Growing up in a town with such traits means regular contact with aunts, uncles, and grandparents as well as other pivotal non-kin adults (for example, ministers, teachers, and a peer's parents) who care about a child's well-being and are actively involved in the collective socialization of local children.[33] In these ways, a small town may produce a positive community or neighborhood effect that helps children develop successfully—that is, to stay in school, develop a work ethic, stay out of trouble, and maintain loyalty to family and community.[34]

To examine what is shared and what differs among trailer-park folk across rural America we followed thirty-nine families—white, black, and Hispanic—all with children, as they chased their dream of a better life from inside a trailer park. The parks we studied were located in Illinois, North Carolina, and New Mexico, representing three distinct rural regions and ethnic populations, where manufactured housing remains common.[35] The social, cultural, and economic structure of each region varied. So did the trailer parks. The large Illinois park where Amy lived was termed the "Cadillac" of mobile home parks by a member of the Illinois Manufactured Housing Association. The parks in North Carolina were smaller and considerably more modest than in Illinois, and those in New Mexico included several low-end parks that visibly represent the economic hardships of resident families and this region.

In all the parks, families owned their homes but rented the land on which those homes sat. This meant that they were simultaneously homeowners and land renters. The decision to focus on homeowners was largely methodological. We wanted to follow families for a full year and anticipated that trailer home owners rather than renters would be more residentially stable. Fortuitously, homeownership emerged as critical to understanding a set of unique tradeoffs that this quasi-ownership status brings to family life. Although our field studies were carried out between 1998 and 2001, the issues we identify remain salient today.

The first chapters of this book concern aspects of life inherent to mobile home park residence and homeownership. Each trailer park is unique, shaped by its size and layout, history and ownership, regional regulations, and the population it serves. Yet as privatized solutions to a public need for housing, virtually all trailer parks today exist in a market context. Chapter 1 provides an orientation to the entrepreneurial markets of trailers and trailer parks—something we term the "mobile-home industrial complex." Chapter 2 contributes a detailed examination of trailer-park housing costs and finances of the working poor rural families who live there. Both chapters supply a critical context for understanding the case studies that follow.

The second part of the book provides a window on trailer-park life across three rural regions of the United States: the Midwest, the Southeast, and the Southwest. Our field studies were carried out in a similar manner, but the results were regionally and culturally so different that we chose to emphasize distinctions rather than to compare them closely. Illinois white families dream of social mobility to the middle class, and their park choice reflects that; North Carolina black families require that their housing provide ready access to kin, a church, and jobs; despite a dismal job market, New Mexico Hispanic families desire to remain in the community where they have generational roots, and especially important, an extended kin network. We describe those distinctions and consider how these aspirations shape the daily routines of park and family life. Because neighborhood and community provide crucial supports for families raising children, we pay particular attention to whether a land-lease park in each rural place supports a sense of community among families who reside there or whether this is something people actually desire.

Following the case studies, in part III we turn to focus more specifically on the children and youth growing up in a trailer park. How park children fare developmentally provides an important gauge of whether a rural trailer park has a negative, positive, or neutral community or neighborhood effect. In chapter 6 we explore the outcomes for park children by drawing on their own reports as well as school records, observations, and the insights of their parents.

Chapter 7 discusses the implications of our findings for policy that addresses how to reform the mobile home industrial complex to make it more fair and equitable for the poor families that are its target market. The conclusion returns to our key questions and compares the three park case studies to examine the social and financial implications of living in a rural trailer park and how that life affects park families' ability to achieve their housing dream.

Our book makes the case that an owned mobile home on rented land in a rural trailer park offers working poor families at best a downscaled version of their housing dream. Trailer-park residents are well aware that the wheels beneath their home violate the central tenets of permanence and stability associated with conventional homeownership. That their home, likely their most valuable asset, sits on someone else's private property brings a loss of rights and freedoms routinely experienced by families. Trailer-park residence is not a lifestyle choice for these families, as the crude jokes imply. Rather, it is an optimistic attempt to grab hold of something better for themselves and their children. While park families truly believe in the tantalizing possibilities their American housing dream dangles before them, for most, as we will show, that dream remains just that—out of reach, as it does for Amy.

> *A few weeks after Amy's planned move from the park, that dream was deferred. Things with Jack had not exactly worked out. And the sale of her home had fallen through when the park owner would not approve her buyer. With boxes half unpacked, Amy puts dinner in the oven. "Yep. We're back," she remarks with resignation.*

The term singlewide in the book title highlights the reality of ninety percent of the study families owning this trailer form, the smallest type of mobile home, and what is affordable on their modest incomes. "Galvanized ghetto" is a powerful term for a trailer park that influenced our study. We heard it from a youth in one of the study parks (see chapter 3). We use it understanding that all trailer parks do not function as rural ghettos. But some trailer parks do. As the three case studies unfold, it will become clear to the reader which constitute a ghetto, which do not, and what factors account for the differences.

All the names for people and places used in this book are fictitious. We do this, as standard practice in ethnography, to honor the assurance of confidentiality given to the people we interviewed or observed.

Part 1

GOING MOBILE IN A RURAL TRAILER PARK

THE MOBILE HOME
INDUSTRIAL COMPLEX

For rural families of modest means similar to those of Amy in Illinois, Ms. T. in North Carolina, and the Vegas of New Mexico, trailer home ownership is appealing because of its affordability and accessibility. And these buyers find few alternatives for affordable housing in rural America. Experts, in fact, are calling the affordable-housing shortage a "quiet national crisis."[1] In 2015 an Urban Institute report found that *no* county in the country had enough affordable housing to meet its rental needs.[2] Thus for families in rural areas with modest resources and a housing dream for a better life, buying a trailer in a rural trailer park is a logical housing decision.

When Ellen Adams found herself suddenly single with two school-aged children, she went in search of housing. The family had been living in a metro-area mobile home park, but it was time for a change, and that change needed to happen on a budget. "I was a single mom and didn't have anything like a down payment." Ellen took home roughly $12,000 a year as a receptionist, yet she was eager to gain access to the homeownership central to her housing dream. And, as Ellen explained, "At least my money is going for something."

The purchase of her trailer and the subsequent siting of that home in Prairieview Manor entangled Ellen with the cast of players who make up the "mobile home industrial complex" (MHIC, explained below) Those players, involved in the manufacture, finance, and sales of trailers along with ownership of trailer parks, together create a system that flourishes by milking a market in which buyers of lower incomes have limited options. A successful urban trailer-park entrepreneur owner of one hundred parks in sixteen states succinctly describes the circumstances that families like Ellen's, at the margins, face for affordable housing: "We're the Dollar General store of housing. . . . If you can't afford anything else, then you'll live with us."[3]

Here we provide an essential framework for understanding the mobile home industrial complex—a term we coined to capture the interlocked markets that make up this relatively misunderstood but commonplace rural housing form. For the mobile home industrial complex entrepreneurs, trailers and trailer parks represent highly lucrative investments, which have attracted prominent investors. Key to the investment attraction, as we will show, is that the homeowners bear a personal risk—greater than that borne by the entrepreneurs who control the various enterprises that families encounter when they buy a mobile home. A trailer home carries high burdens both financially and structurally for buyers. Their greatest risk, as landless buyers, is incurred by needing to place the trailer, their most valuable asset, on land that is owned by another. We heard many resident complaints, particularly in Illinois, about park owners' greed, the quality of a mobile home's construction, and high financial costs for home loans and site rent in the trailer parks we studied—where rural families of modest means own their mobile homes and rent a trailer-park site. Park families do not readily acknowledge or perhaps not fully anticipate how they become caught up and often trapped in what is fundamentally an expensive private solution to the national public need for rural lower-income housing.

Key Terms of the Mobile Home Industrial Complex

"Trailer" or "mobile home" and "trailer park" are familiar labels. The industry and park owners, however, prefer the terms "manufactured home" and "manufactured home community," which perhaps equate better with conventional housing or communities. Park residents, we learned, realistically refer to their homes as trailers and their neighborhood as a trailer park or a trailer court. Given that all these labels are common, we use them interchangeably. Technically, a trailer park emerges when a developer or landowner clusters three or more mobile homes together on a single tract of land. We do not know how many trailer parks exist nationally because the US Census does not collect data on trailer parks, only on mobile homes. But the Manufactured Housing Institute (MHI) of the industry estimates that there are upwards of fifty thousand parks in the United States.[4] This number may actually be low, because the smaller, often older "mom and pop" parks are not apt to be included since they do not need or buy membership in this national trade organization. The MHI incorporates all entrepreneurs of the mobile home industrial complex and politically represents the industry. The 2010 Census reports that twenty million people live in mobile homes, while the MHI estimates that perhaps half of those homes are sited in a trailer park. Therefore, it is a housing form that shelters many families.

Five distinct types of mobile home communities or trailer parks are found across the United States, which vary according to residents' homeownership arrangement. In a "land-lease community" (37 percent), residents own their home and rent a site for it from a park owner. These parks range from those with large lots for newer, doublewide homes to those with only older, singlewide units on smaller lots, or the lot sizes may be mixed. Land-lease parks are the type we studied. In a "rental community" (estimated at 6 percent), the landlord owns the land and the homes and rents both to tenants. This type of trailer park perpetuates the negative stereotype of parks as transient places that house a fair share of residents who are hard-living, poor, not always well educated, and subject to job instability. A "seasonal community" (included in the land-lease 37 percent) is populated mainly by snowbird retirees from the Midwest, East, and Canada who spend the winter in Sun Belt states such as Arizona and Florida. These communities house residents who traverse a circular migration route on an annual basis to this type of land-lease park. In Sun Belt states retiree parks also house permanent residents. These parks offer recreational and other amenities to attract retirees and are more upscale. A newer and proportionately smaller variation of the land-lease type is a "subdivision community" (7 percent), where residents own both their home and the land but the park is privately owned. A "cooperative community" (1 percent) is a new form that functions as do co-op apartments. Nearly half, 49 percent, of the nation's mobile homes are sited singly on the owner's private property, not in a park.[5] Our three study sites represent a range of land-lease park sizes and have both local and absentee owners. Ellen Adams took up residence in a rural Illinois, a large land-lease park with a local owner.

Land-lease trailer parks for many years had policies that excluded recreational vehicles (RVs). But RVs are now found in these parks nationwide. The owner of the land-lease park in Illinois, for example, changed his policy to capture a new profitable income stream. A decade after the original study, MacTavish observed a half dozen RVs in the park, despite their small size relative to even an older singlewide trailer.

The mobile home industrial complex provides a needed and affordable product to rural America. Four major players control the complex domains: the manufacturers, the home financers, trailer-park owners and operators, and the municipalities where parks are located. Of these, the first three players are investor-controlled businesses. The fourth player represents rural municipalities—small cities, small towns and counties—responsible for the zoning policies that govern where rural parks are located, regulate local mobile home sales, and oversee park functions such as water and electrical systems. The fourth player uses zoning and other mechanisms to allow or exclude nearby trailer parks and their operation.[6] Trailer buyers who become homeowners are an important fifth player and the market for the other four domains. But as buyers and eventual trailer owners, they stand outside the MHIC complex and hold control only over their original choice in each business domain—to purchase, finance, and site their trailer. Once a landless family makes the choice to become a trailer home-owner, the players from the three business domains gain much control over them and their purchased home.

Mobile Home Manufacturers

In a tour of Palm Harbor Homes, a large home manufacturer provides an example of the sales pitch aimed at the retirees' upscale market. But this pitch is similar to the sales methods smaller dealers employ to sell to prospective buyers of low-end manufactured homes, as well as used models.

> *The tour at Palm Harbor Homes opens with a short film. Three Little Pigs each construct a home in an effort to defend themselves from the Big Bad Wolf. Footage then shifts to focus on a Palm Harbor Home still standing after Hurricane Andrew has flattened every other adjacent structure. "Superior construction techniques," the film's narrator explains, "make the difference."*
>
> *Once the movie ends, the tour heads to the actual production facility. The building itself is massive, large enough to accommodate the factory line assembly construction of multiple homes at a time. From an observation deck, every step of the building process is visible. Tour guide Piper Lee highlights distinctive features of the homes: exterior walls are constructed with two-by-sixes; water and electrical lines are carried in separate flexible polytubing; fiber rather than sheet metal ducting eliminates the old "ping pong" of air exchange; insulation in the walls and ceiling exceeds standards for site-built homes and is made of recycled materials to which borax and cornstarch are added for extra fire retardation and pest control; and Hardi Plank siding finishes out construction. Lee concludes, "For the money, these homes are more structurally sound, include stronger, safer and environmentally friendly materials, and pass a rigid testing and inspection process."*

Having heard this, an older couple on the tour seems pleased with their selection of a Palm Harbor Home. The home will be sited in a Palm Harbor–owned park—a housing solution they define as a good compromise between their stick-built home and a retirement facility. "The park seems like such a small, close community. I think we'll be safe there and have plenty of people to enjoy our older years with." The couple heads back to the model home and the selection of upgrades such as higher-end kitchen appliances, a bigger and deeper bathtub ("garden tub"), or a skylight.

The national US recession that began in 2008 became a consolidation period for the home manufacturers' industry. As a result of the consolidation, by 2015 almost 68 percent of the manufactured home industry became dominated by three major producers and their subsidiaries: Clayton Homes, Inc. (with a market share of 41percent), Champion Home Builders, Inc. (15 percent), and Cavco Industries, Inc. (12 percent). In the consolidation, Cavco acquired well-known brands including Palm Harbor Homes.[7] These major producers are not as likely to be in the limited markets of rural areas, however, where smaller producers are still found.

Important to our story, for *rural* homeowners and renters, manufactured housing is *the* major source for unsubsidized, low-cost housing.[8] Its major advantage for a rural family who cannot afford a "stick" home is that a mobile home provides instant housing with all the basic necessities built in. Retired households like those on the Palm Harbor tour are the market for the newer high-end doublewides with all the bells and whistles. We found, however, that the younger rural families with fewer resources in our study bought lower-end or used models that on average had been constructed twenty years before the study. At our three study sites high-end manufactured homes were a small minority of trailers: of eighty-two Illinois households, three homes (3 percent); of the sixty-five North Carolina households, four homes (6 percent), one of which was a repossessed home bought at a bargain; and of the seventy-nine New Mexico households, no homes.

Manufactured housing is now a major industry, which grew from humble beginnings as small tourist travel homes in the 1920s. Starting in the 1930s it gained a reputation as group housing for those down on their luck. In part, this was due to the federal government's use of trailers (or small recreational vehicles) and trailer parks as temporary or emergency housing for New Deal WPA workers in the 1930s, World War II defense plant workers, postwar soldier-students, and refugees from natural disasters. Reminiscent of their being employed for temporary occupancy, until the 1960 Census mobile homes were grouped as an "other" form of housing, along with houseboats, tents, and converted railroad cars.[9] In all three of our study sites, trailers are required to display a license plate (for which they pay a registration fee) on one end of the home, a remnant of trailers' classification as vehicles—a requirement of the Housing and Urban Development Act of 1968. Manufactured homes and trailer parks have since evolved from such humble, transient—and at times unsavory—uses.[10]

In his 1970 address to Congress, President Richard Nixon acknowledged that trailers satisfied a pressing need for affordable homes and proposed that they be considered houses rather than vehicles.[11] In 1974 the U.S. Congress passed the National Mobile Home Construction and Safety Standards Act (better known as the HUD Code), preempting any existing local codes for mobile home construction and safety. Home foundation standards, however, remained under local control.[12] The HUD Code is the only federal housing building code, and its standards regulate manufactured housing design and construction, strength and durability, transportability, fire resistance, and energy efficiency. The industry originally resisted the HUD Code. Ironically, dealers today advertise that manufactured homes' uniquely regulated construction provides the consumer an advantage because producers are held to a higher standard than in conventional home construction. The manufactured home industry tends to fight new regulations proposed by the federal government to enhance the structural integrity of the product, even though such regulations can be used in marketing the product.

Despite the 1974 HUD Code, the industry has encountered a long history of serious quality and safety problems, according to consumer groups. In a survey of mobile home owners by the Consumers Union, 82 percent were satisfied with their homes, but a majority (including those with homes less than five years old) had experienced a least one major structural problem.[13] One-fourth had the particle-board subfloor swell when wet. More than one-third had plumbing problems such as leaky sinks and showers. Almost one-third had experienced leaky windows, doors, or roofs that affected home heating or cooling. It is possible, however, that the Consumers Union captured more low-end trailers in its research.

When a manufactured home is a high-end model, its quality is comparable to that of a conventional home (albeit of lower price), with "thicker exterior walls, steeper roof pitch, higher rated insulation, double-pane windows, residential sheet rock walls, higher quality carpets, superior brand name appliances, wood cabinetry and Energy Star packages . . . and [it] doesn't look like a mobile home," according to an industry analyst.[14] Low-end manufactured homes, in contrast, are more cheaply constructed, plain in design, and show substantial deterioration after five years.[15] In keeping with the 82 percent satisfaction rate the Consumers Union found despite the structural problems it documented, homeowners of the majority low-end trailers in our study also reported satisfaction with their homes. Our study's younger park families' satisfaction must be viewed in light of the fact that they were enjoying ownership of their first home. And their perspective was shaped comparatively by prior experiences with a low-end rented apartment or home. Thus pride of ownership is an important component of a rural family's satisfaction with their trailer and may override other housing concerns.

Manufactured homes' affordability, according to the industry, results from efficiencies gained by the factory-built process, which eliminates typical issues encountered in conventional home construction. This process produces a home that is cheaper by the square foot than a site-built home. Up to the 1960s trailers were modest in size and features. Later-built trailers grew larger, possessed more amenities, and were, as a consequence, less mobile than previously. Nowadays, a new singlewide home is comparable in size to a small apartment, averaging 600–1,200 square feet (8 to 14 feet wide, 40 to 90 feet long); a doublewide home equals the size of a modest home of 1,700–1,800 square feet.

The required transport of a factory-built home, on its own wheels and axles or on a flatbed truck, accounts for some of its design features and inherent structural features and problems. For example, the roof slope of the mobile home is typically less than that of a conventional home simply because during transport the home must fit under highway overpasses. Similarly, both the truck size and what typical rural roads can accommodate limit the width of a single-wide. Hence the mechanism for obtaining more home width is the doublewide, which is actually two singlewide halves transported separately and assembled together on site. More than two units can be and are aggregated.[16] According to the industry, more new doublewides are now sold than singlewides, and they hold their value better.[17] While originally made with wheels for transport, most homes are now so large that once they are installed, the wheels are removed. Structural damage may occur during installation (hence the industry's advice not to move them once sited). A homeowner has difficulty getting vendors to take responsibility for any structural problems experienced—with the transporters, installers, and the manufacturer each blaming the others for the problem. Tellingly, most dealers offer only a one-year warranty on a new manufactured home.

Materials used in the construction of manufactured homes involve air pollution risks greater than those of a conventional home. These homes typically are constructed making extensive use of pressed wood products such as plywood and particleboard. Because federal guidelines require mobile homes to be airtight, these homes have higher concentrations of pollutants such as formaldehyde than do other home types.[18] A large California survey of mobile home residents found elevated indoor formaldehyde levels to be related to such physical symptoms as burning eyes and skin, fatigue, sleeping problems, dizziness, chest pains, and sore throat. If residents are smokers, the airtight homes and the interaction of tobacco smoke with other common pollutants mean the possible health risk for children in particular can be high, especially in seasons when families are more often indoors.[19]

A trailer potentially poses another potential health risk related to its construction. Mobile homes have twice the rate of fire deaths of all other home types combined, and the likelihood that a fire will be fatal is high.[20] Because of their propensity to burn quickly to the ground, trailers built before 1976 especially (common to rental parks), are often referred to as "matchsticks" or "firetraps."[21] Smoke detectors in mobile homes, unlike conventional homes, provide little protective effect because of the home's small size. And the use of a high proportion of flammable materials allows a fire to build quickly. An older home increases the fire risk. An Illinois park woman reported her major concern was fire. "My brother was burned severely in a trailer fire. If it had been a house, they said the extent would not have been so bad. They said trailers just burn faster." Again, the risk of a fire-related death is higher in a trailer than in all other housing if a resident smokes or consumes alcohol.[22]

Wind mobility may be what is most mobile about a contemporary mobile home. When a trailer is properly secured or tied down with cables anchored in concrete footing, it is less likely to sustain wind damage. Whether trailer tie-downs are required is a local municipal issue, however, for they are not governed by the 1974 HUD Code. A major HUD study found that over a ten-year period, a manufactured home when exposed to normal wind conditions was five times more likely to incur structural failure than a conventionally built home. Because of their size and wide use in tornado-prone states—Florida, the Carolinas, Oklahoma, Missouri, and Illinois—mobile home parks have been reliable indicators, not attractors, of tornadoes.[23]

In 2001, the national median age for trailers was about 20 years. Compared with conventional housing, with an expected useful life of 100 years or more, manufactured homes have an average useful life of 57.8 years, according to the manufactured housing industry, while nonindustry estimates project usability for as few as 22 years.[24] Structural issues are exacerbated as a manufactured home ages. Even in newer mobile homes (those less than five years old), our park surveys found that homeowners incur high costs for repair or replacement of basic structural features like doors, windows, floors, and roofs. The rapid deprecation and physical deterioration of mobile homes and high utility bills due to poor insulation constitute substantial hidden costs for mobile home owners.[25]

But park folk keep a sense of humor about their structurally vulnerable homes: "Do you know what rednecks and tornadoes have in common? They both can spot a trailer park a mile away," joked a forty-year-old truck driver, father of three, from the Illinois trailer park.

Mobile Home Dealers and Financers

Given these problems why do our study families buy mobile homes? A mobile home is decidedly affordable when compared with a site-built home (table 1.1). While rural areas are not separated out in the Census breakdown of home prices, a study focusing on rural regions indicates the median price of a new single stick home with land is three times that of a new manufactured home. Affordability and the rural prevalence of mobile homes explain why rural America has higher homeownership rates (76 percent) than does the nation as a whole (69 percent). One estimate finds manufactured housing accounted for almost three-quarters (72 percent) of new homes for low-income buyers between 1997 and 1999, when Illinois park families purchased their mobile homes, though the majority of them were purchased used.[26]

Rural buyers in the market for either a new or used manufactured home face a relatively limited number of nearby dealers. Rural people like Ellen Adams in Illinois therefore settle for a local dealer if their needs are met rather than shopping around over a larger region. For the same reason, rural dealers typically arrange for the financing.

TABLE 1.1   2011 relative cost of U.S. housing by type

COST	TOTAL OWNER-OCCUPIED UNITS	OWNER-OCCUPIED MANUFACTURED/ MOBILE HOMES	RENTER-OCCUPIED MANUFACTURED/ MOBILE HOMES
Median purchase price	$110,000	$30,000	Not available
Median value	$160,000	$30,000	Not available
Median year acquired	2000	2001	Not available
Median monthly cost[a]	$1,008	$508	$660
Median cost as % of income[b]	21	21	35
% housing-cost–burdened[b, c]	32.4	34.1	59.9

Source: U.S. Census Bureau. "American Housing Survey for the United States 2011." Current Housing Reports, Series H150/11. Washington, DC: U.S. Government Printing Office, 2013.

[a]Excludes households reporting no cash rent.

[b]Excludes households reporting zero or negative income and those reporting no cash rent.

[c]Housing-cost burden occurs if a household spends 30% or more of monthly income on housing.

Ellen Adams's housing search led her to Warrington Homes, an off-the-highway dealership she had passed many times on her commute to work. A community legend, Craig Warrington got his start in the manufactured home business in the mid-1950s when a post–World War II housing boom was transforming the national economy and mobile homes and trailer parks were evolving from purely transient housing to a more permanent housing type. The large sign above the Warrington Homes dealership declares, "Quality Homes at Affordable Prices" and is clearly visible from the highway. The deal that Craig worked out for Ellen was for a gently used slate gray singlewide with three bedrooms and one bath totaling 670 square feet. Craig explained that at roughly $400 a month, the median monthly cost of an owner-occupied manufactured home would be significantly less for Ellen than the just-under $700 a month a conventional home would cost. Craig Warrington also handled the financing end of Ellen's trailer purchase, steering her to a no-down-payment loan with Countrywide Financial, a then-national leader in mobile home financing and a high-profile subprime lender. Throughout the 1990s subprime lending fueled growth in mobile home sales. Countywide, through a program called "House America," worked hard to qualify an increasing number of Americans for home loans. The financial giant's efforts were successful, and between 1982 and 2003 investors earned a 23,000 percent return on their stock. Ellen's deal included a twenty-year loan that called for a $240-a-month payment.

The family of three moved in with their modest possessions. Once settled, Ellen realized there was no way they could survive the sticky heat of an Illinois summer without air conditioning. She recalls going back to Warrington: "Then after we moved in I went back and said we had to have air conditioning—I was about to die. I didn't have any money then to pay for it, but he said he could just add $20 a month onto my house payment. He said, 'Can you handle that?' and I thought 'I can do that' so we got air."

When a study family buys a new or used manufactured home with little or no cash for a down payment, their concern is whether the proposed monthly loan payment is manageable on their budget. If, like Ellen, they feel the loan payment plus the lot rental is doable, they tend not to negotiate the interest rate, nor do they examine how much the loan will cost over its fifteen-, twenty- or thirty-year term.

Clayton Homes, the nation's leading builder of manufactured homes, is vertically integrated—which allows it to offer one-stop shopping for a home, from financing to insurance.[27] No one in the trailer parks we studied, however, purchased a home from a megadealer like Clayton Homes. Rural families like Ellen's buy from a small local dealer who, if it is also a park owner, is able to operate a small-scale vertically integrated business. For example, we observed that some park owners, like the one in Illinois, offer buyers a package deal for home financing along with free site rent for some months or a year in the dealer/owner's own trailer park. In this way a dealer gains a tenant as well as a buyer. Families find the arrangement convenient. Unlike the major players, small rural mobile home dealers sometimes struggle to stay afloat while juggling sales, financing, and park management. Theirs is a riskier enterprise than is the Clayton Homes operation, which makes more from the financing of mobile homes than it does from manufacturing them.

In 2014 the average price for a new singlewide home was $42,900 and for a doublewide was $79,500, in contrast to a site-built home's average price of almost $269,000 plus about $80,000 for land.[28] (Table 1.1 shows similar 2011 costs.) Price was a major factor in making mobile homes the fastest-growing housing form in the country during the 1990s. Between 1950 and 2000 mobile housing grew from just over 300,000 to nearly 8.8 million—an increase of about 2,700 percent.[29]

FIGURE 1. A Palm Harbor Homes model home site located off Oregon's busy I-5 corridor. Like its competitor Clayton Homes, Palm Harbor Homes is a vertically integrated organization offering buyers one-stop shopping for a new home, insurance, and finance at their model sites. Source: K. MacTavish.

Rapid growth of this market slowed in the 1990s, however, when the overexten-
sion of the credit market for mobile homes crashed in ways similar to the burst-
ing of the conventional housing mortgage market bubble around 2008. For our
discussion we draw on a fine investigative piece by Alex Berenson of the *New York
Times* about the mobile home financial bubble.[30]

Unlike with a conventional mortgage, backed by land as its collateral, a landless mobile home owner (85 percent) typically must use a personal property loan,
or "chattel loan," to purchase their home. According to lenders, lack of landownership provides the strongest rationale for the chattel-loan monopoly. Chattel
loans are easily obtained by low-income manufactured home buyers, like Ellen,
with little or no cash for a down payment. But these loans carry extremely high
interest rates of up to 13.5 percent and over, compared with conventional mortgages. Despite federal efforts, current lending practices for manufactured homes
remain dominated by high interest rates.[31]

Chattel loans involve other shortcomings for trailer buyers. A chattel loan
lacks the foreclosure protections available with a real property home mortgage.
Trailers can be repossessed as quickly as a car—the other major market for chattel loans. And like a car, a mobile home loses value with time rather than gaining
equity. Rural mobile home buyers lack many of the other quality credit or affordable mortgage options that exist in cities or suburbs. Rural places have fewer
financial competitors, except for a proliferation of subprime lenders.[32] Rural
buyers of a new or used trailer, therefore, opt for what is recommended by their
local dealer, as Ellen did.

Prior to the 1990s manufactured home boom, standard mobile home loans
typically were for fifteen years. Mobile home sales peaked during this decade
and accounted for 27 percent of all subprime loans, of which 40 percent carried
interest rates above 10 percent.[33] The market boom was in part driven by the fact
that thirty-year loans became more common for the low-income mobile home
buyer with limited financial resources. And the subprime industry was willing
to extend credit with little concern for a borrower's ability to actually make the
loan payments. It is important to note that a thirty-year loan lowers the monthly
payment slightly but greatly increases overall interest costs throughout the loan's
duration and stretches out repayment on the principal.[34] (See table 1.2.) We
found thirty-year loans to be relatively rare in our rural study parks.

The 1990s mobile home market bubble anticipated the conventional home
real estate bubble of the early 2000s, with a similar reliance on a high volume of
risky loans with securitization, which for the mobile home bubble was based on
the meager collateral that a trailer on rented land represents. Forty percent of
1990s mobile home loans were financed by Green Tree Financial, a prominent
Minnesota subprime lender. (Almost everyone in the large Illinois park reported

TABLE 1.2 Costs of fifteen-year versus thirty-year loan for manufactured home

COST	15-YEAR LOAN	30-YEAR LOAN
Loan amount	$50,000	$50,000
Interest rate	13%	13%
Monthly payment	$632.60	$553.10
Total payments	$113,868	$199,116
Interest paid	$63,868	$149,116
Interest paid in first 5 years	$30,325.45	$32,226.40
Principal paid in first 5 years	$7,630.55	$959.60

Source: Conseco Finance, cited in Berenson, "A Boom Built upon Sand."

having a Green Tree loan.) Viewed by Wall Street as a growth stock, Green Tree was bought by Conesco in 1998. But as in the conventional housing boom in the following decade, the profits and growth reported by Green Tree were a fiction, made possible by "gain-on-sale" volume financing. In the late 1990s trailer repossessions were so high that even the industry acknowledged that loans were being made to many who could not afford them. By 2001 Conesco projected repossession of one in five manufactured homes it had financed.[35]

After the real estate bubble of 2008, when conventional home loan interest rates fell to all-time lows, conventional homeowners widely refinanced at the historically low interest rates of below 5 percent, even on a fifteen-year mortgage. In contrast, trailer homeowners who rented a site in a land-lease trailer park—our target population—did not refinance their high 13.5 percent chattel loans.[36] Mobile homeowners are prevented from the refinancing option because they hold a chattel loan and own a home that is worth only about half its original price after three years, far less than what is owed on it.[37] Lenders justify their reluctance to refinance by pointing out that manufactured home owners, especially those with homes installed on leased land, are more likely to default than are conventional mortgage holders. After decades paying on a chattel loan, a family has accrued little equity on its investment because the home loses value even as the loan must be paid on (table 1.2 reflects fifteen- and thirty-year loans as examples). For example, Ellen Adams's loan payment of $260 a month (including $20 for the air conditioner added on), with her twenty-year loan would eventually total around $62,400 paid for a used singlewide worth about $10,000 when she bought it. Her added-on air conditioner would cost her $4,800 (of the $62,400) over twenty years.

Although the interest on a chattel loan, like that on a conventional loan, is a potentially deductible cost, the study families either did not know about the tax credit, or if they did, were not knowledgeable about the complex documentation involved to obtain the deduction. No park family related having concerns about the high interest rate on their twenty- or, more rarely, thirty-year loans, which greatly inflated the cost of their mobile home (see table 1.1). They cared mainly about whether they got a good deal or a bad deal and whether their monthly cost was manageable.

The rural manufactured home market is made up of inexperienced first-time buyers who assume that their trailer accrues equity, as does a conventional home. And indeed, equity is a selling point typically promoted by mobile home dealers. According to an Illinois park resident, the best thing about their newly purchased singlewide is "We actually get a chance to own it as opposed to paying rent. We have a chance to build equity." In reality, a trailer homeowner builds little or no equity, although a trailer eventually can be sold for some financial return. Our park families did not express concerns about the real long-term costs associated with their decision, and especially the costs associated with needing to place the home on rented land. But because of these financial pitfalls, a manufactured home bought with a chattel loan represents an expensive trap for park families.[38]

A financing alternative to the chattel loan, used to privately purchase a trailer that we encountered, is the "contract-for-deed sale." Essentially this is a rent- or lease-to-own arrangement in which the seller-owner finances the loan (even if not owning the home outright) and the buyer agrees to a monthly payment to the seller—typically it is a used trailer purchase. Sometimes referred to as a "poor man's mortgage," a contract-for-deed sale, which carries no fees, formal application, or closing costs, is faster and cheaper to execute than the conventional chattel loan. It promises eventual homeownership to a family who cannot qualify for other forms of loans.[39] This loan form, at least until recently, has operated outside the domain of the mobile home industrial complex.

Typically, a rural trailer-park family uses a contract sale for a mobile home bought privately—whether from a relative, a friend, or acquaintance. In such cases, the parties may not formally write a contract but essentially make the agreement with a handshake. In New Mexico such arrangements are characterized as informal because people simply take over the loan payments from the previous owner. Buyers, in these circumstances, must rely on the seller's honesty to fulfill their part of the contract-for-deed agreement. For example, Darlene and Ron Vega, the New Mexico park family profiled in the introduction, were on the verge of losing their mobile home because the seller took their monthly payments but did not make his payments to the bank on the original loan. The bank threatened repossession regardless.

The buyer faces a host of problems with the easily assumed contract-for-sale arrangement. First, financing might be easy, but the default process is also easy. If a buyer misses one payment, the seller has a right to cancel the contract even if the home is almost paid off. In case of default, the buyer has a narrow window, sometimes only sixty days, to find a new home before eviction. Second, under the contract terms, the buyer assumes full maintenance of the home, including any unexpected or hidden home repair costs. And monthly payments are not amortized, which means that they are not structured to pay the debt off by the end of the loan term. At the maturity date a lump sum principal payment occurs. The risk is greater with nonamortizing loans because the home's value may fall while the principal on the loan remains unchanged. Also, the contract may include a final "balloon payment" that further challenges completing the contract. An objection raised about contract-for-deed financing, apart from its association with nefarious equity-stripping scams, is the reputation these agreements have for giving little legal protection to a buyer who has limited ownership rights or control over the property while making payments to the seller—as in the case of the Vegas.

A buyer might enter a contract-for-deed agreement in the hopes of repairing a credit history, but these arrangements do nothing of the sort. A seller, who retains all legal rights to the property, may sell the home or encumber it further with loans until the obligations of the contract are fulfilled. And a contract-for-deed sale also excludes the buyer from using the federal mortgage-interest tax deduction.[40] Contract-for-deed loans have recently become popular among Wall Street investment firms (who buy up foreclosed homes in lots cheaply and turn around and sell them to lower-income families at substantial prices) because of the ease of eviction in case of owners' default, in contrast to the lengthy process involved in a foreclosure.[41]

Prevalence of contract-for-deed sales is difficult to track as no formal reporting is required. In 2001, 5.2 percent of owner-occupied manufactured homes nationally were estimated to be financed by contract-for-deed sales. These sale arrangements are more common in minority populations. Nationally among Hispanics in owner-occupied homes, contract sales make up 8.7 percent of loans, and for blacks they comprise 7.7 percent.[42] We identified 25 percent of such agreements in North Carolina and a lower 11 percent in both the New Mexico and Illinois parks. But families in all three of our rural park sites had a higher proportion of contract-for-deed agreements than are found nationally. Park families with a successful contract-for-deed experience consider it a good deal.

The Trade-Up System

It is in the best interest of rural mobile home dealers (and loan financers) who are also park owners to lock in a buyer as a park tenant for the long term and thereby assure themselves a reliable, regular cash flow. Park owners/manufactured home dealers, therefore tend to encourage established residents to "trade up," by providing easy financing for a newer, albeit more expensive unit. If like a car dealer, a mobile home dealer keeps the new monthly loan payments the same as the old ones, a park family does not feel a financial pinch. But the financial costs are steep for using the trade-up option—because it involves a new fifteen-, twenty-, or thirty-year loan. The policy tends to promote the owner's short-term cash-flow goals rather than the buyer's long-term dream of a buying a conventional home.[43] For a park owner, the trade-up system also enhances the appearance of the park itself—newer homes are more attractive to a prospective tenant.

A trailer homeowner receives little when trading in a used unit because of its rapid depreciation. And another chattel loan on a new unit requires long-term repayment on the new, rapidly depreciating unit, causing the chattel home loan to go "under water." An "underwater mortgage" is a home purchase loan with a higher balance than the free-market value of the home, which prevents the homeowner from selling the home unless he or she has cash to pay the loss out of pocket. This means that the homeowner owes more than the home is worth after just a few years.[44] Thus a mobile home purchased with a twenty-year loan or a secondary trade-up option with a new twenty- or thirty-year loan mires a land-lease park family in chronic debt. If a family cannot make their monthly mortgage payments, they may quickly lose everything and face homelessness.[45] Thus, mobile home ownership fosters neither the accumulation of household equity nor the housing savings potential mobile home buyers are led to expect.[46]

Older homes are often moved out rather than retained by a park owner who arranges a trade-up deal for an established park resident. The Illinois park owner ships his older, traded-in units to Kentucky or Tennessee, where mobile homes are more prevalent (than the 3.2 housing proportion of Illinois) and a market exists for older, used units among a poorer rural population. In the North Carolina site (where mobile homes constitute 16.4 percent of all state homes), county ordinances require that units be no older than ten. New Mexico (where trailers constitute 16.8 percent of all homes—second highest in the nation) lacks regulations on the age of mobile homes. Consequently, southern New Mexico's mobile homes are often ten years of age or older—in all likelihood transported from Arizona or California, which both have statutes governing the age of units.[47]

The high-interest chattel loan customarily used to buy a trailer is an antiquated policy perpetuated by powerful financial interests. Industry investors, dominated by a few key players like Clayton Homes, who benefit greatly from the status quo, have made a concerted effort to compromise the few lending regulations for manufactured homes enacted by the Dodd-Frank Act of 2010.[48]

Such investors seek to protect their market for high financial profits squeezed from those with chattel loans who need to live in trailer parks. On December 13, 2016, a final ruling was made by the Federal Housing Finance Agency (FHFA) on Fannie Mae's and Freddie Mac's "Duty to Serve Underserved Markets," including manufactured housing and rural areas, by "improving the distribution and availability of mortgage financing in a safe and sound manner for residential properties that serve very low-, low-, and moderate-income families in these markets." The ruling helps affordable housing on the whole, especially expanding and making more robust the situation in rural areas. Implementation of the rule is in the works for 2017.[49] This ruling is the sort seen as a potential threat to the established system, dominated by large lenders who are happy with the high-interest chattel loan status quo.

Park Operators: Trailer Parks Operated as a Real Estate Commodity

Because little funding has been provided for new public housing since the mid-1990s, fewer units of subsidized housing exist now than in 1995. And federal spending on rental assistance programs remains flat, despite the housing-related recession of the early 2000s.[50] A trailer park therefore represents a major form of accessible housing for rural folk of modest means. For Ellen Adams, with few financial resources and narrow housing options in her rural area, owning a used trailer sited in a land-lease trailer park represented "getting something for my money."

> Craig Warrington transported Ellen Adams's trailer to Prairieview Manor, the land-lease park adjacent to the small town of Prairieview, where Craig had a longtime working relationship with Joe, the park owner. The park offered Ellen a lot in a well-established neighborhood with amenities like paved roads, off-street parking, a playground, and a swimming pool. While those amenities mattered, Ellen remembers choosing the park for its access to the good schools of Prairieview. Her oldest, a son, had met with challenges in the racially mixed metro schools nearby. She wanted to avoid that for her daughter: "I would not have my child go to school in the [nearby small city] schools. I mean, they're okay for the first five years, but when Trinity was ready for sixth grade we moved here so she could go the Prairieview schools."
>
> In Prairieview Manor, the trailer was tied down to a cement slab and hooked up to the park's water and sewer systems. The park's location outside the jurisdiction of Prairieview proper allowed Joe to essentially act as

his own water company, as is often the case nationally. Phone and electrical service came in from the county. Lot rent in the park, water and sewer included, added another $180 a month to Ellen's $260 basic housing costs, plus the air conditioner. The total monthly cost for her trailer home, now $440 a month, consumes half of Ellen's monthly take-home pay. She soon learned that the lot rent increased by $10 annually, stretching her budget even more.

Ellen Adams's experience of seeing her lot rent rise annually so that it consumed over half her low monthly income is common and illustrates how families can find themselves at the mercy of a park owner's policies. A nationwide affordable housing gap—like what motivated Ellen to the trailer park solution—is capitalized on by entrepreneurs like Sam Zell, the Chicago real estate magnate. Through his REIT (real estate investment trust) Zell holds a controlling interest in 370 US land-lease manufactured home communities with 140,000 sites, which target the retiree market.[51] Zell—like Warren Buffet, who bought Clayton Homes—is a major investor in trailer parks because of the market's robust financial potential.

Land-lease parks represent a market in which the most investment action occurs. These trailer parks are attractive to investors because the resident homeowners care for their own homes and bear the risk inherent in putting their greatest asset on land controlled by a park owner. Not all land-lease trailer parks, however, are operated in the same manner. Park ownership represents a diversity of management styles, goals, and commitment to residents' well-being. We outline a set of ideal management models—ideal in the sense that no actual park we observed is exactly like the ideal models, and in reality park owners combine trait from several types. Park owners display a range of commitment to residents, profits extracted from a park, and management of a park's infrastructure.

We are indebted for the basic ownership-models idea to Charles Becker, a Duke University economist also involved in studying trailer parks.[52] We made modifications and expanded on Becker's original concept, based on our findings.

Mom-and-Pop Model: Such trailer parks are older and smaller and were developed by the original owner, who may live in the park or nearby. In rural areas these typically were developed on family farmland. Mom-and-pop park tenants are well known to the owner, and management may operate in a paternalistic manner—flexible and even compassionate toward tenants. Becker thinks these owners might cut a little slack to tenants who hit a hard patch financially. Mom-and-pop parks are the source of growth for other types of models as they are bought up by investors across the nation as the original owners age and wish to retire.

Benevolent Model: Owners are committed to building a sense of community, have a concern for tenants' well-being, and aim to do right by them. Parish Manor, located in Raleigh, North Carolina, exemplifies this model, according to Becker. A father-son team founded the park on family land. They also are a manufactured home dealer. The owners manage with an eye to residents' welfare by doing such things as background checks of prospective tenants; high monitoring of the park; and the provision of many amenities such as sidewalks, paved streets, a pool, a well-equipped playground, picnic grounds, storage areas, community gardens, and community activities. The founders have won significant awards for their dedication to community, residents' needs, and their parks' appearance.[53] To a certain extent this management style resembles some aspects of the mom-and- pop model but writ large.

Walmart Model: Park management is corporate, uniform, and sterile. It is a stripped-down product but clean, neat, and well run—albeit by arm's-length ownership. Management keeps costs low and removes any amenities like laundry or recreational facilities associated with a previous mom-and-pop ownership. Owners like to expand the park's home sites because money is made on volume. Thus, parks of this model may be fairly large. This model is detailed below as a guide for investors who buy older mom-and-pop–owned parks and update them with infrastructural improvements to increase profitability. Operation is standardized and impersonal.

Corporate Model: Operators minimize their inputs and costs and extract every penny possible from tenants. These parks may be neglected—even desolate and rundown. Owners provide little in the way of maintenance like upkeep on streets, landscaping, lighting, or other features that make life more pleasant or safe for tenants. What makes a park a better place to live is not what concerns these investors. One scenario for this model has investors keeping a park running in anticipation of the land's being purchased for redevelopment as a higher use of the land. Lakeside Park in North Carolina provides an example of this model (see chapter 4).

In mom-and-pop parks the owners live in or nearby the trailer park they developed and continue to manage. These parks tend to be older and smaller than parks of the other models. Existence of the mom-and-pop ownership model, like those in study park of Illinois and several in North Carolina and New Mexico, is in decline as the original owners age and heirs are not interested in being owners. These parks are now in demand for purchase by the Walmart-type operators/investors capitalizing on a flourishing market fostered by the Internet.

Investors buy these older parks cheaply, renovate the facilities, and raise the lot rents.[54] If the original owners had let things deteriorate, the residents may welcome the new management even if their rents are raised. Absentee owners of the one hundred to two hundred site parks we observed in North Carolina employ residents as managers. This management form functions more like a mom-and-pop operation because the managers tend to also be residents.

The benevolent model is relatively rare among park types. A park like Parish Manor resembles an expansion of the mom-and-pop model, for the owners are the original developers and remain personally engaged in running the park despite its large size. The Parish Manor website features the rich and varied activities regularly provided, including a foundation that sponsors events and services for residents. The Illinois study park began with this model. The owner lived in the park in its early years, and residents were provided a laundry room, playground, swimming pool, and meeting room. There were also community activities, such as a Fourth of July parade and a park newsletter. But gradually many of these amenities disappeared or aged after the park owner moved out of the park.

Industrialization of Trailer-Park Investment and Management

A cottage industry of guides and short courses exists for how to invest in the purchase, sale, or operation of trailer parks. Mobile Home University (MHU) was profiled in the *New York Times Magazine*.[55] Its operators advertise MHU as boot camps—or short courses that offer practical advice, based on the practices of the MHU entrepreneurs' land-lease park investments in more than ten states, including Illinois. The MHU operators themselves have made millions by buying and upgrading mom-and-pop trailer parks for resale. "There's more money in decent than slumlording," one comments. They advise operating a trailer park according to the Walmart model, and according to the philosophy, that the best-run parks are those where the owners live at a distance. "You don't want to know the names of your tenants or about their families. You don't really want them to know yours."[56] Investors are advised after buying a park to strip out all amenities—from laundry rooms and vending machines to play areas or pools—to eliminate both operating expenses and liabilities.

MHU's founders have park tenants pay on average at least 20 percent of their incomes on rent. Like families we studied, tenants are typically the working poor, two-income younger families. Rents are raised annually—a practice they advised for investors. Although these tenants might be struggling, the entrepreneur says they can absorb the rent increases because they "can always pick up extra hours" working for minimum wage at Taco Bell.[57] The annual return, on the hundred parks the partners own, is a robust 25 percent. They are "doubling their money every four years."

Trailer parks have become an investment commodity—using the corporate model—with ownership of multiple parks. As early as the 1970s one Chicago real estate investor reported having consolidated thirty-one parks with twelve thousand home sites. By 1994 trailer-park investment was featured in *Forbes* magazine. Said another entrepreneur, "There's an incredible amount of stability in this business. We've got around 15,000 families supporting our income stream. If you had an office building with ten tenants and two of them leave . . . you have to spend a ton of money on improvements to attract another tenant. With manu-factured home communities all we have to do is . . . plant flowers in the spring, we cut the grass, put down fertilizer, and maintain our roads."[58] John Grissim, an industry analyst, characterizes trailer parks owned by large corporations as having "no souls. Some are quite good, others awful to the point of being preda-tory. These companies exist to make money for their shareholders and one way is incremental annual rent increases (usually in the 4 percent–5 percent range) that in a few short years can really put tenants living on fixed incomes in a bind."[59]

MHU entrepreneurs promote mobile home parks as "the best kept secret in commercial real estate."[60] Land-lease trailer parks in particular (like those in our study) are touted as a "gold mine."[61] "Of the 50,000 parks in the U.S. . . . 40,000 of them are basically owned by moms and pops. . . . When you find a park where you can walk in and either easily cut costs or raise the rent, then you are look-ing at a great investment." An apartment renter or conventional homeowner can readily move, but trailer park tenants are a captive market—an advantage touted as beneficial for investors. An *urban* MHU entrepreneur gives an example of his strategy after buying a mom-and-pop trailer park:

> I bought a park in Grapevine, Texas, [near Dallas]. . . . His tenants were paying one hundred dollars a month . . . when the going rent was at least $300 in the area! So I bought it and sent a letter to all the tenants telling them that they had been getting away with paying next to nothing for years, and in 60 days I was raising the rent to $275. . . . Sixty days later, I almost tripled the rent, and everyone stayed. I didn't change anything else, except that I put up a nicer-looking sign.[62]

Investors are able to hike trailer park rentals, especially in urban areas, because they and the residents know the cost for a two-bedroom apartment rental in their area. Because the mom-and-pop parks they buy are typically rundown, these investors do put money into upgrading the infrastructure, particularly roads.

FIGURE 2. An aerial view shows the typical density of a trailer park as homes are clustered hitch end toward the park streets. Source: Google Images.

That trailer-park site rentals are tied to local two-bedroom apartment rental rates is consistent with practices found generally in the industry, according to Becker.[63]

Investors other than benevolent model owners are seldom concerned about ambience or tenant privacy. Among all the park layouts we observed, trailers are arranged by placing them perpendicular to the street on the home's smaller hitch end, to squeeze the most units possible on a tract. The typical layout aligns all windows on the long sides of the trailers shaped like shotgun-style homes to face those of like-positioned neighbors.

To achieve a modicum of privacy, tenants must keep their windows covered; otherwise neighbors can look directly into all rooms. Except in the Illinois study park, we saw little in the way of public spaces provided, and sidewalks are uniformly absent. Car traffic dominates park streets, which walkers, bikes, and children playing must also share. All park land is made financially productive to maximize an investor's cash flow.[64] Some parks—such as the subdivision park in North Carolina—have larger sites, which is also related to the requirements for septic tanks. There tenants do have more privacy.

Because a trailer park is private property and few states have statutes regulating evictions, residents are subject to eviction without due process. For example, MHU advises that investors begin eviction proceedings on a tenant as soon as local laws allow, even if a tenant is just two or three weeks late in paying the rent. "Ours is a strict 'no pay, no stay' policy." Such a practice MHU advises helps "rid their parks of bad seeds and ne'er-do-wells." A newly evicted family meanwhile has to simultaneously think about finding a new place to live while facing the possibility that they are about to lose any equity they have in their trailer.[65] Evictions also occur for other reasons: conflict with the park owner or neighbors; sale of the park to new owner; or sale of the land to a developer for another, higher use. Easy evictions demonstrate that trailer-park tenants, in reality, have limited control over their property despite their being homeowners.[66]

Municipalities and the Market Scarcity of Trailer Parks

The urban park entrepreneur observes that few new trailer parks are being built, yet the demand for affordable housing is increasing. He believes that the numbers of the nation's trailer parks are unlikely to grow because municipalities dislike them: "The supply is static even as the demand for cheap places to live is high."[67] Occupancy rates are at a high 90 percent nationally. Southern California, for example, has restrictive zoning laws that keep the supply fixed. "It's just an absolutely great time [2014] to be in the mobile home business, with all the people who have been displaced from their homes because of foreclosures or they've lost a job or what have you," according to an operator of another park investor's seminar.[68] Despite this increase in demand, potential park tenants are stymied by the limited supply of vacant sites in existing trailer parks or the development of new parks. An inadequate supply and high demand for trailer sites in parks allow owners to charge more rent.

Data supporting the decline in parks in mid-2014 come from the manufactured homes mortgage market. This sector showed the largest unit drop among all housing during 2012, for example.[69] Much of the reduction in new manufactured housing placements is associated with barriers that now exist for the development of new trailer-park sites across the nation.[70] Land and zoning issues explain many of these barriers.[71] Municipal objections to allowing development of new trailer parks are that parks are threats to real estate values, that they are a blight on the landscape, and that they house those of questionable moral character. Municipalities also argue that the concentration of households in a trailer park produces high demand for educational, police, and fire protection services while generating insufficient property taxes to pay for them. The tax issue is a controversial one. The industry argues that mobile home communities may actually save local governments money by assuming costs for sewage, water, trash collection, and road maintenance. But mobile home parks lack few advocates other than the industry.

Restrictive zoning and high land costs are factors in the gradual marginalization of trailer parks to more remote rural locations. As early as the 1970s zoning practices generally forced trailer parks into undesirable areas. As a consequence, the parks are often zoned as commercial-industrial and not regulated as are the conventional residential areas in or near the same place.[72] Older mobile home parks situated originally on what was the urban fringe are now particularly threatened by suburban sprawl. In a suburbanizing landscape, particularly one of upscale developments, manufactured housing is not viewed as the highest or best use for a community's land.[73] Thus, local zoning (or lack of it) tends to squeeze mobile home parks into places that, because of weak building codes and regulations, are unlikely to be resistant. And when parks are sold out from under tenants, they have no recourse and experience challenges finding a new home site in a rural market narrowed by these sales for a higher use. Correspondingly, a lack of surplus park home sites and the weak remedies available to tenants being evicted potentially favor abusive management practices such as dramatic hikes in lot rent and the abrupt cancellation of leases—which are simultaneously considered wise investment practices.[74]

A basic democratic right of voting locally may be denied trailer-park residents if the nearby rural community does not annex the park. Termed "municipal underbounding," the practice defines a town that does not incorporate a place that, except for housing "undesirables," would be a logical choice for annexation.[75] By not annexing a concentrated and discrete housing enclave—a trailer park on its fringe, for example—a town uses underbounding to systematically disenfranchise a particular group from voting at the local level (although the right to vote in state, county, and national elections is unaffected). The large Illinois trailer park exemplifies how underbounding works to exclude a population deemed undesirable. Such a policy may represent a response of the town feeling threatened by the 1,500 residents of the park on its perimeter. Control over park residents is also exerted if a municipality has a lax legal system for the protection of their rights in cases of eviction or redevelopment of park land. Although the North Carolina parks had been annexed by the adjacent small city, one resident manager felt the city administration discriminated against her park. For example, she had to fight to make the community provide the trailer park the same trash collection services that nearby upscale subdivisions enjoyed.

Trailer parks, as a consequence of the above trends in trailer-park management and municipal policies, reflect emergent rural social divisions and/or the persistence of previous rural social inequities but in a new context. For example, mobile home parks, as the only affordable housing available in a rapidly suburbanizing area, tend to lodge the workers who occupy the service jobs that support the affluent lifestyle of second-home owners, upscale subdivision dwellers, rural tourism, or retirees. Trailer parks thus enhance income inequalities in rural places even if they are populated by new or high-end doublewides. They represent a spatial expression of the social inequalities in rural places, which define who belongs to a place and who may be excluded or seen as beneath the status of the wider community.[76]

FIGURE 3.   A sign advertises "Lots for Rent" in a land-lease park. While the availability of lots varies by region, the national shortage of mobile home sites favors the supply-side economic model that makes a mobile home park an attractive and profitable investment. Source: K. MacTavish.

A recent *Bloomberg News* article describes the surprisingly hot "asset class" that trailer parks have become for former hedge fund investors.[77] These new players in the mobile home industrial complex are drawn by the favorable supply-demand equation that the scarcity of trailer parks represents. Until 2008 most park families like those in our study, were moving up into homeownership for the first time. Since 2009, half the mobile home buyers are families moving down from conventional homeownership into a land-lease park, a scenario that reflects the middle class becoming poorer. Because the Walmart model strategy of the new investors is to upgrade the shabby parks they buy (as advised by MHU), communities may begin to look more favorably at trailer parks as a solution rather than a problem.

Trailer-Park Families' Engagement with Nearby Communities

A trailer home sited in a land-lease park is a rational purchase for a poor rural family. Uniformly our study families said they strongly preferred rural life, and a trailer park was the realistic and affordable way for them to achieve their desired living place. Ellen Adams, living in an unannexed park on the outskirts of an Illinois community, regularly felt that her upscale neighbors treated her with scorn.

> With half of Ellen's monthly income going toward housing costs, she has no savings: "We cannot even consider that. We're living paycheck to paycheck." Furnishings are a mix and match of items either bought at garage sales or handed down from Ellen's mother. Her appliances are all used. "They're from yard sales. They were junk when I got them." The family lives modestly. The small wooden deck at the front door is always tidy. A sleeping bag unzipped and stretched wide serves as both curtain and insulation for the living room window. Boxed food items, stacked high on top the kitchen cabinets, are a bulk-buy effort at keeping food costs down. A large-screen TV, purchased on her credit card, seems the only luxury.
>
> During her daily interactions in the town of Prairieview Ellen encounters disdain reserved for trailer park "free riders." But for Ellen, that her children gain access to its good schools is a worthwhile trade-off for her daily humiliation and indebtedness.

We found variation in the acceptance of trailer-park families by the adjacent community across the three sites. If a rural area undergoes upscale suburbanization, as did our Illinois site, a mobile home park is in all likelihood the chief housing accessible for a family with few financial resources who wants to live where they were born and raised. And trailer owners consider life in a land-lease trailer park preferable to the rentals available in rural areas. For poor rural families in southern New Mexico, a trailer offers better housing than, for example, a crumbling adobe dwelling. Likewise, a trailer is often better than a midwestern shabby and drafty wood-frame or an old southern tenant farmhouse—other rental housing that may be available to a rural poor family. We learned that despite the negatives associated with trailer-park life, young families like Ellen Adams's view their trailer purchase on the whole positively—even if uniformly they regard it as only temporary.

A mobile home is typically the first home the majority of the working-poor rural families have owned. They have a pent-up hunger to express through consumption their individuality and respectability—unfulfilled while they were renters. Mobile home ownership for the rural poor, therefore, represents to a certain extent the freedom to consume like others above them in the local status hierarchy.[78] Satisfaction with their sometimes poorly built trailer is rationalized by the privacy and ownership pride a stand-alone home provides, albeit one with wheels. That park management or a nearby town makes and enforces the rules that govern their most valuable asset—their home's upkeep and appearance—and their daily lives leads to frustration with time.

The hallmarks of US small-town life, idealized by the young families we met, diverge in critical ways, however, from the reality of rural trailer-park life.[79] Trailer parks uniquely shape family circumstances by hidden processes that color everyday existence for a park family: landlessness, disenfranchisement, stigmatization, ghettoization, and segregation. In the three distinctive park case studies that are the book's core, we explore how or whether these five processes produce a social and environmental context that enhances social mobility or depresses it. Of these processes, landlessness, disenfranchisement, and ghettoization are directly related to the mobile home industrial complex and to internal trailer park issues that function similarly across rural regions. But stigmatization and segregation are more a function of social choices by a rural community adjacent to a park—whether to be inclusive or exclusive—that shape the social environments families and children encounter outside the park proper and help determine whether the park where they live functions as a rural ghetto.

It is clear that mobile home parks have an expanded role to play in providing affordable housing in rural areas. The reality of how the mobile home industrial complex operates, however, keeps the housing dream that park families chase tantalizingly out of reach for all but a few. For the majority of the rural working poor whose modest assets are tied up in a mobile home sited in a rural trailer park, it means being caught in an expensive financial trap. But a mobile home purchase is also a life changer for the young rural families of modest means we studied. Despite its shortcomings—structurally and financially—families told us that trailer ownership provided them more stability as well as pride, especially if they had previously only rented housing.

The manufactured home industry has long promoted trailer parks as functional communities. Industry publications have painted trailer life in glowing terms, including testimonials from happy, satisfied residents.[80] In reality, trailer parks exemplify the intentional production of a "community" for use as an investment commodity. Community as a commodity produces built-in challenges for residents' development of the ownership, responsibility, or relationships that fundamentally underlie a socially integrated neighborhood. Thus, the sentiments of the forty-year-old Illinois park mother: "We don't feel like we belong to any community here. It's a roof over our heads and a place to live, and that's all."

MAKING ENDS MEET
Park Family Finances

Over the past few decades, the affordability of mobile homes explains how rural families of modest incomes have improved their housing and realized home-ownership. By detailing the household expenditures of North Carolina African American rural trailer-park families, we highlight the constant struggle families experience to make ends meet. Achievement of homeownership on a modest income does not provide an escape from living on the financial edge, and in some instances ownership enhances the challenge.[1]

> *Georgia Walker, a North Carolina divorced single mother thirty-nine years old and her two young daughters moved into their singlewide, now only five years old, in the Shady Grove Trailer Park. Georgia bought the trailer, furnishings, and appliances as a package deal from the park owner, who is also a mobile home dealer. She took a twenty-year loan on the entire package.*
>
> *When she bought the mobile home, Georgia was desperate to move from her rental situation in a remote rural area of the county. "I was tired with where I was living at. It was after a flood. . . . We always had rats. I thought it was below myself. I wanted to buy a house, but the bank told me that*

The detailed household financial data from North Carolina families in this chapter draws on fieldwork materials gathered by Michelle Eley, Community and Economic Development Specialist, North Carolina A&T State University.

I had to wait a year. . . . I would have qualified for a lot of housing subsidy programs [e.g. Fannie Mae] but I didn't want to wait a year." Buying a mobile home was just easier. Georgia was also looking to improve the quality of her daughters' education—a priority for her. Living in the Addington trailer park "entitles my children to go to better schools. . . . I want my girls to do better than I have done."

Georgia has a four-year college degree but is underemployed for the only job she could find. She works as a nurse assistant at a nursing home. Her annual income is $15,000, $1,250 a month. On this low salary she pays $550 a month for housing, which includes her mortgage, lot rent, and utilities. Georgia is "housing-cost–burdened" because her housing expenses consume a hefty 44 percent of her income. In addition to having fifteen more years to pay on her home loan, Georgia also is paying on a car loan. Transportation takes 20 percent of her income for gas and insurance on the car. Food to feed the family takes 6 percent of her income. She also pays for cable television and some special phone services, and the girls have a computer. She avoids credit card debt by not having any cards.

Georgia's strong attachment to a small storefront church involves a commitment to tithe, at the traditional 10 percent of her income. Thus, about 80 percent of her salary is already committed each month, leaving little to cover an unexpected emergency or need. Georgia realizes that to reach her housing dream she has to "manage my finances properly, save my money, and get my credit in order. . . . It would be nice to own my own lot. I hope I'm not staying here fifteen years from now. . . . You know, owning my mobile home without my own land doesn't do me much good."

Financial Realities Faced by Trailer-Park Families

Park families feel strapped financially, just like Georgia Walker's. Their modest incomes, debts, and housing costs together put them at risk each month. As James Baldwin famously observed, "Anyone who has ever struggled with poverty knows how extremely expensive it is to be poor."[2] Here we detail the various factors that account for park families' monthly struggle to make ends meet.

Why families choose to live in a rural trailer park is explained by the two-thirds of park residents we interviewed who identified themselves as rural people who preferred life in rural or small-town America.[3] But the decision to work and live in rural America involves specific financial costs that account for our finding that almost three-quarters (71 percent) of Illinois park residents lived in a prior mobile home, and 12 percent had traded up to their present mobile home in the same park.

Housing Costs

A household is considered housing-cost–burdened by the federal government when housing costs consume more than 30 percent of its monthly income; if housing costs are above 50 percent, a household is severely cost-burdened. Across the three land-lease park sites 89 percent of families own their trailer, and about one-third own their home outright.[4] The other two-thirds pay on a mortgage, or a contract for deed, or rent to own. And the monthly rent for a park site adds to their housing costs, as does the cost for electricity. Electricity is rarely included in the basic site rent in these all-electric trailer parks. For about one-fifth of the study families (19 percent) housing consumes 30 percent or more of their monthly income (table 2.1). This proportion of cost-burdened households exactly reflects the situation of rural manufactured homeowners nationally.[5] This close correspondence gives us confidence that the study family finances reflect the general financial situation of those who live in rural trailer-park housing.

Of the families studied in the three sites, those in Illinois were the least housing-cost–burdened because salaries are higher there (table 2.2). Study families tended not to carry the severe housing burden of more than 50 percent of income, although some did. For example, like Gladys Turner's in North Carolina, a household may temporarily take on a severe cost burden—to trade up to a larger trailer, to pay off a loan more quickly, or to relocate to a more desirable place. Full ownership of a home does not guarantee avoidance of a housing-cost burden. Among the thirty households who owned their mobile home free and clear, 41 percent were still burdened when their lot rent and utilities costs were factored in.

Once a mobile home is purchased, reality dawns for a family about the costs and obligations inherent in siting the trailer in a land-lease park. Park owners may add extra fees for children, parking, or pets—hidden costs imposed once

TABLE 2.1 Housing-cost–burdened park households

STUDY SITE	COST-BURDENED HOUSEHOLDS	PERCENTAGE OF SAMPLE
Sample total (n = 175)	33	19
Illinois (n = 66)	7	11
North Carolina (n = 53)	10	19
New Mexico (n = 56)	16	29

Data source: Survey of randomly selected sample of trailer-park households. Sixteen (of 82) households in Illinois, 23 (of 79) in New Mexico, and 12 (of 65) in North Carolina declined to provide income and/or housing costs, for a total of 51 missing cases, n = 175 of the total sample of 226 households.

Note: A household is considered cost-burdened when it spends more than 30% of income on housing costs. This table excludes utilities, which are not always included in the site rent.

TABLE 2.2   Household socioeconomic status across the three park sites

SOCIOECONOMIC STATUS	ILLINOIS (N = 82)	NORTH CAROLINA (N = 65)	NEW MEXICO (N = 79)
Highest educational attainment in household			
% less than high school graduate	6	11	20
% high school or GED[a]	44	36	43
% some college but no 4-year degree	41	45	16
% households with at least one college graduate (4-year degree)	9	8	20
Income status			
Median income[b]	$28,650	$24,500	$17,355
% households "in poverty"[c]	9	16	39
% households in "relative poverty"[d]	51	6	34
% households receiving public assistance (food stamps, Temporary Assistance to Needy Families, disability)	17	5	27
Job status			
% households with at least one "good" job[e]	54	58	47
% households not working (retired, disabled, unemployed)	11	3	26
% households of "working poor"[f]	35	3	11

Source: Survey of randomly selected sample of trailer park households.

[a]GED, or General Educational Development, is a test that if passed earns learners a high school equivalency credential. The GED Testing Service, a joint venture of the American Council on Education (ACE) and Pearson Education, is the only nationally recognized source for the GED test.

[b]Median incomes are converted to 2000 dollars to provide a standard year for comparison with the study years of Illinois, 1998–1999; New Mexico, 1999–2000; and North Carolina, 2002–2003.

[c]An income below 100% to 125% of the poverty threshold established by the federal government.

[d]Jensen and Jensen, "Poverty," define "relative poverty" as income less than 50% of the *local* family median income.

[e]Smith and Tickamyer, introduction to *Economic Restructuring*, define a "good" job as full-time, stable, year-round work with decent pay and benefits. Percentages do not include households without jobs.

[f]Brady, Fullerton, and Cross, "More Than Just Nickels and Dimes," suggest using a contextual definition for working-poor status in comparative research. We thus define as "working poor" those who work full-time but earn less than 50% of the *local* median income.

a family settles into a park and is less likely or able to move. And, as we saw in chapter 1, the lot rent is often raised annually by the owner. The Illinois park owner charged around $180 to rent a site (including water) when the study was done. More than a decade later the rent is a higher $250, which is a $70 increase. However, $180 is equivalent to $260 in 2016 dollars, which indicates that the rents have about kept up with inflation.

Rural Jobs

We found that almost all park mothers and fathers work in the formal labor market. If unemployed they consistently search for work, driven by their strong work ethic. Rural employment is described as either a "good job" or a "bad job." A good job is one that is stable and offers year-round, full-time employment, decent pay, benefits, paid vacation and sick leave, and a regular schedule or one that at least allows a worker some control over it. A bad job, in addition to being unstable, provides only seasonal or part-time employment and minimum or low wages, lacks benefits, and has an on-call schedule that varies day to day as well as week by week, with little or no worker control over it. Rural jobs are often of the bad variety.[6] Because they fall out of work periodically, bad-job trailer-park households have less predictable or reliable incomes, and as a consequence are more on edge financially. If a trailer-park household has at least one good-job holder, the family is comparatively better-off as a result of the benefits received.

Because rural economies have undergone massive transformation in the past forty years, labor demands and markets are also changing.[7] Agriculture, mining, other extractive industries, and manufacturing that formerly provided good rural jobs have all declined. Manufacturing, in particular, provided better wages for rural workers with only a high school education or less. But in a globalized economy such good jobs are increasingly scarce. As a consequence "fully three-quarters of today's rural jobs are in the service sectors."[8] Rural service-sector jobs (e.g., waitress, janitor, housekeeper, health aide) are notoriously bad jobs with low wages, even when a person is employed full-time.[9] (See tables 2.2 and 2.3.) Rural people are also often underemployed—as seasonal (e.g., in road construction or tourism

TABLE 2.3 Profile of job types held by park adults in the labor force

JOB CLASSIFICATION	ILLINOIS (N = 109 JOBS)	NORTH CAROLINA (N = 92 JOBS)	NEW MEXICO (N = 77 JOBS)
% professionals	3	3	5
% technicians	2	3	2
% sales workers	14	12	6
% administrative support workers	13	9	14
% craft workers	9	14	9
% operatives	29	11	12
% laborers and helpers	5	0	14
% service workers	26	48	38

Source: Survey of randomly selected sample of trailer-park households: New Mexico, n = 79; North Carolina, n = 65; Illinois, n = 82.

Note: Classification system: U.S. Equal Opportunity Commission, EEO-1 Job Classification Guide, which maps 2000 Census job codes and titles into the ten EEO-1 survey job categories.

services), temporary, or part-time workers. Underemployment and bad jobs mean that rural workers, even those with full-time employment, may earn less than the official poverty threshold, and certainly well below half the local median wage.[10]

Employment varies across rural America according to the presence of a dominant industry that directly provides jobs or indirectly generates jobs through associated employers. Or a rural region may be distinguished by the absence of any significant industry, such as the county of the North Carolina site. Park adults hold jobs that vary predictably according to distinct regional characteristics.[11]

Because Illinois is relatively urbanized, rural people typically can work in one of the five midsized cities that dot rural central Illinois. This area also has a diverse economy based on several large manufacturers like Caterpillar in Peoria and Mitsubishi Motors in Normal and on many small manufacturers that supply the big plants. As a transportation crossroads of major interstate highways, the region is also home to numerous trucking firms. Central Illinois park folk are able to find jobs, even change jobs readily because of the robust regional economy, although rural poverty rates even in the Midwest became more like those in urban areas over 2010–14 as a result of deindustrialization in this rural region.[12]

Eastern North Carolina is a rural region with few small cities and relatively high poverty. Even good service-sector jobs involve a substantial commute. Jobs are available in rural North Carolina but not with the abundance, diversity, or convenience of the Illinois labor market. Tourism to the Outer Banks is important to the local economy, but it is seasonal and offers largely service-sector employment. Southern New Mexico is the most rural region compared with the others, and it is a poor region that never had a manufacturing or strong agricultural base. Little employment is available outside small, locally owned businesses, a small college, or the public sector (about one-third of the workforce). When park folk find a job, almost any job in southern New Mexico, they are reluctant to look elsewhere or even consider other options.

These different regional labor markets when studied portray a distinctive profile for trailer-park adults' jobs in the formal economy.[13] (See table 2.3.) Illinois's relatively robust rural labor market means that almost 30 percent of jobs are in the "operatives" category—manufacturing and trucking—good jobs typically held by men. Illinois women's service-sector jobs are those of waitress or housekeeper. Only about one-quarter of Illinois jobs are in the service sector, compared with almost half of North Carolina jobs and near 40 percent of New Mexico jobs. In North Carolina service-sector jobs are primarily in hotel and restaurant work, because the county is a gateway to a popular tourist destination. But, unlike Illinois, these jobs, held by both men and women, also tend to be management positions, good jobs that come with benefits. In New Mexico, service-sector jobs are more likely to be low-end health care workers or hotel room cleaners—jobs without benefits. Here "administrative support workers" mainly indicates public-sector jobs. New Mexico's greater numbers of laborer and helper jobs—temporary, seasonal jobs that are also bad jobs—tend to be held by men. Women in New Mexico hold better jobs than men, particularly those that require a college degree. Few trailer-park adults (5 percent) across the three sites (table 2.2) are employed as professionals, reflecting both their modest educational levels and their rural location.

To highlight the socioeconomic status of park adults across the three sites, table 2.3 compares their job status, educational, and income levels. New Mexico has the greatest proportion of adults at both the high and low ends of the educational spectrum. One in five New Mexican households includes at least one adult with a four-year-college degree, a proportion well above that of North Carolina (8 percent) and Illinois (9 percent). That few jobs are available in southern New Mexico accounts for the lowest proportion of park households with at least one good job. The high proportion of New Mexican park adults with low education means that no household adult has either a high school diploma or a GED (an earned equivalent of the diploma). Lack of education, along with the fact that one in four households (26 percent) reports no formal job for adults, accounts for the 39 percent of New Mexico households living in actual poverty. The New Mexico poverty rate is well above that of Illinois (9 percent) and North Carolina (16 percent).

North Carolina and Illinois park adults hold proportionally more good jobs than do New Mexico adults (table 2.2). Illinois is highest in those households defined as the working poor because less education translates into lower-wage work there. Accordingly, Illinois has the highest proportion of households living in "working poverty" (35 percent), defined by working full-time but earning less than half the local median income. In North Carolina, even service-sector jobs seem to keep park households above the poverty status. Not a single North Carolina park adult holds a laborer's job, which is by definition a bad rural job (table 2.2). Only in a few cases across the three sites did a man's good job—for example, as an electrician or carpenter—mean that a woman could be full-time homemaker. And typically such couples have more than two children, making the trade-off of child-care costs versus a second income reasonable.

North Carolina and Illinois share higher education levels, with a large majority (89 percent) having a high school degree and 94 percent respectively with at least some high school or higher. Despite having similar educational attainment, Illinois households hold 4 percent fewer good jobs than those in North Carolina (table 2.2). Although the good jobs levels are comparable, more Illinois households have disabled adults, and more than one-third (35 percent) hold jobs that provide low incomes even when people work full-time. It is plausible that land-lease, trailer-park housing differentially attracts the working poor in rural Illinois and a slightly better-off population in rural North Carolina. Or it may be that central Illinois, as a consequence of a regional labor market saturated with well-educated people (multiple institutions of higher learning), represents a more challenging labor market for those with less earned education (tables 2.2 and 2.3).

Table 2.2 provides cross-site indicators for household financial stability, an important aspect of socioeconomic status. In New Mexico a significantly higher proportion of park households depend on public assistance than at the other two sites. In part, many older single men are on disability in New Mexico, but also single mothers need the extra support that food stamps offer. Rates of public assistance are lower in Illinois and much lower in North Carolina. Park folks in North Carolina, with access to more good jobs and wages that lift them above actual and relative poverty, seem less needful of federal income supports.

We use multiple terms to broadly characterize the financial status of park households—such as "working poor," "lower income," and "modest means"—to capture the nuanced financial situations of families living in similar circumstances. These terms all describe the park populations, although actual median income varies across the three sites. Illinois has the highest median household income of $39,967, and the lowest median income is that of New Mexico ($24,210), while North Carolina is in the middle at $34,178 median income (these amounts are corrected to 2016 dollar values compared to table 2.2). In reality these terms incorporate a contextual status that reflects folks working full-time but still earning less than half the *local* median income (table 2.2). The working poor in Illinois (35 percent of park households) are working poor not because they earn less than park folk in the other regions but because they earn less given where they live— where higher salaries are common. Cost of living differs for the particular county represented by each regional site and helps explain why trailer-park households hold a similar financial status despite some disparity in actual incomes.

Cost Burdens Due to Living in Rural America

Trailer-park families may be lured into believing that rural living is a better bargain than urban living. While rural housing costs are somewhat lower—at 80 percent of urban housing—other living expenses are significantly higher, reducing any rural advantage.[14] For younger families with children, the price for living in rural America includes higher costs for energy, transportation, food, and day care.

Electrical Costs

All study parks are completely electrical for the operation of home heating, lighting, and appliances. High energy costs, especially if a family owns a poorly insulated older mobile home, easily stretch a household budget during a cold

Illinois winter or a hot, humid North Carolina summer. A startling example of exorbitant rural-energy costs was found at the North Carolina site. Families paid between $200 and $300 in monthly electricity bills for a three-bedroom single-wide home of approximately 1,100 square feet. These high costs were due to the recent construction of a regional nuclear power plant and the heavy debt load of the rural utility company, which it passed along to its customers. The Addington city manager expected the excessive utility costs to decline in about ten years as the bonds were paid off for the utility company's debt load. But ten years is a long time for a family living on limited means.

Transportation Costs

Because by definition rural refers to places with low population density, park families must travel substantial distances to work, to shop, or to obtain services. In addition, the three study site counties lack public transportation, which is typical in rural places. For travel, trailer-park folk must rely on personal transport—a car or a pickup truck. If several adults work outside the home, each needs a vehicle. Car trips for rural folk average 40 percent greater in distance, compared with similar trips for urban folk.[15] That only a single Illinois park household surveyed was identified without a vehicle (aside from elderly residents unable to drive) and that a similar situation was found in the North Carolina and New Mexico parks reflects how critical a vehicle is to a rural park household's ability to sustain itself. Personal transportation is expensive, however, particularly if a vehicle is purchased used (and often needs repair), insurance is required (in all three states), or gas prices are high (another rural hazard). Driving long distances to sustain and provision a household also causes more vehicle wear and tear.

When gas prices are high, the cost of a lengthy commute to work rises to the extent that a rural park family is potentially transportation-burdened.[16] Among the North Carolina thirteen-family sample, one lacked a car as they could not afford one. The five single-parent households each owned one car, while the six households with two adults each owned two vehicles, and one owned four. Their transportation costs—including car payments, fuel, and insurance—ranged between 2 and 45 percent of household income, with an average of about 18 percent. With a slightly higher income, there is a greater likelihood that a North Carolina park family owns multiple vehicles.

Food Costs

Feeding a rural family on a limited budget is a challenge. Rural food costs are higher than those in urban places because of less competition, smaller food stores, and greater transportation or other costs incurred by suppliers.[17] Food prices in close-by small stores are therefore probably higher than in those found in the nearest larger city.[18] In New Mexico, for example, to obtain cheaper food and better selection families drive about fifty miles to the closest Walmart. Their perceived cost for the cheaper food bought there, however, tends not to factor in the gas and car costs, which in reality add some $20 to each trip, especially if the car is a gas guzzler.[19]

Given that any rural trailer-park site provides some land around the home, we asked whether a park family used it for a kitchen garden. Remarkably few households cultivate a garden to supplement their food budget, although not all park rules allow a garden. In the Illinois park many grew flowers to beautify a home site, but only a handful chose to raise a few vegetables—tomatoes the most common choice. Rules in the North Carolina parks essentially discourage gardens, although in the largest trailer park, two gardeners managed by keeping their gardens small and inconspicuous. New Mexico parks lie on dry, wind-swept places not conducive to gardening, which requires substantial water. It does seem, however, that gardening either is a lost skill or falls victim to yet another park rule that favors management convenience over residents' well-being.

Child-Care Costs

Affordable, quality child care is problematic for rural trailer-park families. For the many single-parent, female-headed households—19 percent in Illinois, 23 percent in North Carolina, and a high 30 percent in New Mexico—child care is crucial to their working. The large park in Illinois supports three licensed child-care providers, with the park owner's approval. North Carolina's largest park has one provider. But these convenient providers are unusual. Women holding low-paying or bad jobs in a dual-earner family sometimes abandon work when children are young because they earn too little to afford child care.[20]

If a park household has close relatives living nearby—a mother, grandmother, or a sister—kin babysitting is used, especially for very young children. In this distinctive, widespread rural practice, family caretakers are depended on because organized day care (center-based or certified home-based) is either unavailable or unaffordable. On the whole, a kin network offers a degree of trust and support that rural parents tend to think is superior to organized day-care centers.[21] An informal or casual reciprocity is depended on with kin even if such support allows a woman to participate in the formal labor market.[22]

Rural low-income families spend an average 9 percent of household income on child care, compared with the lower average of 8 percent paid by their urban counterparts.[23] For an employed, low-income rural mother, using organized child care for an infant or toddler may cost more than one-third of her earnings. Nationally, rural children in the year prior to starting kindergarten are underrepresented in center-based child care other than Head Start.[24] In some rural areas a free Head Start program is the only formal care available to low-income families with preschoolers. Lack of public transportation also makes access to child care outside the home challenging for a rural parent. Dispersed rural places and limited child-care resources erect unique barriers to finding quality and affordable preschooler child care for rural trailer-park families. For these same reasons, we found park children six to eleven years of age at home alone after school.

Household Income Supplements

The Informal Economy

To supplement their modest household incomes or to compensate for lack of local services, trailer-park folk, like rural people in general, depend on the informal economy. It is a livelihood strategy that augments household formal-economy salaries, rather than substitutes for them. The informal economy involves wide-ranging activities in which goods and services are exchanged for unreported cash or bartered directly for other goods and services.[25] Families regularly draw on informal economy providers—in their park, among kin or friends—to obtain such services as child care, auto and home repairs, home painting, yard work, or haircuts.[26] But if trailer-park folk fall on hard times, the informal economy may be relied on as an alternative income strategy for getting through a lean period.

Rural men growing up on a farm or in remote areas learn a variety of repair, construction, or mechanical skills. Families rely on the informal economy to maintain their older trailers or to renovate a shabby trailer bought used. Kin, friends, or neighbors do home repairs such as roof or floor installation and window or door replacement. Older cars under repair are a frequent sight on trailer-park streets. Park women work in the informal economy as a child care providers, housecleaners, hairdressers, seamstresses, or cooks. In fact, rural households with skills or resources to barter are more often those involved in the informal economy.[27] People may also self-provision by cultivating a small kitchen garden, but only rarely. At times the line between self-provisioning and recreation is blurred, as when neighbors hold a joint yard sale or men fish or hunt together. In the North Carolina Shady Grove trailer park, a river running behind it was regularly frequented by park men for fishing.

The Kin Network

As a way of life, trailer-park families, like other blue-collar or poor families, are deeply embedded in networks of kin, neighbors, or friends.[28] A large kin group living nearby provides potential resources that serve as both social and financial safety nets. The less well-off a household, the more likely it is to depend on its kin network.[29] When one household receives a windfall (e.g., money, food, or goods), it is shared, gifted, or loaned among network members.[30] In addition, a reliance on the kin group may be critical for life crises such as illness, death, military service, incarceration, or migration. "What goes around comes around" describes a pattern of indirect reciprocity that exchanges givers and takers over the course of a lifetime.[31] North Carolina park families, in particular, are distinguished by large sibling networks with rich resources exchanged. A trailer-park household without kin nearby appears isolated and vulnerable.

The kin network and the informal economy are both critical to trailer-park families' ability to get by. Each is used to piece together sufficient funds to support the household in an enhanced daily life and in emergencies or, if need be, to substitute for a formal-economy job.

North Carolina Trailer-Park African Americans' Household Economics

Park families say they live paycheck to paycheck and regularly have little to tide them over until the next payday.[32] Almost all are stretched thin by the burden of their high housing costs and other debts. We found two income-management styles despite financial overcommitment: those who manage by using cautious budgeting and those who make reckless choices that perpetuate their fragile situation. What helps the thirteen North Carolina black families make ends meet each month is rich support from their kin or church networks. Without these supports, some of these families would face greater financial vulnerability.

While we describe detailed financial information from thirteen North Carolina families, their household finances highlight what we observed across the three sites for park families struggling to make ends meet.

Typology of Household Financial Status

Two-thirds of the sixty-five North Carolina households surveyed identified themselves as lower-middle or middle-income. Despite the reality of their modest incomes, the perception of class status is fundamentally connected to their achievement of mobile homeownership. In addition, their belief that they will eventually ascend the housing-tenure ladder is associated with their holding good jobs.[33] One homeowner of two years (who bought a repossessed mobile home at a bargain price) holds a modest job as a hotel housekeeper but considers herself middle-class: "I found a better living status when I selected this home. I got more room. It's luxury. I've got a Jacuzzi. I've got a master bedroom."

We illustrate the range of financial circumstances of the thirteen African American families by classifying them based on their income, housing debt, and employment status. The two lower-income groups together include five families. Better off, although of modest income, are the eight families in the two higher-income groups.

The Poorest or Impoverished Group

Two households fall into this group. Alberta Reynolds is a single mother with one child and unemployed during part of the year. The three-member Wilson household has two unemployed adults, who are raising a grandchild. Because of his poor health, Mr. Wilson is on SSI (federal Supplemental Security Income/Disability). Mrs. Wilson can work only sporadically as a housekeeper because of caring for her husband. Annual income is $12,000 and $16,000, respectively, for these two households. Each household lives in a singlewide home bought used. Ms. Reynolds is purchasing her home with a lease-to-own arrangement.

The Working-Poor Group

The working-poor group has three households. Two are single-female–headed households, each with two children, one of which is Ms. T. The third household, the Bankstons, has two parents and two children. This group's annual incomes hover slightly above the poverty threshold, at $15,000 to $21,000 annually. They are termed the working poor because all the adults work full-time, year-round but maintain incomes only slightly above the poverty line (i.e., between 100 and 125 percent of the poverty threshold established by the federal government). They work hard to get ahead, play by the rules, but struggle to make ends meet. Each family lives in a singlewide home, two of which were bought used. One singlewide home was purchased new by Georgia Walker, a single mother of two.

The Low-Income Group

The low-income group includes four households.[34] Two households have two earners, one with two children and the other with one child. The remaining two households are headed by single mothers, one with two children and the other with one. Their modest annual incomes range between $24,000 and $36,000 but still fall below 200 percent of the poverty threshold. Two households live in a singlewide bought new; the other two households purchased used singlewides.

The High Low-Income Group

The high low-income group has four park households. The Henry and Roberts households each have two working adults earning combined annual incomes ranging between $43,000 and $63,000. The Robertses have one child and the Henrys have two. The Donner household has two parents with two children, and the remaining household has two parents and one child. All four households live in a mobile home bought new: two are singlewides and two are doublewides.

The typology is also representative of the income range and household financial arrangements found in both the Illinois and New Mexico trailer parks. That is, we believe the typology describes income patterns found generally in rural, land-lease trailer parks where families own their trailer homes. In addition to income, other household factors account for the families' position in the typology.

Factors Accounting for Household Finances

Education

Most adults in the thirteen families are high school graduates, while three-quarters have some college education, including a single female who heads a household in both the poorest and the working-poor groups. These two female breadwinners are both underemployed. The single mother in the poorest group has three years of college (laid off for part of our study because of a national chain-store closing). Georgia Walker, the single mother in the low-income group, has a four-year college degree. In contrast, the Bankstons, the working-poor couple, both hold good jobs with benefits, although they are only high school graduates with some college years earned. Thus, higher-income or good jobs, especially for a woman, do not necessarily equate with greater investment in education. The challenge of finding a rural job—even a job for which one is overqualified—explains the work status of these underemployed single mothers with higher education.

An interesting educational pattern for two-parent households typifies the two higher income groups. One household in the working-poor group and in all four two-parent households in the high low-income group, including the Henrys, have women with more education than the men, who are not even high school graduates. But these men hold good craftsman jobs in construction or carpentry, and one is a custodian. Because the five men have a marketable skill, they obtained good jobs. Their better-educated wives work in management—one, Cora Roberts, is a self-employed beauty salon owner.

Jobs with Benefits

Eleven of the thirteen households are supported by at least one adult who holds a job with medical benefits, even if that person earns low wages. In the working-poor, low-income, and high low-income groups, four families have one adult with a good job (three wives, one husband), and five households have two adults with good jobs that carry some medical coverage. Of the two poorest households, the unemployed female-headed household of two is covered on her husband's military insurance because, although the couple is separated, they are not divorced. The Wilson household, the other poorest family, has a disabled breadwinner, who is on Medicaid. (Before he was disabled, his skilled job lacked medical benefits.) Only two of the thirteen families, one each from the low-income and the high-low income groups, hold jobs without medical benefits (prior to passage of the federal 2010 Affordable Care Act). Of the households with medical benefits, fewer also have dental insurance (six of eleven) or are covered for long-term disability (only three). Eight of the nine good-job households (excluding the unemployed woman on her separated husband's plan) with medical coverage also have a retirement plan. Thus, most but not all of the families have at least one good job that carries some medical and some retirement benefits.

Debt Load Carried

The thirteen families across the board carry housing debt except for the Henry family in the high low-income category, who bought their new singlewide with a ten-year loan and readily paid it off. The poorest two households with incomes below the poverty level, despite their buying a used singlewide, nonetheless are severely housing-cost–burdened. Housing takes 85 and 55 percent of their respective monthly incomes. In the working-poor category, although the families employed different home-purchasing strategies—one traded up to buy a used singlewide and Georgia Walker bought a new singlewide—both carry the same high housing-cost burden of 44 percent of their modest monthly incomes. An even higher 61 percent housing-cost burden is carried by another single mother, Ms. T., who bought a used singlewide with a six-month, short-term contract, which heavily taxes her modest income. Thus, all three working-poor households are severely housing-cost–burdened, and Georgia Walker, the single mother with fifteen years remaining on her twenty-year loan on her new, fully furnished sin-glewide, will remain so burdened for a long time.

Contract-for-deed agreements were used to buy several of the used trailers. The single mother in the poorest group had a month-by-month rent-to-own agreement with a mobile home dealer. The working-poor householder, Ms. T., had a contract-for-deed with the previous owner, with terms that required she pay-off her home in six months. It may be that since the post-1990s crash of the mobile home financial market, the change to tighter mortgage rules makes con-tract sales more accessible than a chattel loan for these single-parent households of limited means.

A single family in each of the working-poor, low-income, and high low-income groups is locked into a thirty-year chattel loan for a manufactured home purchased new. It is an expensive decision over the long term, although the loan made the home purchase possible for a family with little or no cash for a down payment (chapter 1). In the low-income group, a couple purchased a new single-wide with a thirty-year term loan and gained a housing burden of 30 percent. A high low-income couple bought a new doublewide with a thirty-year loan, but their housing-cost burden is only 15 percent since both hold good jobs.

Monthly loan payments for the thirteen households range between 3 and 50 percent of total housing costs. When utilities are included, however, the actual income proportion of housing costs ranges from 8 to 85 percent, with the high utility costs in the North Carolina site. Of the five housing cost-burdened house-holds, three are headed by single mothers, whose income differentially must go toward housing. The poorest-category Wilson family coping with a disabled pri-mary breadwinner and little income is at 55 percent housing-cost–burdened. The remaining cost-burdened household from the working-poor group upgraded to a newer mobile home, making the choice to be cost-burdened at 44 percent for only three years, but as a two-income family, they are more able to handle it.

Trailer-park families learn to cope with limited financial resources, but some families manage financial security better than others. These differences are clear when we examine household choices with discretionary income that remains after monthly housing, transportation, and food expenses are paid.

Consumption Choices and Cost Burdens

To an outsider, park families seem to struggle, living from paycheck to paycheck. In addition to their housing costs most carry credit card or car loan debts. They tend not to view such circumstances as perilous, for they are accustomed to being stretched financially.

Trailer-park households who earn modest incomes even with good jobs reflect the recent national rise in debt load among those living at the margins. In addition to the high-interest chattel loans on a trailer, families may also buy a car with a chattel loan, which causes them to slip into "a cycle of debt" that keeps them more deeply in debt than those at a higher income level in the nation.[35] Amassing credit card debt along with car and housing debt characterizes those who can least afford it. But credit is used to enhance their lives and perhaps bring the illusion of social mobility.

Like other Americans, trailer-park families are avid consumers; consumption, after all, is central to the American Dream.[36] Two of the thirteen households admitted that to improve their credit histories, they once had to consolidate their debts. Only one household practices frugal household management. Odette Henry (high low-income group) explains, "If we get something, I don't use credit. I could, but I don't want to. I want to find new furniture for the bedroom and we need new carpet. But I don't want to pay monthly payments." Credit debt, she realizes, would threaten the family's financial stability. The other eleven households (Georgia Walker has no credit cards, nor have the Wilsons) carry over credit card debt monthly and consequently are saddled with penalties and interest charges of as much as 12 percent. Ten households pay monthly debt obligations not only on credit cards but on the penalty payments for the carryover balance. Most (eight of thirteen) also pay on at least one car loan. Only a few seem to manage credit card usage well; for example, one low-income group woman with three credit cards carries a balance on only one. Families citing credit card and other debt are not those cost-burdened, however. The five families classified as housing-cost–burdened have no credit card debt. Of the three study sites, avid consumption is less true for New Mexico families, where incomes are the lowest and the local economy is marginal.

The poorer the household, the less debt it is able to accrue. The poorest and working-poor groups' five families do not use credit cards. Yet they hold other debts, such as a car loan. Ms. T., a single mother from the working-poor group, says, "I usually work extra hours at work to deal with money emergencies." For unexpected expenses, the other working-poor group single mother, Georgia Walker, reports she must juggle loan payments for her car and home: "I haven't learned to budget. I rob Peter trying to pay Paul. If something comes up, I postpone a payment of one to pay the other. In a real emergency, I can depend on my father or my sister to support me." Ironically, among the five households in the two poorest groups, we found greater generosity. For example, three families including Georgia Walker's are active church members who pay a church tithe, which customarily represents 10 percent of household income. Among the eight families of the two higher-income groups, only one from each group pays a church tithe, despite attending a church. One explanation for the six households' reluctance to tithe is in all likelihood their use of multiple credit cards (between three and five) and a propensity for accumulating debt on each, which takes all their disposable income. Or alternatively, these households prefer to spend their modest incomes on themselves.

A low level of savings is typical for the thirteen families, with the exception of the high low-income Henry family, who allocate half their monthly budget to savings. Their singlewide home bought new is owned in full, and they are saving for a conventional house with land—a goal close to being achieved. Odette, from this blended family of five, learned through past experience of the downside to credit card debt:

> I like for my money to be accounted for . . . to the last penny. See, before when I used to work, I used to spend my money on clothes every week when I got paid. But that was before we were trying to buy a house. Now, I like to put my money in the bank and I just take out enough for what I need for the week.
>
> I try to work on the weekend—on Saturdays and some Sundays. . . . I work down at the beach at a time-share condo. My father and mother work as housekeeper supervisors there. . . . As a housekeeper, I can make the same amount of money in two days as I make in a forty-hour work-week. . . . I used to work as a cashier at Walmart so I know basically know how much you can clock in during the week.

All thirteen families lived as a household before moving into the trailer park. Thus they did not furnish their present trailer completely from scratch. Four families used furniture from a prior residence or found used pieces and are on the whole less indebted. A single mother of this group recounts how she furnished her present living room: "My mother had furniture that she was not using. She's got a room in her house that is like a living room, but no one ever sits there because there is so much stuff. . . . I got some [other] furniture from her brother. . . . I'm truly a blessed individual. I don't have to go through what other people have to go through."

Furnishing a new or used trailer is a common debt incurred, however. Six of the thirteen families own new matching living room and/or dining room furniture sets, bought when they moved into their trailers. While half the families quickly paid off the furniture sets purchased on credit, two high low-income households purchased a package deal—a new, fully furnished mobile home. Georgia Walker from the working poor group used such a deal and took on a twenty-year housing loan to pay for it. Two other households are also in debt for their furniture, having bought it on credit. One man explains, "We had some furniture when we moved in here, but we waited about a year before we . . . got new furniture all throughout the house. We are still making payments on the furniture." Furniture debt, added to a high interest for a chattel home loan, however, is a bad bargain for a park family.

Beyond the basic necessities of shelter, food, transportation, or tithing, families sometimes make expensive choices with leftover discretionary funds. They spend their modest monthly resources on expenses, like eating out, cable/satellite TV, or special phone services (e.g., caller ID, call waiting).[37] Most of the thirteen families own one or more of these "luxury" items, which also represent their recreation. Slightly over half the families own a computer, which requires Internet service. Despite their modest means, they want their children to experience the digital world. But all these choices strain their modest household finances.

Excepting the one frugal household, the Henrys, the other twelve park families carry substantial debt, in addition to a home loan, and have no savings. Those burdened with a high level of debt have few assets to leverage if confronted by a financial crisis. The two poorest families provide examples of the financial peril faced when an unforeseen crisis occurs. The single mother who lost a good management job (when a chain store closed), and the main breadwinner in the Wilsons' household, was forced permanently onto disability by a serious health issue. Alberta Reynolds has little family backup—her parents are dead. Her housing burden for the contract sale she took on, utilities, and lot rent takes $850 of her monthly income of $1,000. The Wilsons have a monthly housing burden of 55 percent of their income—a somewhat better situation because they do not own a car. The Wilsons belong to a church that has provided them with generous, substantive support. But given that these poorest households must meet their monthly debt costs and other housing costs, both are perilously close to homelessness.[38]

While the thirteen North Carolina park families are proud of their mobile home ownership, their debts trap them in a home that falls short of their housing dream. Two of the thirteen families traded up in the same park as the only pathway they saw to obtain better housing. Nor for the thirteen is their homeownership the foundation for financial security. Mobile homeownership's financial peril for families raises questions about a core US value, especially relevant since the 2008 national conventional housing–triggered recession—whether everyone is better off as a homeowner. The Nobel laureate economist Paul Krugman, for example, sees a downside to homeownership—the risk, debt, immobility, and high commuting costs that characterize rural park households—as not being worthwhile for low-income families. He sees their being tied up with a twenty- or thirty-year chattel loan on a home that quickly loses its value as risky and tying down this population. Would not renting be a better option for this population?

economists ask.[39] Economists, of course, ignore the critical symbolic value of pride and respect that homeownership holds for our trailer-park families of modest incomes.

In part II the voices of trailer-park residents—in the Illinois, North Carolina, and New Mexico park case studies—show the meaning, the value, and the reality for trailer-homeownership and life in a trailer park Although each field study followed the same research procedures, we highlight diversity across the three sites. Each site of trailer-park homeowners follows its own American housing dream for a stick home on owned land, in the context of its cultural ideals for what a better life entails.

Part 2

CHASING A HOUSING DREAM ACROSS THREE RURAL REGIONS

THE ILLINOIS PARK
Closer to Middle Class

Prairieview Manor residents differ from North Carolina and New Mexico trailer-park residents by their tendency to measure themselves with residents of the adjacent town of Prairieview, which over the course of forty years was transformed from a farm town by the development of upscale subdivisions.[1] Many, although not all, park folk strive to emulate their wealthier neighbors. Homeownership and education are values park folk share with the "subdivision people." But their efforts are scorned, they believe, by the townspeople, who stigmatize them as trailer trash because of where they live. The town views the trailer park as the bottom of the social order, while park families, as homeowners, consider themselves above the bottom—occupied by renters or those in subsidized housing. Said a park man, "What kills me is—it's not where you live, it's who you are." A mother related, "The mobile home park itself—that's not a good thing for us. A lot of people . . . [say] if you excuse my French, we're trailer trash. We don't like the fact that the kids have to deal with that, but we do our best." A widow in her sixties says she's made peace with living in the park: "At the beginning there were remarks . . . but you get over it. I used to think that this was a second-class neighborhood. But I know that I'm as good as anyone else."

Prairieview Manor Trailer Park

Prairieview Manor was called "the Cadillac of Illinois parks" by an Illinois Manufactured Housing Association board member.[2] A thirty-acre land-lease park, it houses some 1,500 residents—a population that makes it larger than many Illinois small towns. Of the park homes 62 percent are singlewides and

TABLE 3.1   Residential status of Illinois park households

RESIDENTIAL STATUS	PERCENTAGE
Ownership	
Own home in full	38
Own home, making mortgage payments	48
Buying on contract sales	11
Renting home	3
Tenure	
Previously lived in a mobile home	73
Define home as "permanent"	48
Prefer rural or small-town living	82
Structure	
Singlewide	62
Doublewide	38
New	46

Source: Survey of randomly selected sample of trailer-park households (n = 82).

38 percent are doublewides (including two modular homes) (table 3.1). Unlike Prairieview's upscale subdivisions built on cul-de-sacs radiating from the older downtown, distinctively the trailer park's streets follow the rectangular grid, originally platted in the nineteenth century. Corn and soybean fields surround the trailer park on three sides, with a busy road on the fourth side.[3]

Joe, as he is known to all, developed the Prairieview Manor trailer park in the 1970s, outside the town of Prairieview on some of his family's farmland. He began the park with about two hundred sites but eventually expanded to the current six hundred-unit capacity. It is a large size for rural Illinois, where trailer parks are relatively uncommon. Joe Johnson is also a mobile home dealer. When a family buys a new home from him, he throws in a year's free lot rent. He calls himself a "hands-on developer."

Four factors account for the appraisal of Prairieview Manor as a Cadillac trailer park, and Joe cites them in marketing it. First, the large lot size of eighty by one hundred feet and the rental of $180 month are bargains relative to the national average rental of $230 month for a typically smaller lot. By 2016 the lot rent became a higher $250, which roughly kept up with inflation (chapter 2). A woman who chose the park as a compromise location between her and her husband's jobs remarks, "This is a nice park. It's clean and quiet, and the lots are spacious."

Second, park amenities, while modest, are more generous than those provided in any other park we saw. Monthly rent includes a concrete pad, the required trailer tie-downs, utility hookups, a paved driveway, a streetlight, and a small front yard. In addition, Joe promotes the ball field (used by the Little League),

FIGURE 4. With homes arranged on long, straight streets, better trailer parks offer amenities like paved driveways and streetlights. Source: K. MacTavish.

a playground with swings, tennis courts, a basketball court, and a small swimming pool. All park streets are paved. Large mature trees stand throughout the park and shade every unit. A cement-block building standing at the park entrance houses the management office, a mailroom, a coin-operated laundry, and a meeting room available for rental, but where Scouts and Brownies meet for free. The soda-pop machine out front is heavily used by park children and adults.

Third, Prairieview Manor is as close to country living as the rural working poor can afford. Over three-quarters of park adults say they prefer rural or small-town life. "It feels like country out here. I like that. It's not like a busy city at all," commented a young woman. "Both my husband and I want a lot of land so it'd be quiet—not a lot of people or hustle and bustle," said another woman. Most residents work in nearby central Illinois cities with no public transportation available. But for these self-identified rural people, a work commute of fifteen minutes or more is a worthwhile trade-off for living in an affordable place with a small-town feel.[4]

Fourth, and most important to younger families, is that living in the trailer park gives their children access to quality schools. "That's why we live here, because I want my kids to go to Prairieview schools," explained a park mother about her choice. Prairieview Manor's parents value a good education as much as do their upscale subdivision neighbors.

Park amenities as advertised, however, disappoint tenants. They grumble that except for the pool, the recreational facilities suffer from neglect. A single mother and two-year resident disparages the common areas: "The tennis courts and basketball courts they talk about, well they're filled with [broken] glass. The swing sets are down. It's bad there." Explained another mother about her disenchantment, "When we moved in we were told about the pool and playground, snow and trash removal, and the clubhouse. . . . But things didn't turn out to be as nice as that. I don't think I've [ever] seen a snowplow. . . . Everyone drops their kids off at the pool, no matter how old, and leaves them there. . . . I can't leave my kids there. I would never use the clubhouse for a party. . . . It looks just like what you'd expect at a trailer park." Joe claims that he constantly repairs the recreational facilities but that park teenagers vandalize them. Residents counter that only the pop machine always works. "Well, he makes money off the pop machine. He doesn't make any money off the swings," cynically commented a mother of two.

Joe's constant presence means Prairieview Manor does not suffer from neglect, although residents readily relate a host of complaints about the management. A retired resident thinks Joe views himself as a "tough but fair" manager but in reality acts as "a lord would run a serfdom . . . the park is his little fiefdom . . . If he doesn't like you, he'll tell you to leave. Groused another, "You don't have any rights here except to pay the rent. . . . That owner is something else. He didn't get rich being nice to people." Both Joe and the residents know that given the expense for moving a mobile home, all they can do is gripe.

Park Owner's Management Practices

Joe has management rules that attract people to his trailer park. A liberal pet policy is a draw—44 percent of park households (possibly more, although we did not systematically count pets) have a least one pet, most commonly a dog. Among the sixteen families we knew best, over half own one pet, including cats and dogs, rabbits, tropical birds, turtles, guinea pigs, and an iguana. One singlewide home of a family of five is crowded with four cats. If neighbors complain about a particularly aggressive dog, however, owners must get rid of it or move. Illinois park families bear considerable expense for pets, given their modest incomes (see table 3.2).[5]

TABLE 3.2   Population traits of Illinois trailer park and town

TRAIT	TRAILER PARK	PRAIRIEVIEW
Ethnicity		
% households white	98	98
Age		
Median age	25 years	34 years
% householders 65 years and over	12	14
Household type		
% family households	58	83
(% female-headed, no husband present)	(19)	(9)
Average household size	3.07	2.95
Income		
Median household income	$28,650	$57,574
(in 2016 dollars)	($39,967)	—
% below poverty	9	4
% reporting public assistance	17	<1
Educational attainment, all adults[a]		
% less than high school	13	3
% high school graduate (includes equivalency)	53	23
% some college or associate's degree	30	36
% bachelor's degree or higher	4	37
Occupancy and tenure		
% owner-occupied	97	82
% renter-occupied	1	18
% in home for 1 year or less	32	22
% same home 5 years prior	37	46

Source: Trailer-park data come from the survey of a randomly selected sample of trailer-park households (n = 82); town data from U.S. Census Bureau, "DP-1 Profile of General Demographic Characteristics: 2000"; "DP-2 Profile of Selected Social Characteristics: 2000"; "DP-3 Profile of Selected Economic Characteristics: 2000"; and "QT-P20 Educational Attainment by Sex: 2000."

[a]Educational attainment data for the park sample include all adults 25 years of age and over. Similarly, U.S. Census data include adults 25 and over only.

Joe is flexible about tenants' landscaping a home site. An older, longtime resident chose Prairieview Manor because she likes to garden: "It's the only mobile home park I've run across that . . . allows you to landscape your yard. And that was a huge selling point. . . . During the height of the flower season . . . it's literally like living in a park."

Joe is also liberal about tenants' operating a full-time or side business out of their trailers. His office maintains a list of residents who provide household services along with a bulletin board holding cards that advertise who offers painting, mowing, or home repair work. He considers it an asset that three park women are licensed home day-care providers. Yard sales are also permitted. Only auto repair as a business is discouraged.

Prairieview Manor residents uniformly agree that "as trailer parks go, this is one of the better ones." Over three-quarters of households (82 percent) say the trailer park provides satisfaction for their hard-earned money. But residents still object to certain of Joe's business practices, such as raising lot rents almost annually (during the study's two years, rents increased $20 from $160 per month) without explanation.[6] In this regard the park owner is simply following the advice advocated by park investors (chapter 1). Tenants also report that Joe is "quick to tack on extra costs," such as $10 for a large dog, or $2 per child for a season's park-pool tag. If a family hits a rough financial patch and is behind on rent, children are publicly punished by being denied pool privileges.

As a mobile home dealer, Joe encourages families to upgrade to a new, larger doublewide. Some 12 percent of park households had used their previously owned mobile home to trade up. The remaining one-third purchased a new or a used singlewide either from Joe directly or from a family trading up to a better unit. Over one-third (38 percent) of households fully own their homes (table 3.1). Almost half (48 percent) have a monthly mortgage payment; a few carry expensive thirty-year term loans. A minority (11 percent) are de facto renters (buying on contract sale) through informal arrangements between an owner and the tenant. All households are responsible for the monthly site rental, water, and electrical service.

Residents' Complaints and Concerns

Because tornadoes are frequent in Illinois, many Prairieview Manor residents have safety (44 percent) or weather (24 percent) anxieties. One middle-aged woman says, "I just worry the whole place will blow away." But Joe said all trailers are tied down, according to Illinois state law. The park by Illinois law must provide a tornado shelter—the pool's cement block recreation building is supposed to be it. Yet a mother of three said, "When we moved in we were told in case of tornado to go there. . . . Whenever there's been a tornado I load the kids up and drive over there. But there's no way to get in." The building is kept locked.

Everyone complains about the park's water system, which is owned by Joe. Despite an annual quality inspection by the Illinois Department of Public Health, people say the water tastes bad and that its color stains their laundry. If a rent payment is missed, management turns off the water within five days and charges $25 to turn it back on, plus what is owed. Another concern is too few fire hydrants for the park's large size. "There are only two. . . . And that whole area to the north—they shut those off years ago and never turned them back on," complained a couple. The husband remarked how the owner cuts corners on park operations and county officials ignore it because "he's in cahoots."

Residents also grumble about mud problems—without a park drainage system, water from rain or snow has nowhere to go and lingers for a long while. Finally, management posts speed signs, but these are largely ignored and never enforced, say residents. Speeding on park streets and mud, however, are actually complaints we heard in all the trailer parks.

Life in Prairieview Manor does not always live up to the small-town idyll pitched to entice prospective tenants—of a peaceful, quiet rural lifestyle with all the conveniences and advantages of city life. Things were better, old-timers say, when the park opened forty years earlier, and both Joe and Craig Warrington, another mobile home dealer, and their young families lived there. Craig organized park-wide activities, including a monthly newsletter, a "House of the Month" prize of a month's free lot rent, Fourth of July park parades, activities at the poolside recreational center, and a Neighborhood Watch system. These made the park feel more like a community. Now, explained a widow and long-time resident, "People just come and go. They aren't real neighbors. . . . People don't want to be involved with each other. . . . Thirty years ago people were warm and friendly. Now people don't want to bother."

Families with children, despite their pride in achieving homeownership and on the whole being satisfied with the park, harbor feelings about being cheated by Joe and his management team. These younger families, however, tend to consider the park a temporary address and hope to move on in five years (52 percent) to a stick house on its own land, out in the country. In contrast, over three-quarters of the older, retired, or the poorest homeowners over fifty-five years of age say Prairieview Manor is their permanent address. They are less negative about the park.[7] (See table 3.1.)

Park Life

Park streets vary in vitality by the season. Frigid prairie winds howl down the streets in winter, and quiet descends. Few adults or children venture outside for long. "Once it starts to get warm and everybody is outside again, we'll meet [new neighbors]. It's hard in the winter to meet people, but once summer comes I'm sure we will," commented a couple. After being cooped up indoors all winter in tight quarters, everyone's mood improves with spring. The warm weather brings families outside for picnics, car repairs, and walks. Children ride bikes, play basketball, or skateboard in driveways, yards, or the streets. With windows and doors opened to catch a breeze, the sound of televisions is pervasive. It is the background music of park life.[8]

Except for the thundering traffic from the highway alongside the park, early evening summer sounds resemble those of any neighborhood: girls giggle, basketballs thump, dogs bark, and a lawn mower hums. On a home's back deck adults sit watching kids jump on a trampoline while a radio blares. In front of a trailer several children use chalk to color the walkway, while others ride small bikes. A group of Little Leaguers dressed in blue and white uniforms gather in a backyard and toss a ball back and forth before they head to town for a game. A family sits outside their trailer enjoying a dinner of hamburgers; the adults gather around a table on the deck, the kids at a table in the yard. Commonly a family car or truck parked in the driveway has a man working under its raised hood. The park at these times feels like a neighborhood with a small-town ambience but with a greater density of homes.

FIGURE 5. Even older, modest trailers often include a small planting of flowers. Sheds aid in keeping a neat appearance by providing storage for bicycles, a lawn mower, tools, and other household items. Source: Image taken by a park youth.

Park families are house-proud, as is signified by the well-maintained exteriors of most trailers. Owners readily boast about their home improvements, like replaced windows, doors, furnace, toilets, roofs, or floors. Yards around most homes are landscaped with shrubbery and flowers, and lawns are neatly trimmed. Some are embellished with yard ornaments like a pig, a kerchiefed goose, or a miniature windmill.[9] Few cultivate fruit trees or vegetable gardens that could supplement a food budget. Only a small minority of trailers have yards littered with the clutter of overflowing garbage bags, used diapers, broken toys, squashed beer cans, or cigarette butts—emblematic of trailer-trash stereotypes.

A common grumble is that children often cross through carefully tended yards, trampling the grass or flowers. The park has a 10:00 p.m. evening curfew for youth to be off park streets and the same rule for quiet time, when noisy music or activities are supposed to be hushed. Older residents think both rules are honored only in the breach and are rarely enforced by management. "People out here like to play their stereos too loud, past curfew time. You can't get nothin' done [about it]. You call the county.... [but] they're not getting through to those people," said a disgruntled man whose complaints were echoed by others. He continued, "The park owner, all he wants to do is collect the money from the park.... They make the park rules, but they don't enforce them."

A husband recalled how his wife served as a lifeguard at the well-used park pool but quit. She tired of the "riffraff"—youth using profanity and "out-of-control." Such behavior he felt was inappropriate for this better park.[10] Residents say the park needs a place for teens to gather. But for various reasons, although the park is the size of a small town, residents cannot or do not mobilize to make a teen gathering space happen.[11]

Prairieview Manor's layout, with trailers parked closely parallel to one another, actually approximates urban density when compared with the spatial openness of midwestern small towns' home lots and public spaces.[12] One man philosophically blames this density as a source of the park's social problems: "Some people in town look down on us out here. They say this is where all the trouble in town is. But I always say that if you took other neighborhoods and squashed them together . . . as close together as you have in the park—then you would have just as much trouble."

A Vietnam vet who rated his neighborhood as "somewhat undesirable" complained about the crowded conditions, noisy children, and loud music: "[It's] the only place in the county that you'll find slums . . . rural slums." A woman derisively called the park a "tin jungle." A young father bemoaned the lack of privacy in the park: "Hell, all you have to do is sit on the porch to know what's going on. Voices just echo off all this aluminum. You can hear a conversation three streets down. And people just thrive on all the scuttlebutt." Again, these are the common grievances heard in small towns, where residents know everything about everybody. [13]

A Sense of Community?

Though the large trailer park may superficially resemble a midwestern small town, it comes up short for the factors that are crucial in providing a sense of community. Despite its large size, for example, the park lacks requisite public spaces for the informal gatherings essential to being a real community—shops, a coffee shop, hair salon, or barber shop.[14] Park people do improvise public gathering spaces. Mothers and children sit around the park pool chatting on hot summer evenings. Teenagers hang out in the street in front of a friend's home, at the basketball court, or around the park office pop machine. Remarked one teenage girl about her favorite place, "I go to the pop machine and then like two hours later I finally come home, and my mom says, 'You met someone and was talking, didn't you?'"

Because it is only forty years old and its residents are somewhat transient, however, the place lacks a shared history. Yet some subtle indicators of community are seen. Three third-grade girls were seen taping signs around the park and at a pickup store's pay phone (just outside the park) to advertise a show they planned for the next week and expected neighbors to attend. A grandfatherly man says that kids in his neighborhood know they can turn to him and his wife for help when needed. His wife gives an example of their helping two small children caught in a rainstorm and locked out of the house. She took them in, dried them off, fed them, and then called their mother. They believe supportive networks do exist in the park. "Those little kids . . . I think most of them know who says 'hi' and where can I go 'cause I need help,'" explained the man.

This large trailer park is experienced mainly through residents' immediate neighborhood—typically one's own street and the adjacent streets. A distinctive "grapevine" pattern for how gossip travels results from the rectangular streets with trailers sited hitch end to the street in parallel rows: "The neighborhoods are streets and there are no back-fence neighbors. . . . Word travels up and down, but not back and forth," explained a woman.[15] "Everybody minds one another's business . . . everybody on the block knows what's going on with everyone else. And there are drugs and trouble on this street. . . . When the police come, everybody asks, 'What's going on?'" A mother remarked, "It's the kids who really know what happens in the park. . . . I have two kids in school and they find out everything that goes on through the school." Households with children also know their neighbors better. "My kids [girls seven and eight] had friends here before we even got the truck backed up," commented one father about their move-in.

Common gossip highlights that all park residents do not necessarily share common behavioral standards. Some gossip is indicative of residents' trying to enforce more middle-class norms. Adults often gripe about nosy neighbors.[16] A grandfather and twenty-five-year resident says the park rumor mill works remarkably well: "I used to go to the park office and ask the manager what the latest rumors are about me." A woman and her twenty-year-old daughter, who dress in black Goth style, complain of the nasty gossip about them. "People say we're witches," which causes small children to run past their trailer holding their breath out of fear. A fifteen-year-old youth related his group's gossip about park neighborhoods: "We always say that the other end of the park is the bad area and the other end says this end is bad."

A final indicator of community is that neighbors discipline one another's kids and readily report bad behavior to the offenders' parents. For example, a mother whose family is having a picnic hauls out two neighbor boys throwing rocks at them from under the hedge separating the two homes. She yells at her daughters, who quickly come to watch: "Get back over there and eat your dinner. I'll handle this." After she finishes scolding the boys, she grabs them and makes her way to their home. She knocks and explains to their father about her disturbed dinner. Their dad motions for the boys to come inside. The girls sing out, "Somebody's gonna get busted!" All behave as if these are normal occurrences. In another instance, a third-grader appears at the park pool with her hair cut very short. "Head lice," announces her little sister. "Now you don't need to be telling personal information like that. That's nobody's business," scolds the pool guard—a mother and park resident.[17]

As the park ages, several factors may combine to integrate it more as a community. First, the locking-in of families with long-term mortgages and trade-ups functions to retain families as permanent residents. Second, these working-class families' preference is to live near kin. If Prairieview Manor families gradually build extended kin networks of several generations through indebted homeownership, chain migration, and marriage, the park may come to function more like a village. High transience, on the other hand, may work against these community-building factors.

Neighbors and Neighborhood Concerns

Prairieview Manor residents consider their trailer park middle-class because "everybody owns their homes." A park woman remarked about her family, "We're not lower-class, but lower-income." In fact, park households tend to rank their incomes as higher than they are in reality: 45 percent report themselves as middle-income, 26 percent as lower-middle, 4 percent as upper-middle, and only 20 percent as lower-income (table C.1). Most, but not all, park residents like to regard themselves as similar to the citizens of the town of Prairieview.[18] Middle-class norms for property are reflected in tidy yards and quiet lives. Self-perceptions about class color interactions with neighbors whom other families identify as lower-class or trailer trash. That is, whether a neighbor is labeled bad depends on a park family's own class-based perspective on lifestyle, social mobility, and acceptable behavior. That the park is home to families who essentially think of themselves as from different classes leads to misunderstandings and conflict among neighbors.[19]

> *"We live in the park but are not of it," Laura and Tom Martin say. Laura is in her thirties and Tom is about ten years older. They met while students at the community college. Both hold good jobs with benefits. Their four children range from thirteen to seven years of age—two older boys and two younger girls. The Martins do not want them to be latchkey children, left at home alone. So the parents split their shifts—Tom works days and Laura nights. Everyone is in bed by the time Laura returns at midnight. "Since I've been working nights, I'm just always tired," she comments. They live in an immaculately kept new doublewide decorated with new, matching furniture. Its exterior is neatly maintained, with flowers planted around the home's foundation.*
>
> *From a social perspective, the Martins liked their previous location better, on the other side of the park. "We lived in a piece-of-junk house, but we had good neighbors." Four years ago they bought this new doublewide and crammed it on the only available larger lot. "The house is great but the neighborhood stinks. We have neighbor problems next door and across the street." The girls say, "Our dad doesn't like them. They smoke and play pretty loud music when they're home." Laura warns the older son, who plays ball with the neighbor boys, that she expects him "to act like a gentleman" and avoid using bad language.*
>
> *"Everyone here thinks we're stuck-up snobs because our kids aren't running the streets. We don't let them," says Laura. The girls don't know their neighbors. Strict parental rules limit their exposure to the park's "bad influences." The older girl says, "I'm not allowed to ride my bike beyond our street," unlike most of the third-graders we observed riding all over the park.*
>
> *"We try to stress school. The kids know we value education," explain the Martins. The parents are involved in school activities. "Tom even went on*

a class trip to Chicago last year," says Laura. They feel, however, that the Prairieview schools are biased toward "excellence," which works against their children, who are average students. And they feel the school too readily classifies park children as problem learners, like their older son, and it "destroys their self-esteem."

Because Prairieview Manor is a trailer park, Laura says the town thinks "that everyone living here must be trailer trash—white trash." Explains Tom, "It doesn't make that much of a difference as long as it doesn't affect the kids. . . . I like to think it hasn't yet but it might be getting to the boys. . . . Our older son had a friend who had been his friend since way back. This year the boy decided not to be his friend anymore because he lives in a trailer park."

Bad neighbors or a bad neighborhood is a recurrent complaint voiced, in particular, by park residents without children. Recognizable "bad streets" are explained by their housing unruly children, youth, or even adults. There are the adult "partiers" who, especially in the summer, are out every evening drinking beer, playing loud music, and yelling rather than talking, say their neighbors. "I love you, man," shouts one such bearded and pierced man to his friend and neighbor. A single man reports that his neighborhood deteriorated after an older couple moved out and partiers moved in: "They like to celebrate. Every night they have something to celebrate." One couple identified themselves as former partiers and "hard livers" until they became religious. "We used to have a lot of friends [in the park] when we were into drinking and partying," commented the husband.[20]

Rather than speak directly to offenders, neighbors on a bad street readily resort to notifying local authorities, even when the culprits are young children. An older man, for example, complained that "the girls in that trailer [pointing] threw rocks, onions, fruit, and eggs [at my home] for no apparent reason." His response was to call the police, which resulted in the young girls being taken to juvenile detention. He considered his action justified. Older people like this man readily report families they consider bad to the DCFS (Department of Children and Family Service). Reported parents express great anxiety about encounters with the DCFS; major repercussions occur after charges of child neglect or abuse. If a formal supervisory hearing results, a parent must by necessity miss work to appear. Multiple DCFS hearings can mean loss of a job for a parent. For a single park parent especially, eviction, homelessness, or even loss of parental rights is a possible outcome.[21] A mother of four living in a new doublewide was reported by a neighbor and now considers the park an undesirable place to live: "Because everybody is in everybody else's business . . . calling DCFS every time my seven-year-old plays in the yard by hisself. . . . It's illegal for a seven-year-old to be outside by himself? That's ridiculous." One young mother reported by a neighbor to DCFS for a transgression that embarrasses her quickly had her life fall apart. "The hoops that they make you jump through with DCFS—I couldn't keep a job after that." Such serious repercussions from a call to authorities may not be fully realized by a neighbor, or perhaps such reports are considered a solution to be rid of an undesirable neighbor.

An older woman—always a longtime resident—is typically pointed out as quick to call the authorities about incidents her neighbors regard as minor offenses. "People are callin' the law for no reason," said one couple, the heavily pierced partiers, who just eighteen months before had bought their shabby singlewide trailer from the wife's sister. They say the older lady next door calls the police "all the time" for loud music. The husband pointed out loud music coming from the next block, commenting that the neighbor would probably call the police and blame it on them. "It makes the whole trailer court look bad. . . . The right thing to do is for her to come over and ask us to turn it down, and we would," the wife said. The husband explained, "You get a $75 ticket if they come out two times."

Neighborhood deterioration is generally attributed to "renters." Despite a management rule prohibiting renters, they arrive as "subletters." Renters occupy homes not readily sold, repossessed, or exchanged for an in-park upgrade. A grandmother explained, "Your biggest problem out here would be your renters. The ones that just scrape up enough money to get in. They're gone in six months. They just can't make it." Commented another person on the park's transient renter problem, "That's where a lot of these no-gooders, these fly-by-nighters are coming from." Homeowners are contemptuous of others they deem lower in status—as giving Prairieview Manor a bad name. A woman who lives near some partiers says, "I've lived here fourteen years and don't even know my neighbors—don't care to know them. . . . I don't have to bring myself to their level."

A longtime woman resident is philosophical: "Neighbors move in, neighbors move out. Sometimes it's bad, then better, than bad again." Another elderly woman, a resident of long standing, observed about the transients on her street, "[It's] like a pendulum, back and forth—right now it's good." A middle-aged man reported that his strategy for dealing with a bad neighbor is to act more neighborly. He makes a point of introducing himself when new people move in. He also makes an effort to talk when they casually meet while outside. But he is fatalistic about the inevitability of getting a bad neighbor. "We did have several dopers here. But they [management] cracked down on them and made them move. But you can get that even more so in town. It doesn't make any difference—you get good and bad wherever you live."

Family Lives in the Illinois Trailer Park Detailed

Here intimate family stories are drawn from the observations and interviews of the sixteen park families in the Illinois family sample whom we followed during much of the field-study year. For larger patterns we draw from the entire park sample, which represents a onetime interview with eighty-two randomly selected households.

Although Prairieview Manor residents self-identify as rural or small-town people, their lives diverge from those of midwestern small-town folk, who are typically landowners, residentially stable, and socially embedded in their community.[22] Park family residential histories reveal push (motivational) or pull (beneficial social and financial) factors shaping a trailer's purchase and their placing it in the trailer park. About two-thirds of families (61 percent of eighty-two households) cite a trailer's affordability as a strong pull factor. Another pull factor for over one-fifth (22 percent) is kin-related—whether to access support, to gain proximity, or to provide care (e.g., for elderly relative). The good Prairieview schools are cited as a strong pull by over half the park households with children (54 percent of fifty). And another 7 percent are drawn by the park's rural setting. "For the size of the lot, and the amount I pay a month, it's the cheapest place to live in the country," said one man. Commonly a cluster of these reasons explains a family's land-lease trailer-park choice. But the fact that families own no land is crucial to their choice.

Family stories consistently reveal that the mobile home park was the best solution among other unattractive options for "convenient and available" housing. A shelter imperative was the major *push* factor (57 percent) motivating Illinois families toward park residence. As one woman recalled, "We were kind of in a bind when we bought this place." Another family explained the urgency behind their decision: "We didn't have another place; the landlord took our house." Immediate accessibility was a plus, and homeownership provided more security against facing such a crisis again. Another 39 percent were pushed to the park by divorce, illness, pregnancy, marriage, retirement or job reasons. A small 4 percent alluded to financial difficulties landing them in the park. Affordability was the major benefit factor to *pull* 61 percent to the park, kinship explained another 22 percent, while the remainder was drawn by the schools (10 percent) or the rural setting (7 percent).

Stretched-thin finances and borrowing from parents to buy a trailer are a common pattern, especially among single mothers. Carrie Williams, a single mother of two, had long held a wish for a place of "my own" during the years she rented or shared a home with a sister. Although buying the used doublewide was a move that stabilized her previously highly mobile family, she holds mixed feelings about their living in a trailer park. "The house is in my parents' name. I had to do it that way to get it financed. But they don't pay anything on it. I pay it." A community college degree enabled Carrie to hold a good job with benefits. She borrowed from her retirement fund for the down payment. Her budgeting management: "I get what we absolutely need. There's never any left from my paycheck. We always live paycheck to paycheck." She has a checking account, but "I empty it out week to week." For big purchases "I wait till tax [refund] time." And she is on food stamps.

After a second divorce another single mother of two reluctantly returned to Prairieview Manor, where she had grown up. Pushed into the park by a personal crisis, she was also pulled by her need for affordable housing: "I really don't like living in a mobile home. It's better than an apartment. I won't live in an apartment. . . . I need my own yard. It's second best. . . . Until the kids are gone it's the best I can do. . . . If I had the money, I'd be outta here today."

About half the sixteen families had already lived in one or more trailer parks (including Prairieview Manor) before buying their present home. Close to half used their previously owned mobile home to trade up to their present larger, newer, or better home. A pattern of sequential mobile home ownership is indicative of the narrowed financial options created by the indebtedness associated with the original loan taken on. Substantial debt remaining on a chattel loan makes trading in one trailer for another the most affordable way to improve a family's home quality, get more room, or obtain a better park address. When Joe the park owner offers a trade-up (appliances added on to the loan) through his mobile home dealership and throws in a year's site rent free, families recognize that they may "get stuck" in his trailer park.

Several households regretted not doing more careful calculations before trading up or buying a new trailer and becoming trapped in the park. If she had added her mortgage costs to the monthly site rental, "I could have afforded a real house," claimed one woman. In another case, a single middle-aged woman chose her doublewide home because it was new and larger than the singlewide she had lived in for twenty years. "It was easier to get credit for this than for a home . . . but I forgot about lot rent." With hindsight she realizes that for the $400 a month loan payment plus the monthly lot rent of $180, she could have afforded a conventional home. Although she has no complaints about her new home, "I would just like to have it on a piece of land." The park's rural setting is a typical trade-off for the higher living costs for a family: "[I] just like bein' out in the country quiet. . . . Here's close." Not becoming landowners is what these families bemoan.

Another factor that traps a family in the park is the challenge of selling an older mobile home to anyone but the park owner/home dealer on a trade. A planned move to a conventional home prompted a couple to put their trailer on the market. But after their three-year-old mobile home attracted no buyer, they found themselves stuck in the park. Susan Bachman and her husband custom-ordered a high-end doublewide from Joe. Now, only a year and a half later, Susan questions the finances of their decision. "It seemed like the best deal. Turns out it probably won't be." They had neglected to do the math for the new home, furniture payments, plus the monthly site rental. The miscalculation may hinder their plan, once the kids have graduated three years down the road, to move to a log cabin home, perhaps in rural Colorado.

How did mobile homeownership in the Illinois trailer park affect the lives of the sixteen families? Taking into account that some families were previously mobile home park residents, three-quarters (twelve) essentially made a parallel move from another park to Prairieview Manor, which they regard as a better park. For two households, the move to this park represents downward mobility from conventional homeownership as a result of divorce, job loss, or financial difficulties. For another person, the move to the park from a rental apartment represents upward mobility because homeownership stabilized a formerly highly transient life. Another family, a couple in their early thirties with two children, lives in an older singlewide bought for them by the wife's father. Problems with keeping jobs or paying rent had forced ten moves during the previous five years. For them, subsidized trailer ownership in the park brought household stability to the family, although it meant the assumption of a dependent status. A young wife explained that they bought their trailer from her aunt, who had previously rented it out. "She had to evict the tenant, who didn't take care of it." This couple, because of the financial and school problems of the student-husband, had moved four times in the previous five years. When they bought the aunt's used trailer as a fixer-upper, it needed lots of work. But it allowed them entry to homeowner-ship despite few resources. "She [the aunt] helped us out and we helped her out," explained the wife. We also observed two or three generations living together in a trailer. In one case, a mother is the homeowner and her teenage son, along with his fiancée and baby, live with her "to help" with her medical problems. The young couple is likely to remain caught in the trailer park because of poor finances and employability problems.

Over one-quarter (28 percent) of park householders represent the second generation to live in Prairieview Manor. Both adults were born and raised in the park as park residents married and had children. There were two instances of three-generation families. A third-generation young husband explains how the park shaped his marriage pool: "We were next-door neighbors, we grew up together."[23] Despite being a third-generation resident, he, like other young families, considers Prairieview Manor only a temporary way station. A second-generation young father has his parents, sister, and brother all living in the park. Although his children were born in the park, he also views it as a temporary home—for "five years tops," he says. Like this father, younger park couples cherish their housing dream of a conventional home on owned land—a goal manifest in their ease with mobility, even rootlessness, and lack of attachment to the trailer park as a place to call home.

Of the 55 percent of the park sample with relatives living nearby, 38 percent have kin living in the park, and 17 percent have kin in Prairieview or another central Illinois small town. Those with kin living in or near the park typically represent a chain migration—after one family moves there, other relatives follow. For example, a young couple after the birth of a child were the first to move into the park, followed by the wife's mother and the husband's sister and brother-in-law. They are now a kin network of three related households. In another pattern, an older relative moves to the park or has lived there for many years, and subsequently a grandchild, niece, or nephew moves in or buys the relative's home after he or she trades up or dies. The many chain migrations to the Illinois trailer park indicate the interdependence of low-income kin networks as well as kin members not rooted elsewhere by property ownership. Thus a trailer in Prairieview Manor may represent a kin network together accessing homeownership for the first time.

Almost half the sixteen park family parents have one or more grandparents or parents from rural Appalachia—Kentucky, Tennessee, or southern Illinois—originally drawn to central Illinois soft coal mines (now closed) between the 1930s and the 1960s or to this prosperous agricultural region as farm laborers. For example, Doug Riley, a single father of four, described his family as "country people" from Kentucky. "My mother's mother came from Hardin County. . . . I'm just a dumb hillbilly." His Appalachian grandparents and parents were either farmers or coal miners. Having these rural Appalachian roots means that the park families descend from poor rural people whose itinerant, landless status persisted until this generation established some stability with trailer home ownership in Prairieview Manor.

Nearly every able-bodied Prairieview Manor park adult holds a job, especially in the younger households with children. Overall these jobs are relatively low-skilled, bad jobs that pay minimum wage or a bit higher, lack benefits, and hold little chance for advancement. Work histories are a succession of jobs found through a newspaper ad or, as one woman explained, when "I walked in and applied. They hire any and everybody." Kathy Smith, a waitress/hostess at a Central City restaurant, recruited several other park mothers to waitress with her. Working together they could pool driving as well as have some social time.[24] A handful of nurses (about four or five—several retired) are in the park because of downwardly mobility—for example, after a divorce—although they hold good jobs.

Although many have bad jobs, among the sixteen families two-thirds have at least one adult with a good job (with benefits, a regular schedule, and chance for promotion), and several have two adults with good jobs. Adults holding good jobs tend to remain in the same job longer. For example, Carrie, the single mother of two, worked ten years as a small factory receptionist, a job with good benefits. She then trained on the job as a forklift operator to improve her take-home pay.

Park parents with bad jobs seem untroubled by readily walking out or being fired. When the job is waitress, housekeeper, cashier, or truck driver, they simply move on to another job just like it. If a boss is uncooperative or inflexible when there is a family illness or similar circumstance, a parent quits. Because central Illinois has five small cities within commuting distance of the park, parents count on easily finding another minimum-wage, dead-end job. A single mother left one job because an administrator rubbed her the wrong way. Another woman became pregnant and decided the job had health risks (despite her own smoking). Explains a single mother of two, "My shift changed. The boss wouldn't let me off for half an hour to pick [my son] up from kindergarten and take him to the sitter, so I had to quit." When a woman's boss changed and she did not get along with the new one, she abandoned the job.

Perhaps it is the hard jobs they work, but job-related disabilities are high among the sixteen families. The single dad, Doug Riley, a gifted car mechanic, worked at an elite foreign car dealership but quit his job because the chemicals "made me sick." Women report body stresses from repetitive work tasks; others have work-related back or feet problems. In addition, some are obese and have the associated health problems, such as type 2 diabetes.

Complex Family Histories

Among the adults from the sixteen families, their relationships, residence histories, and children's childhoods are distinguished by complexity. If the parents of park adults had chaotic lives before or after they became parents, their children's lives are similarly chaotic and suffer various disruptions. Housing plays an important role in the stability or lack of it in life histories.[25]

Divorce is a common thread in the fabric of their lives. Except for Doug Riley, the other adults in the sixteen families are the children of divorced parents. Dubious mate choices, shotgun weddings, fragile marital unions, serial cohabitation, single parenthood, and alcoholism repeat across generations. Marital failures among the previous generation are echoed in the rocky marital outcomes of their offspring.[26] Of the total of twenty-four adults who make up the sixteen households, eight are from four married couples, eight are single parents (one father and seven mothers), and the remaining eight adults are split between two common-law couples (five to eighteen years of cohabitation) and two couples made up of women who each live with a man they call their fiancé, although the fiancés refer to them as girlfriends. Children are accustomed to breakups among their parents or parents of friends. They become matter-of-fact about marital fragility. A youth's friend lived nearby but "I haven't talked to him in a while. . . . His mom just moved to Indiana, so now he lives [here] with his dad." Divorce leads to both high residential mobility and multiple schools for children.

Of the twenty-four adults that make up the park family sample, nine mothers and one father (two-thirds of the twenty-four adults) as children were bounced back and forth between separated or divorced parents and their successive fragile relationships. Children bear the consequences of unpredictable parental breakups, divorce, or the custodial parent's serial coupling. They typically remain with their mother, who moves them around as she serially forms and breaks relationships. A child with one such mother recalls, "We moved a lot. . . . My parents would get together and break up." Circular transitions became a pattern as the mother moved in and out of her parents' home with a new relationship or fell on hard times and returned to her parents' place. "It got to where we'd just register ourselves. We went to the [school] office and they were like 'Oh, you're back,'" she reflected on her unstable childhood. As adults, those who had tumultuous childhoods tell of lives with a chain of bad choices: teenage pregnancy, dropping out of high school, early marriage and subsequent divorce. Some mothers moved in and out of short-term relationships during which a child was conceived, prior to settling in Prairieview Manor. Four of the fifteen mothers became pregnant as unwed teens.[27]

One woman boomeranged between parents who eventually divorced. Her life history reflects this chaotic childhood, starting with her dropping out of high school. At one point she was homeless, an alcoholic and on drugs. But she righted herself after some time in jail. Eventually she earned a GED (an alternative to a high school diploma) and a community college degree in bookkeeping. Each of her two children has a different father. They recently moved in with her fiancé (met at work) in his Prairieview Manor trailer. "My kids have been through a lot, and seen me with a lot of different men. They feel stable and safe here. They call this home, and they call him Dad." She feels guilty about her past: "I was not raised to be lower-class. I was brought up to be upper-class. I made some bad choices in my life. That's how I ended up here." Although the fiancé drinks, because of her children's sense of security she is committed to making this imperfect relationship work.

The Harwood family consists of two parents in a stable marriage, a sixteen-year-old daughter, Miranda, and an older son, Nick. Neither parent nor any adult in the extended family had completed high school. Education is clearly not a family priority. Already as a ninth grader Miranda hates school and was kicked out a dozen times in one year. "I don't even go to school. I get in trouble for the littlest things," she explains. During the study she ran away to her boyfriend's home in the park and became pregnant. Explained her mother Peggy sadly, "We're having a lot of trouble with her right now." Abortion was never discussed despite Miranda's young age. Eventually she had a miscarriage and moved back home.

Doug Riley heads the poorest household. Finances are tight because he quit a well-paid auto mechanic job and is in the midst of retraining at the community college. "I had a good childhood as far as learning stuff," handyman and mechanic skills taught by his dad and stepdad in rural Kentucky. Doug runs his household with definite rules and consistent routines. He cooks dinner daily and eats with his four children together at the table. Rules are observed by the family, such as waiting for everyone to be seated before the meal begins and not leaving the table before all are finished. In contrast, half the other fifteen families lack a daily routine, although for some it is a consequence of a parent's irregular work schedule.[28]

For other families, household disorganization seems especially prevalent during the summer, when school does not impose a regular schedule. Five families rarely sit down to eat dinner together. Commented a mother when we asked to observe a meal, "We don't really do family meals." Her daughter's teenaged friends take priority over her family: "I'm always out," she says. She and her friends like to hang out at the park pop machine: "That's my place. It's like my best friend." Despite their not sitting down together for meals, it is a stable household headed by parents together for almost twenty years, although never married. Another family eats together on trays sitting in front of the television; they are fans of Monday night wrestling.

Despite experiencing a tumultuous childhood, some park women find a good mate by luck or by choice. Such unions provide steadiness for children and break a disorganized family pattern. For example, in the almost twenty-year common-law union above, their two children have attended only one school, in contrast to their mother's having attended a school in each of five different towns. "Nothing is the same," she says about her current family-focused life, compared with the unpredictability of her own childhood. "I have more sta-bility." An additional component of family stability is that the mother's large sibling group lives nearby; one lives in the park. She and a sister work as motel housekeepers, which brings them together every day. Like blue-collar families elsewhere, this mother describes her social life as among kin, not friends.[29] Liv-ing in their second Prairieview Manor–owned home (after trading up to a better one), having two parents around, and attending one school are factors central to the security and stability she believes her children have experienced.

Several parents act as steady support to their daughters living in the park—who are single mothers. After Amy Armstrong's mother died, the money she inher-ited as an only child of divorce allowed her to pay in full for a new singlewide in Prairieview Manor. Owning a home stabilized her dysfunctional life, which had included being a school dropout at thirteen, having a first child at seventeen, and experiencing homelessness. Eventually Amy earned a GED. Throughout these ups and downs, her father, who never remarried after his divorce, provided consistent child care and support from his trailer in the park. Amy, raised by a mother (a college graduate) who moved them about erratically, never learned what normal family life involves. Her trailer has a highly disordered, even trashy, appearance, with garbage and toys strewn about the yard. The family also has a random daily schedule. During the study, Amy's second husband, father to her younger child, moved out. She formed a temporary union with another man that ended when her husband moved back. But their trailer home is a constant in her children's lives.

Mobile home ownership thus functions for some families to stabilize their lives. Parents explain that the steadiness homeownership brings is a conscious choice. One single mother of two borrowed $200 from her grandmother for the down payment on a used singlewide. Having bounced around as a child between divorced parents, she plans to stay in the park for her children's sake: "I want the kids to be in one place until they graduate. I want that for them." Another single mother of two lives with her divorced fiancé and his children. A product of a stable marriage, the fiancé remains close to his supportive extended family. His "rich" sister lent the couple half the down payment for a new doublewide to house their large blended family of seven.

Buying a mobile home, carefully choosing a mate, and belonging to a church (seven of sixteen households) are all indicators of how some park families adopt middle-class priorities to break from the past chaotic life in which they were raised or that they created for themselves. For a woman whose youth was spent weekly shuttling back and forth between divorced parents, the military was her stabilizing force after a troubled adolescence: "I started going down. I was hanging out with the wrong crowd, doing drugs." She had a son at fifteen but married a military man and eventually joined the military herself. In her early twenties she tutored herself, earned a GED, and then completed some college work. She has cultivated a steady and organized life. Her family eats together and is active in a church, and the parents follow their children's sports. Church was similarly a stabilizing force for three other families. Two fathers reported hard living as alcoholics before turning their lives around through church engagement.

Finances are stretched thin for all sixteen park families, and they depend on kin to be a safety net. Such support comes typically from parents rather than siblings, as it does in North Carolina. Carrie Williams "really counts on my parents" for both emotional and financial support. Unlike Carrie's parents, who only signed for her home, in two other families their parents bought the mobile home and the woman or the couple pays them a monthly rent. Amy Armstrong says that in an emergency, "I'd have to turn to my dad."

Of the sixteen families, the two-thirds with at least one good job (nurse, welder, lab technician, dispatcher) or two good jobs are less stressed financially and own better trailers (larger or newer) than those owned by the eight single parents or those with two parents holding bad jobs. Work and residential histories for both men and women with better jobs reflect lives less stretched financially and more stable. A common dream of the single mothers related by one is "That we'll have a better place to live. . . . That I'm financially stable . . . and married again—I'll have to be to be financially stable. That's my goal." Single mothers envision marriage as the solution to help alleviate the stresses of their lives. Park children grow up aware of family finances and what is possible for parents to manage.

Family life is not all stress and angst for park families. Many trailers have large-screen television sets dominating the living room—a popular Christmas gift purchased on credit. Television is on day and night, even when no one watches. Soap operas, talk shows like *Oprah,* or cartoons drone on. A common women's leisure activity is weekend "yard saleing" in nearby towns, where they troll for clothing, furniture, or kitchen equipment. One woman shared a passion for yard sales with her mother before she died: "Every weekend that's where we'd be. . . . We would go to every one we could. When in high school I prayed every night for a leather jacket. . . . Then one day we were driving to the grocery and there was a yard sale. We stopped and—this is so amazing—there was a leather jacket just exactly like I wanted, and just the right size, for ten dollars. . . . I'll never forget that." Park women also shop at the Salvation Army or Goodwill. Some visit the local food pantry, "Helping Hands," to stretch their limited budgets.

For some families their church provides a rich social life; others have hobbies or follow children's sports. Several women indulge themselves after work when they "stop on their way home to tan." Peggy Harwood maintains an elaborate manicure, such as purple nails with bunny pictures. Another family is proud of a Beanie Baby collection numbering over one thousand, which they expect to be valuable eventually. Hunting and fishing are common male leisure activities. Families regularly use the nearby county park to hike or bike together. One dad's hobby is carving miniature wooden log cabins to give as gifts, returned to him when a relative dies. It is poignant symbolism that he builds model "real" houses, which symbolize the family's housing dream.

Living with Stigma

When we asked what townsfolk in Prairieview thought of the trailer park, the uniform response from the park residents was "They think we're trailer trash." Trailer-park folk in their routine interactions in Prairieview experience stigmatization through no fault of their own—other than being poor with a trailer-park address.[30]

Carrie Williams, the single mom in her thirties profiled earlier, lives in an older, well-landscaped doublewide, always neatly kept. She holds a good job in a factory that does not draw on her community college degree in child development—that made her more educated than anyone in her family. Carrie jokes, "I developed two children." She must spend "almost everything" of her salary on housing.

Carrie is close with her parents, who live nearby in the city. "We have contact about five times a week, with half of that on the phone and the other half face-to-face." After her divorce, her parents were her safety net when she moved in with them. "It was pretty bad, but that's the only place I had to go. I had to stay there until I could get on my feet again." She stayed two years and then moved to a rental home with her sister. Carrie finally realized the first place of her own in the Prairieview Manor trailer park. "At least here my monthly payment is getting me something I can keep." And the move to the trailer park stabilized the family.

Carrie grew up in Prairieview and attended the local high school. Although her family was working-class, she remembers that she and her classmates all considered Prairieview Manor to be a bad place. "The trailer-park kids were singled out—by both teachers and kids. They were seen as the trouble causers—the bad kids. I can't say for sure that they were, but that's how they were seen at school."

Carrie explains how folks in Prairieview react if you live in the trailer park: "People look at you like you're trash. . . . We do live in Prairieview but that's not how the people in town see it. . . . When I went to school here I remember hearing . . . 'Ooooh, Prairieview Manor'" reflecting its negative reputation in her voice. "And now here I am, and my kids are Prairieview Manor trailer-park kids," she says, seeing the irony of her downward mobility.

Those who do not keep up their trailers or yards are held in contempt by Carrie, who has middle-class property standards: "I hope that since the management keeps raising the lot rent, that it'll do a better job about kicking some of the trash out of here. I look at some of these places with the trash and junk all piled up in the yard and I wonder how can they allow that?" Carrie explains her plan to not look or act like the town's stereotypes for park residents: "We used to all the time drive past our house, and look and ask, 'OK, do we look like trailer trash? Well that's got to go off the deck and that needs to be picked up in the yard, to be sure we don't live that way.'"

Illinois park homeowners, despite living in a Cadillac park, complain more about where they live than do North Carolina and New Mexico park residents. But their gripes might have more to do with experiencing the sting of the trailer-trash slur than with the trailer park itself.

The trailer park lies adjacent to Prairieview, a town whose upscale subdivisions house professionals from the nearby city.[31] (See table 3.2.) Although Prairieview Manor was built before the upscale subdivisions, its presence outside this now "elite" suburban town is unwelcome. A village official explains the town's elitist attitude: "Most of Prairieview thinks the trailer park is low-income. Most free and reduced lunches in schools are served to children from the trailer park. Most police and ambulance activity comes from the trailer park. Residents there are just never going to pay their way [in taxes], and because of that, the trailer park is the focus of the entire community's wrath."

An almost $30,000 median income disparity between Prairieview and the trailer park (table 3.2) situates park residents in the category of relative poverty. Educational disparities similarly reinforce the social inequalities. In the town, the census indicates that 37 percent have a four-year college degree or higher. Illinois park adults (85 percent) have earned at least a high school education or a GED, but a college degree is rare. Furthermore, for about half of the park households, a post-high school degree is indicative of only a two-year community college degree. Thus mobile home owners are both poorer and less well educated than are homeowners in Prairieview.

The park's population of 1,500 raises concerns in Prairieview, a town of 5,000 people. Some townspeople worry that the trailer park's potential voter pool of the working poor could outvote its wealthy subdivisions on critical issues like property taxation. So the park residents are disenfranchised from voting locally on policies that directly affect them because the town has not annexed the park. The subdivision residents suspect that the trailer park lowers the market value of their homes, a major concern.

In Prairieview, one's address reveals social status. One woman explained, "I say I live in a mobile home and they get this stereotype that I am white trash." A Prairieview Manor woman recalls becoming friendly with another mom during their sons' Saturday soccer games. Her new friend, from a nearby upscale subdivision, persistently probed about where she lived. Giving evasive answers such as "in the country," she was wary about disclosing her trailer-park address. When she finally admitted, "I live in Prairieview Manor," the subdivision woman turned on her heel, walked away, and never again spoke to her. A retired couple from the trailer park shared a similar experience with people they met through a Civil War buffs' club. Once they gave their trailer-park address, they were treated as lowly trailer trash not worthy of basic civility even though they had moved to the park after retiring and selling their main street Prairieview business.

A common sentiment voiced by park families about Prairieview is, "They look down on us." After a move into the park only five months previously, a father already regrets the choice: "I would rather have a house than live in a trailer park. My fifteen-year-old is already hearing it—about the stereotypes. She tells me, 'God, Dad—I don't want anyone to know where I live 'cause everyone is going to think I'm trailer trash.'"[32] Although they love the trailer park, a retired couple in their seventies agrees that Prairieview "looks down their noses at us . . . thinks we don't pay taxes." An observant park mother said, "I don't like the way they treat us. It wasn't so bad for my oldest. She was in first [grade] last year, but it's gotten worse in second. It's really bad for the older kids, the teens. They get treated like they are from the wrong side of the tracks by the others . . . even the teachers, but mostly it's the other kids. It comes from their homes, their parents." When asked about the film *Baby Dance*, which features a brassy surrogate mother from a trailer park, a teenage park girl remarked, "See, it's when they show that kind of thing that it ruins it for all of us! Yesterday when my friends [from high school] . . . were bringing me home, one guy said, 'Watch out, we're in trailer trash territory now.' The other guy in the car told him, 'What do you mean? It's nice here!'"

Park residents are considered free riders who do not pay sufficient property taxes to cover their participation in, for example, park-district activities. Thus, special fees are levied on park people and only on them. Some park families cannot participate in the park district's activities because of the expense involved. A young mother explained, "Because the park is not considered part of Prairieview, we have to pay $45 to be in the baseball program, whereas someone two miles down the road has to pay only $20." In her opinion, it has to do with the town's belief that "we're all trailer trash and a burden on the school system, as if we're rabbits pumpin' them out over here." Commented a park resident self-identified as middle-class: "We're not lax people. You won't ever see us sittin' out on the patio with our big bellies hangin' out and a beer in our hand. You know, you might see my husband out there tossin' back a beer after work once in a while, but you know, it's the general [belief] about a mobile home park that you walk through and there's a bunch of lazy people hangin' out, fallin' all over the place. . . . The ones I know about anyway . . . all have jobs to go to, they all have children to raise." Park adults and youth experience the sting of the trailer-trash stigma from the town. Only small children are oblivious to it.

Park families, we learned, ranked the Prairieview schools as a strong pull factor for choosing the trailer park. It is as significant a factor as the home's affordability. And therefore, the schools figure importantly in their assessment of the town's acceptance of them. A fifteen-year-old girl is unhappy with high school, although her mother is pleased with the education she receives. Her mother remarked, "We're outcasts here. She feels that at the school." Stigma explains the loss of the daughter's best friend: "They used to hang out together. Her mom, well, they're rich. I think she's a doctor or something. Well, she kinda said things to her daughter that her daughter told [my daughter]. That kinda hurt." "Once the girlfriend's parents were going out of town, and she needed a place to stay. So I said she could stay with us. When her mom and her came by, my boyfriend was here. Well, he was smoking. Her mom saw that and the trailer and took her out of here. . . . Her mom couldn't handle that. Now they don't even talk."

"School is the worst thing about living here," remarked Nick Harwood, a high school senior. Peggy, his mother, added, "They do consider this 'the Projects' for Prairieview. There is a difference between those that live here and those that don't in the way they [schools] treat the kids. My niece lived here and then she moved out to a farm. She says the way the school treats her kids [now] is completely different." When the parents of Nick's girlfriend found out where he lived, without even meeting him, they forbade her to see him. "They're still friends, but she has to see him behind their backs," explained Peggy.

Segregation heightens Prairieview Manor park residents' sense of being marked with the trailer-trash stigma.[33] It is understandable that the school district designs bus routes for efficiency. But the fact that one bus exclusively picks up and delivers park children and youth underlines their otherness. Even teachers, perhaps unwittingly, reinforce the negative stereotypes. A mother related this story: "They were going over tornadoes in school and [her daughter] was in second grade. She asked her teacher, 'Well, we live in a trailer, where should we go?' She [the teacher] said, 'Well, you live in a trailer. If you got hit, you'd die.' After that [the daughter] was hysterical every time there was a storm." A park mother of four, owner of a trailer bought new three years ago, is bitter about the Prairieview schools: "I was told that it was a good school system, but I found out different later. I was told that they treated all children like individuals and that they did what was best for each child . . . that they wouldn't judge them but they do. . . . My mother raised ten kids on a farm near here. . . . She has a reputation there of being a good person. But they don't care about that at the school here. . . . Once they hear you live in the park that's it. . . . Right away they label you as trailer trash."

Park parents are resentful that authorities exaggerate problems among park youth and disregard similar problems among town youth. "They're seen as the trouble causers—the bad kids. I can't say for sure that they are, but that's how they are seen at school." Park youth report biased treatment by both teachers and students. A nurse and single mother of a park youth said that though her son makes straight A's in the high school, "Prairieview Manor boys get pegged as delinquents. . . . It just makes me so mad." As for the girls, she said, "They're pegged as 'easy.'"

Proud park parents are insulted if others assume they are impoverished or needy. One mother was offended when her son went to school with scuffed shoes and came home with a note that the school could gladly supply him with a new pair. A Prairieview elementary school principal, well liked by park parents, sees discrimination by the town toward the park. Yet he too has some biases: "When there is an outbreak of head lice many parents are quick to point at the park . . . [but] the problem of lice is less likely to be taken care of by some park families, but that is not from families not caring. It's an SES [socioconomic status] factor. . . . The treatment for lice is very expensive and a poor family is less likely to take the effort and expense required for a complete cure." The principal gives other examples of financially needy park families:

> *Some of those kids really live in impoverished settings. . . . Last year I took several kids home to the park. Some of the homes they live in are really unsafe . . . unhealthy situations with clothes and toys and papers and trash crowding the floor . . . and dirty dishes piled up. . . . One little girl told me a story last year about a possum being in . . . the kitchen drawer! And she told me about it without any alarm . . . said that her mother picked it up and threw it outside. That's the kind of thing that I see.*

Our contact with almost one hundred park households, however, found disorderly and shabby homes rare rather than the rule in Prairieview Manor.

The principal says few park parents attend school meetings. "Many families in the park don't have a car or child care so that makes it hard to get in to the school . . . but that has to do with SES, not the park." But his presumption that park families lack cars is wrong. Among the eighty-two households surveyed, only several frail, elderly widows and one other lack a car. Thus even the principal allows the trailer-trash stigma to color his perceptions about park families.

Assessment of children's abilities may be influenced by stigma in the school district. A case of the school's mistreatment of two brothers was related by several in the park. After their divorced mother's sudden death, they came to live with their father in the trailer park. In their previous school they were in accelerated classes and recognized as bright. But the Prairieview school district immediately assigned them to general classes, assuming without testing that the boys would perform at normal or below normal levels. These boys, and park kids who entered the school district after being successful students elsewhere, "have a hard time," explained a mother. "Kids are calling them 'trailer trash.'" A fifteen-year-old girl reported being hailed in the hall by other students as "Hey, trailer trash. . . . If where you live is where I live, you are nothing," she said. She enrolled in a private church school the year after the study. Doug Riley describes the move to the park flatly as "the biggest mistake I ever made." When they lived with a relative in Prairieview proper, his children were treated well at school. "Now they have trouble." Some park parents would prefer not to live where they are looked down on, but they are determined to stay until their children finish school.

Because they regard themselves as upstanding citizens and homeowners, being stigmatized as trailer trash cuts deeply. Like Carrie Williams, others reveal discomfort about their park address—as if they absorb the negative trailer-trash image. It is perhaps this discomfiture that provokes the overreaction by those who call and report neighborhood adults and children to authorities. Such residents view park violators of middle-class norms as embodying how the town sees them all—as trailer trash.

That stigma shapes a soiled identity for park youth is evident. A divorced nurse was dismayed to hear her fifteen-year-old son say, "I've lived in mobile homes my whole life. I'm a mobile home person and probably will be all my life." She objected, "Don't limit yourself that way. Why do you say that?" (He had lived in Prairieview Manor since he was four.) He replied, "Because it's probably true." Indeed, youthful aspirations may be dampened by the stigma. Such factors help reinforce social barriers keeping status persistent and durable across generations—evidenced by the multiple-generational families in the park.[34]

Prairieview Manor families actually share basic beliefs with their upper-middle-class neighbors in Prairieview. Other affordable housing options are available in the area, which they clearly rejected, in contrast to other working-poor families who chose to rent or to buy on-contract stick housing, albeit old, deteriorated cheap homes (under $10,000) in the shabby town of "Splitville," described by Salamon in *Newcomers to Old Towns*. Choosing the Prairieview Manor trailer park over an alternative low-cost housing option highlights parental priorities—for affordable housing and their children's access to a quality education. But progress toward their middle-class American Dream, realized by homeownership in the trailer park, carries the burden of stigma. Some think the trade-off is worth the cost; others have regrets—the cost is too high in self-respect.

Nick Harwood in his future plans reflects the bitterness of being judged as trailer trash. He realizes that the good education he received in Prairieview schools will foster his social mobility, which might not have happened had the family lived in another park near inferior schools. He remarks, "When I graduate from high school I'll stay in Prairieview. But I'm getting out of this galvanized ghetto."

THE NORTH CAROLINA PARKS
Near Ties That Bind of Kin and Church

Among rural eastern North Carolina blacks still working the land, property and land ownership remain the basis for respect and community status. These same values are shared by their descendants, who migrated to the small city of Addington to find work and live in city trailer parks. These parks serve black families primarily as places to live and to provide them proximity to kin. Kin are important to African Americans both financially and socially. A woman out of work explained this support: "If I don't have the money, I call on my mom and dad. . . . If something goes wrong I go to my family. . . . If they can't do it, somebody knows someone who can do it most of the time." Their social lives take place among large, close-knit kin networks and in churches attended by both park families and their relatives. Kin and church are the twin pillars of rural black family life. Because kin networks and church networks are often overlapping and thus reinforcing, park families have rich sources of support.

> The Bankstons have two sons, one in high school and the other a preschooler. Viola works as a cook at a government facility and James as a credit manager—both hold good, full-time jobs with benefits. The Bankston own an older singlewide home in the Shady Grove trailer park.

This chapter relies in part on the dissertation fieldwork carried out by Michelle Eley, Community and Economic Development Specialist, North Carolina A&T State University.

Viola's door is always open to friends and family. She is close with her three sisters and brothers but more so with four half-siblings from her father's second marriage. They all live in Addington. Viola talks with her mother every morning and afternoon: "Whatever . . . if my mother has it, and I need it, then I have it. She is a blessing. . . . My grandmother does the same thing."

Park neighbors frequently stop by the Bankstons' home. One woman Viola says "is more so like a sister . . . [but] I usually hang with fellas." The Bankstons met their neighbor Donnie when both families previously lived in The Projects. "I see him daily . . . and sometimes I think he lives here." Referring to Robert, another neighbor, Viola says, "We call each other brother and sister. We buy for and share with each other when we need to. . . . If I need something financially, I got it and vice versa. He calls my kids his nephews and they call him uncle." Their tight park network is readily mobilized: "We stick together. We petitioned for the basketball goal." And they were successful at getting park management to provide the goal for their street. The goal is heavily used by the neighborhood.

Because of their work schedules, Sunday is the only day the Bankstons sit down to dinner together. "We normally have a prayer—that's a must." Their park network also gathers most Sundays. They watch street basketball and "I cook dinner, and whoever falls in, falls in," says Viola. She keeps things simple when cooking for the Sunday crowd: "I use as much plastic as possible."

Viola was dissatisfied with the condition of her older trailer. She spends a lot of time in her kitchen, and the cabinetry was worn—with chipped paint and some doors off the hinges. When Robert and his family moved from the park, he and Viola arranged for the Bankstons to get his newer trailer and assume the loan payments. Trading up in the same park with someone they trusted allowed the Bankstons to improve their housing and have friends help with the move.

The Bankstons are weekly attendees at a small Addington Baptist church, which Viola's mother also attends. Their older son, Trevor, benefited from church members' tutoring and mentoring after he had to repeat the seventh grade. His test scores improved so much with this church support that Trevor now considers himself a "good student" at the high school.

Addington, a small city of under twenty thousand in population, has a charming riverfront that attracts tourists traveling to North Carolina's Outer Banks. As well as being the county seat, Addington also has three small institutions of higher learning and a military base just outside the city limits with approximately 1,500 active duty and civilian personnel. Park families, however, do not work in these institutions. Farms dominate the surrounding landscape, along with dense forests that reach the city's perimeter. Tobacco demands that have slumped nationally in particular weakened the North Carolina agricultural sector. African Americans' migration to Addington from remote rural places is related to this decline, combined with an unwillingness to follow their parents into agriculture. With no major industrial employer around Addington, jobs are concentrated in the retail/service sector for which trailer-park folk must drive far to work in the coastal tourist industry or at a government-run hospital, prison, or ship-building facility.

Of Addington county's forty mobile home parks, approximately one-third stand in the city proper located off main streets, tucked behind dense trees in residential areas or along rural roads on the city's outskirts. We studied four trailer parks with a total of 450 sites (91 percent, or 410 sites, occupied): three are land-lease, and one is a newer subdivision park with land-lease and owner-ship options. The three land-lease parks are incorporated into the city, although at its periphery on converted farmland. The fourth, newest subdivision park lies farther out in the county. No study trailer park is larger than 200 home sites, in contrast to the Illinois park, which is triple that size. We combine the four parks, referring to them as a single park for most purposes after finding no significant differences among them (see Appendix B for individual park details). Several Section 8 subsidized apartment complexes are dispersed around the city. One commonly called The Projects features such a poor social environment that it functions as a push factor for African American families' move to nearby trailer parks. Thus it is evident that trailer parks are of higher status than The Projects. Because Addington lacks public transportation, park residents must drive to work, shop, or obtain services, and park children are bused to city schools.

Some African American families who live in the parks migrated from more remote rural places to find work in Addington. Other African American park families, however, have two or three generations of kin previously living in the small city. Addington township typifies eastern North Carolina with its population of over 50 percent African American,[1] and mobile homes constitute 16 percent of the housing.[2] In fact, the South leads the nation in the highest proportion of housing in mobile homes.

Park families are not among Addington's poorest (table 4.1). For example, park families receive little government assistance, adults generally have a least a high school diploma, and they typically earn an income, whether in the work-force or from a retirement annuity. The park population approximates the city's ethnic makeup, in which African Americans comprise 57 percent and whites represent 40 percent of the population. A slightly higher proportion of park adults (80 percent) have earned at least a high school diploma or a GED than have people (82 percent) in Addington, which would explain why the park's median

TABLE 4.1 Population traits of North Carolina trailer parks and city

TRAIT	TRAILER PARK	ADDINGTON
Ethnicity		
% households African American	52	57
Age		
Median age	26 years	33 years
% householders 65 years and over	7	27
Household type		
% family households	62	64
(% female-headed, no husband present)	(23)	(23)
Average household size	4.40	2.39
Income		
Median household income	$24,537	$24,200
(in 2016 dollars)	$34,178	—
% below poverty	16	25
% reporting public assistance	5	8
Educational attainment, all adults[a]		
% less than high school	18	26
% high school graduate (including equivalency)	50	28
% some college or associate's degree	25	28
% bachelor's degree or higher	4	18
Occupancy and tenure		
% owner-occupied	92	50
% renter-occupied	8	50
% in home for 1 year or less	26	25
% same home 5 years prior	34	48

Source: Trailer-park data come from the survey of a randomly selected sample of trailer-park households (n = 65); town data from U.S. Census Bureau, "DP-1 Profile of General Demographic Characteristics: 2000"; "DP-2 Profile of Selected Social Characteristics: 2000"; "DP-3 Profile of Selected Economic Characteristics: 2000"; and "QT-P20 Educational Attainment by Sex: 2000."

[a]Educational attainment data for the park sample include all adults over 18 years of age, while U.S. Census data include adults 25 and over only.

household income is higher than the median income of the wider community. Our random household survey of the four parks yielded a park sample of sixty-five households, of which 52 percent are African Americans, 45 percent are whites, and the remaining 3 percent are Hispanic (table 4.1). For detailed household information we draw on the thirteen African American families in the family sample. First we describe the four North Carolina parks' history and layout and next the management of the two larger parks to highlight each neighborhood's distinctive ambience. Second, we detail kin networks and then the place churches play in families' lives.

The Addington Study Trailer Parks

Development of the four study trailer parks took place after passage of the 1964 Civil Rights Act, which outlawed discrimination in housing. Of the four trailer parks, three are racially integrated, but the smallest and oldest park, Lakeside, is predominantly black. The lot rent is about the same in these parks whether for a singlewide or a doublewide. However, only two of the thirteen families own a doublewide. The average cost of a new singlewide mobile home in North Carolina (2002) is around $29,000, making it a much lower cost than a conventional house in the city of Addington, which runs about $70,000 median cost.[3] About one-quarter of the families in the park sample are full owners, but close to two-thirds pay on a mortgage or contract (table 4.2). The proportion of park families who bought a new mobile home is similar to the proportion who bought a used one, and both groups have lived in their mobile homes fewer than five years, although this time frame might indicate a recent trade-up. The nearly one-third (32 percent) who view their park home as permanent are those who own better, newer homes or are retired.

Shady Grove

Shady Grove is the largest of the study parks. It lies next to a major intersection, between two stick-built home subdivisions and some farmland, along a four-lane road used by residents for all travel. An elementary school and the apartment

TABLE 4.2 Residential status of North Carolina park households

RESIDENTIAL STATUS	PERCENTAGE
Ownership	
Own home in full	26
Own home, pay on a mortgage	41
Buying on contract sale	25
Renting home	8
Tenure	
Previously lived in mobile home	49
Define home as a "permanent"	32
Prefer rural or small-town living	41
Structure	
Singlewide	91
Doublewide	9
Purchased as new	48

Source: Survey of randomly selected sample of trailer-park households (n = 65).

complex The Projects are north of the intersection and the park. Lining the main road is a mixture of car dealerships, single-family homes, a convenience store/gas station, and a bank.

When the park was developed in the late 1980s, the original owner laid out one hundred house sites on a fifty-one-acre tract. Around 1995 the current and second owner added about one hundred additional sites. He lives in Addington. According to the white park manager, an original resident, before the expansion the park was always filled to capacity but since then has never been fully rented. At the time of our survey, slightly over 80 percent of sites were occupied. The park is tidy and homes are well kept. Flo, the manager, accurately estimates that more than half are African American families. "On most occasions I've had more trouble with whites than with blacks," she volunteered.

A tidy office stands at the park's entrance, allowing Flo to see who comes and goes. Mailboxes are outside the office. People stop to chat with Flo, pay rent, or discuss problems when retrieving their mail. Along the park's paved streets homes are sited in parallel, with the hitch end facing the street. The lot size, on average, is fifty by one hundred feet, and each lot rents for $140 month (in the early 2000s). For this rent, a household gets a lawn, utility hookups, and a paved driveway graded on a slope to divert rainwater runoff. The park has city water and trash collection. Most homes are singlewide, with only a handful of double-wides. Park rules were commented on by Flo:

> Pets are supposed to live strictly inside a person's home. . . . We don't allow fences; we don't allow dog houses. . . . There're not supposed to be any firearms or BB guns. . . . [Parents] are supposed to keep reasonable control of their children. You are supposed to keep the outward appearance of your home in good . . . shape. They have to keep their lots clean and uncluttered. . . . Keep your grass mowed. . . . We try to keep things quiet. . . . I've pretty much given up on parking on the grass.

Though 20 percent of Shady Grove sites are unrented, few sites actually stand empty. As a mobile home dealer, the park owner uses the empty lots to display available trailers for potential buyers and make the park appear full. If buying a display home, a family can readily move in. While carrying out the field study, Michelle Eley rented an unfurnished older singlewide from the park owner. He made an exception for her with this older trade-in he owned, as park rules require that tenants own their homes.

The park has a raw, bleak appearance despite being thirty years old because apparently no trees were planted when the park was developed. Small young trees are now planted hopefully throughout the park, and a row of mature evergreens stands along the park's rear perimeter. A new homeowner, a young

African American woman, appreciates that the park is tidy. "You don't see a lot of junk in people's yards. Trailers for the most part look pretty well maintained." Most residents keep their small lawns cut short, while only 10 percent enhance their homes with flowers, a stone walkway, a patio, or a deck. One man related a common opinion about why few sites have improvements: "Because he [the park owner] owns it.... Have you seen the patio blocks that people have in their yards? Well, if you take up his grass to put blocks down, they become his blocks."

Shady Grove, because of its two hundred sites and housing density, resembles a small town. But the park's layout does not facilitate easy interaction. People routinely drive the two main streets to their homes without passing through other park sections. No public gathering spaces are provided. Except for the quick daily visit to their mailbox, residents do not regularly frequent any other park space. The park is a quiet place with noises seldom heard from other homes, even from next-door neighbors. According to Flo, the stillness is due to the quality of the residents: "They're good people and they're quiet." When a car passes through the park, playing loud music, people assume the driver is not a park resident. A black woman who moved from another trailer park commented, "It's quiet. Where I used to live, it was terrible. When I got here, I thought I was in the suburbs."

Most black households describe their park tenure as temporary and their mobile home as a "starter home"—the first rung on the housing ladder to something better.[4] They do not form strong bonds with park neighbors, unless, like the Bankstons, they believe trailer home ownership signifies their housing dream achieved (about one-third; see table 4.2). If bonds are formed, however, friendships are typically confined to the same ethnic group.[5] An African American woman who moved in about a year ago regards the park as her permanent home: "I feel that people in the neighborhood are concerned about each other's welfare. The ones that I talk to are into helping each other. . . . I already knew my neighbor that is behind when I moved here. Other people in the park have said to me, 'If there is anything I can do, just let me know.' . . . I can depend on my neighbors to watch my home when I'm away."

During the fall and winter months, little outside social activity occurs despite North Carolina's mild climate. But with the burst of warm air and the longer days of spring and summer, outdoor activities pick up. A cluster of African American households on the back street enjoy the liveliest social life in the park, centered on the Bankstons' home. They hold frequent parties and cookouts attended by their kin, neighbors, or church friends. "Everyone loves my mother," explains Viola's teenage son, Trevor. Viola knows a white neighbor complained to the manager about their home being a "drug house": "They don't want black people getting along together. They has this home to be a drug house because we party together. And when we cook, we cook together." So distinctive is the heavy traffic of visitors at the Bankstons' home that a white woman living down the street who was unacquainted with them assumed a drug house was the only possible explanation and reported them to management.

Shady Grove's size stimulates informal economic activity by entrepreneurial residents. As one man observed, "This place makes all kinds of money." Parents drop off and pick up children from an unadvertised day-care center disguised as a standard mobile home. On his park walk, a youth pointed out a trailer he and his friends frequent to buy snacks and candy. Male residents mow lawns or repair cars or trucks, fix home electrical or plumbing problems for neighbors. Occasionally, a household holds a Saturday morning yard sale. These informal economic activities, however, are not publicly encouraged by Flo.

In warm weather, front doors are left open to catch a breeze. Outside, people greet one another, chat, do yard work, or wash cars—as in any small town. Men on Eley's street regularly congregated at one home to trade car parts, lend tools, or help with car repairs. Park youth walk in groups, play football on a vacant home lot, ride bikes, or play basketball. They scramble out of the way to allow drivers by. Young children provide an excuse for park mothers to visit. In the evening, Hispanic women (fewer than five park households) stroll down a main street with their children, while Hispanic men often linger outside one home to drink a cold beer and chat. People trust that Shady Grove is a safe place; except for the concern about the so-called drug house, fears about neighbors are never mentioned.

Cedar Brook

The second largest study park was also developed in the 1970s and has 165 lots. Two absentee investors from out of state are its third set of owners. It stands two miles from Shady Grove at another main intersection, across from the military base and beside an upscale subdivision. An Addington middle school is nearby. Cedar Brook's rules resemble those of Shady Grove, and the park is similarly peaceful. Like Shady Grove's manager, Deb, the white manager of Cedar Brook, has lived in the park since its development.

All homes in Cedar Brook are singlewide. The lot size is slightly narrower than those of Shady Grove with homes positioned hitch end and perpendicular to the street. The park is on city water and garbage. Cedar Brook is shady because of numerous large trees, particularly in the original older section. A creek wraps around two sides of the park. At $110, Cedar Brook's monthly lot rent is the lowest among the four parks. Its low lot rent, mature trees, the creek, and the oft-mentioned congenial manager make the park desirable and explain why Cedar Brook park is always filled to capacity. It alone of Addington's parks has a waiting list for home sites. An African American mother of two, a two-year resident, has complaints about the narrow lot size, however: "When I'm in bed at night, I can [hear] the neighbors next door . . . can hear their child crying."

Calvin Roberts, an African American father of two, considers it a desirable park: "If you want some peace and quiet, it is a nice place. A lot of people think that trailer parks are loud, wild, and rowdy. . . . You don't have a lot of noisy neighbors here. . . . I don't have to worry about the law." During the summer vacation, however, his teenage daughter stays at her grandmother's in the country because the Robertses are not comfortable with her being alone all day in the house. That teenage boys attract friends from outside the park to hang out makes him nervous: "If boys knew she was here in the house by herself, it would be an incentive for them to come by when we're not home. I don't want to put [her] in that predicament." Perhaps his concerns are shaped by their previous life in subsidized apartments: "You had to watch who you talked with and what you said—that's why I didn't hang around a lot of people. The law came out there [often]."[6] In contrast, other parents regard the park as safe. An African American mother of a teenage girl said, "It's nice. I trust my daughter here by herself. I trust that nobody will bother her," even though the mother is away all day working.

Hands-on engagement is the hallmark of Deb's management. Her sign posted at the park entrance reads, "No loud music." It is rule violated more by park visitors than by residents, she says. Deb makes an effort to know park children. If she finds a child misbehaving, she assigns a task, such as picking up park trash. "I usually go around the park with them and pick up litter," which allows her "to learn how they are doing in school." A sign in the office window captures Deb's blunt management style: "All children with bicycles stop riding in other peoples [sic] yards. When you are walking in the street, get out of the way of traffic and stop walking in other peoples yards unless invited." When picking up mail inside the office, residents often stop to chat and learn the latest gossip from Deb.

The park's ambience is exemplified by boys playing basketball outside one home, girl groups strolling the paved streets, and neighbors greeting one another outside. Several park men fish together at the river behind the park or play horseshoes at one house. Extended families gather outside on summer Sundays for a cookout under the trees.

A middle-aged African American couple regularly attends a park Bible study group of ten, organized by a neighbor who is a minister. This group extends support to other park residents. "We want to help people in the community. If we give people money, we don't ask for the money back. . . . We have saved $1,000 in four months and the money is in a bank account. . . . We've helped to pay someone's light bill. We've given someone bail money when this person failed to pay their child support. We've helped a person get his car fixed." The Bible study group and the park's general sociability reflect a sense of community among residents.[7]

Northwinds

Northwinds is the newest of the study parks. Because of its newer homes, lot size, and the land-owned section, it is the most upscale of the study parks. Situated outside the city, secluded amid a dense forest, the park has a subdivision ambience. It is zoned as both a subdivision and a trailer park, with half the one hundred lots for rent and the other half available for purchase. How it is designed and operated reflects new trends in the mobile home park industry. According to the owner-manager, "This is a family-owned operation. We—my brothers and my dad—developed the park. . . . We wanted to give individuals a choice. The homes must be fairly new. To own their property, they must have a fairly sizable home—it must be a doublewide . . . [and it] must also have a foundation. . . . Each lot is twenty-five thousand square feet because the county requires that you have a septic tank on each lot."

A benefit to tenants of the septic tank requirement is home sites that are the largest among the study parks. Both singlewides and doublewides are found on the rental side. Renters pay a monthly fee of $165, the most expensive rent among the study parks. More rental sites are occupied (n = 35) than are owned lots (n = 18), with the occupied sites scattered rather than clustered together. Since it opened five years ago, "the tenants have been wonderful and we've had very little trouble," according to the manager, a dedicated salesman: "We feel that there is a need for mobile home parks. It is a great starter home . . . a more affordable home. . . . We don't allow people to rent their mobile home to another person." The park's upscale feel and its secluded location are well known among the other trailer parks. A resident from the rental side explains why homes are widely dispersed: "When someone moves in, they don't want to move right next to someone. . . . Both lots behind me have been empty. The home across from me was the first one to move here [on this street]. I don't consider this to be a mobile home park. I have lived in mobile home parks and this does not feel like one."

Being a newly developed park perhaps accounts for the fact that Northwinds lacks a neighborhood feel. No youth are seen hanging out, for example. A resident confirms that little neighborliness exists: "There is no socializing out here. . . . Even during the summertime, I don't see a lot of socializing. I wave to everyone I see, but people will just look at you." Another resident agrees with his observation: "Everybody kind of stays to themselves. . . . I came from a [mobile home park] where everybody knew you at least by your first name." Northwinds seems more a suburban bedroom community than a small town.

Lakeside

Lakeside is the oldest, smallest, and shabbiest of the four Addington study parks. It lies north of Shady Grove, directly across from an upscale subdivision. It was developed about fifty years ago, prior to when mobile home size became larger. Lakeside has thirty-four home sites on six acres, with a mixture of older and newer (less than five years old) homes packed closely together. Several sites stand vacant. Trailers are aligned hitch end and perpendicular to the single, narrow unpaved street. Lots rent for $125, for which a tenant gets a small yard, no drive-way, few trees, and a patchy lawn. Homeowners create a yard spot for their cars or park on the street next to their homes. There is no resident manager, but the owner lives in Addington. He purchased Lakeside under a foreclosure about fif-teen years ago. It is evident from his lack of interest in upgrading the park that he expects the land to eventually be purchased for a "higher use"—like the upscale subdivision across the road.

A father of two remarks, "The owner always rides through and checks things out around three times a month." He considers the park somewhat desirable: "Sometimes it's all right and sometimes it's rough. Sometimes people are play-ing music loud. And sometimes you hear shooting next door. The owner drives through the park and always asks you, 'Do you have any problems? Is everything all right out here?'" Long-term tenants consider the park vastly improved under its present ownership. "It is a lot better. . . . A lot of the older mobile homes were pulled out and newer ones were pulled in," according to one couple. Another couple with young children agrees that the quality of tenants is now better: "When we first moved here it didn't look anywhere like it looks now. We don't have all the wild people that we did before. . . . People have been evicted. . . . People don't know how to act . . . keep getting in trouble and fighting."

Residents appreciate that the owner keeps the park tidy. According to one father, "The park is nice and clean—no bottles and cans. [Everyone] keeps the grass cut." He thinks outsiders are the worst thing about the park: "I see thugs hanging around and walking around at all times at night." He refers to these outsiders as from the Cedar Brook or Shady Grove parks. "I've had clothes stolen from the clothesline outside . . . and brand new bikes. If you don't keep them locked up, they will walk away." For all these reasons, he is looking into the upscale Northwinds park to move the doublewide home he bought new two years earlier.

Though all the trailers are closely sited along a single street, Lakeside does not function as a cohesive neighborhood. People are familiar with other residents, but the park's layout and size make familiarity unavoidable. Homes are clustered so closely that any conversations from neighbors are easily overheard. "I hardly have privacy. I can hear people knocking on my neighbor's door," lamented an unhappy resident. Residents seldom visit casually outside when they do home or car maintenance or go to the mailbox. Rarely is a family observed having a picnic or entertaining guests. Small children ride bikes back and forth on the street under the supervision of an older sibling, converting the single park street into their playground. Teenage youth also hang out on the street with friends.

For a couple with two children the park's affordability was a major attraction: "It's one of the cheaper parks in the city limits." Gladys Turner, the single mother of two whose older trailer is the first home she's owned, however, expressed frustration with the park's density. For her the park is a temporary way station, and she tries to ignore the undesirables among her neighbors. Other than the affordable low rent, little else seems good about the park to families.

In all four Addington parks the complaint heard most often was about flooding due to poor drainage from the high water table or nearness to a river. "When it rains it floods really bad," said a Shady Grove woman. A man in the same park thinks the owner should "dig out the trenches so it won't flood so bad." In Lakeside a father echoed these sentiments: "I don't like it. . . . The backyard stays muddy. [The owner] should put concrete everywhere so we won't have to deal with this muddy yard." Similarly homeowners in all the parks complain that "kids go through people's yards" and that someone is always playing loud music. Residents in the two larger parks also grumble that stray dogs and cats run loose. But these complaints were also heard in the New Mexico and Illinois trailer parks and seem related to the density of trailer parks.

Distinctively, in contrast to the white Illinois families, African American park families do not invest discretionary income in pet ownership. Only eight households (of sixty-five) keep a pet—six dogs and two cats. Of the eight pet owners seven are white, and a lone black woman has a tiny Chihuahua house dog. Thus, white pet ownership in the North Carolina parks resembles the widespread pet ownership in the all-white Illinois park.

While the two larger parks' rules do not specifically prohibit or regulate home site plantings, residents seem to feel it is discouraged. Two small kitchen gardens are cultivated in Shady Grove. While the gardeners are probably aware that park rules ban gardens, they finesse it by keeping theirs modest. Aside from rules that discourage landscaping home sites, not doing lot beautification highlights that for blacks, park residence is just an address; status and respect are earned elsewhere among families and the church.

Management in the Two Larger Parks

Resident managers in the two large parks by their contrasting administrative styles shape the neighborhood ambience. Shady Grove's longtime manager, Flo, greets people by their first names in her smoke-filled office—especially if they are longtime residents like she is. Flo, a middle-aged white woman, is open, honest, and a talker: "Being manager to me is not a title; it's being a head and looking out for everyone in the park. I think of myself as one of the tenants and we are all neighbors.... It has its drawbacks.... They sort of run over me sometimes." Though Flo appears responsive to tenants' concerns, her tendency to misjudge the demeanor of African American residents creates distrust. She explained to Eley (who is African American), "If I get the impression from how you talk to me that you don't want to be associated with me, then I won't bother you ... especially, you know, with the black community. I've had some come in here and gave me the impression that they would rather not deal too much with a white person.... Then I did business with them and didn't bother them otherwise."

She saw herself as aloof. Several African Americans volunteered that Flo is a "racist," although Eley never observed her discriminate among residents by race. An African American woman thinks that Flo tends to pry and probe for gossip: "It [is] always said that black people are nosy and that they try to get in your business.... [But] the manager tries to get in your business. When she tries to ask me something about what is going on in the park, I tell her that 'I don't know.' It's none of my business what people do in their own home.... To me, she don't know nothin' because she is askin' people questions." The fact that Flo granted an exemption for a white family to the "no fences to house a large dog outside" rule is seen as evidence of her preferential treatment of whites. Blacks note that none of them receives a similar exemption.

Cedar Brook's well-liked park manager, Deb, like Flo, is white, in her early sixties, a heavy smoker, and an original park resident. Her management style is blunt and assertive. Deb describes her philosophy: "To be a park manager, you have to have compassion. You have to be a psychiatrist. You have to be a mother. You have to be a grandmother. It's like being a family.... Whatever the problem whether large or small, you have to treat each problem individually because it's important to the family. You definitely have to love people."

Residents all agree Deb maintains firm control of the park, and little park activity escapes her. Both African American and white residents credit Deb for why Cedar Brook is a desirable park. A black resident reflects residents' satisfaction: "Around here if you need help, all you have to do is ask and 90 percent of the time, you'll receive help. Nobody bothers you. It's a nice park. I think it's because of Deb. . . . She does a background check on people. If you are doing drugs or have a criminal record, she tries to keep you out." In fact, only in this study park did anyone mention doing a background check. A white resident praises Deb as "one of the best landlords you can have. I feel that I am part of her family. If anything happens, she is here to help you. If I ever need to talk to [her] it is as far as it will go. I will never move from this park, unless I've bought a piece of land."

Cedar Brook's residents are unique among study trailer parks in having positive feelings about their manager. Perhaps it is because Deb identifies as one of them: "I don't think I am better than anyone out here. I'm just one of the people living in the community and just guide the ones out here so we can have a better place to live." When tenants are tardy with their rent or ignore a child's bad behavior, Deb describes how she deals with it: "You have good and bad in all parks as far as that goes. This is the first park I lived in and I love it out here. . . . As a person in charge of this many families . . . you've got to be like an actress on stage. You've got to handle each person a different way. There are no two families alike. I've been here for sixteen years. It is best job I've ever had. . . . I check the park every night before I go to bed."

Because of Deb there exists a sense of community in Cedar Brook trailer park not observed elsewhere. For example, under a community watch system Deb initiated, she encourages neighbors to get to know one another and report crime or unsafe conditions. She appointed five "block captains" to help her monitor the park. "If they see something they will call me. . . . In the summer, we have a meeting. In the wintertime, we will talk on the phone." Residents themselves organize regular park-wide flea markets with Deb's support.[8]

Deb believes that Addington looks down on her trailer park. She harbors a visceral dislike of the city manager, stemming from dealing with him since the city annexed Cedar Brook. "[The city manager] wants to do away with us. . . . I don't like him. He's caused me trouble. . . . That's why when [Eley] came in, I was kind of hesitant because I thought you were associated with him and you might say or do something to hurt us." She believes the city thinks the worst of the park and treats it with prejudice: "If something happens at [two upscale subdivisions] it will not get in the paper. However, if something happens over here, it would be in the paper. . . . If you live in [a] mobile home park, that doesn't make you any less of a person. It is better living here than being on welfare. We're just as good as they are. If you live in [a] mobile home park, they, the so-called elite, want to refer to you as 'trailer trash.' . . . We live out here because we have to, not because we want to."

With the exception of the few negative comments about the Shady Grove park manager, Flo, African Americans seldom raised racial concerns about life in their integrated parks. But a young black woman in Shady Grove commented that it took time for neighbors to warm to newcomers. "If people don't know you, they've got to feel you out. I'm the only black in this immediate section." She was touched when her white neighbor volunteered to trim tree branches hanging low over her front door.

Family Lives in the North Carolina Trailer Parks Detailed

Apart from the integrated park where they live and the places where they work, blacks tend to live in a segregated world because of their black church and kin networks. People who still have rural roots return to their black small towns and attend church there. With one exception, the thirteen families attend predominantly black churches. Children experience integration in their schools.

Why did African American families move from their segregated rural roots into integrated trailer parks? The pull, or motivational, factors most often cited by the sixty-five families for buying a trailer and placing it in a land-lease park are location (29 percent) and cost (31 percent). An elderly, single African American woman explains her mobile home purchase: "My mother was living at the time with me and we wanted to get out of The Projects. . . . But I had to put so much down payment at the time for a [conventional] house. I had to get what we could get. So I got a trailer." Another African American woman recalled that necessity motivated her choice: "I wanted to get out of my mother's house. And I moved. . . . I had a baby after being there a year. . . . My roommate and I were paying for the gas, which included the hot water, stove, and heat, and it was $400 and something [a month]. We were killing ourselves. . . . For safety and health reasons, I decided to move into this trailer."

Life events also push black families into a trailer park. Some tire of renting (17 percent), while others suddenly need a place to live (12 percent). A social network is a strong pull factor: 11 percent married a park resident, had a relative already living in the park, or knew someone residing in the park. About half (49 percent) of the sixty-five households are living in their second mobile home (table 4.2). For the other half this mobile home is their first, especially those who were previously apartment renters. When compared with the white residents living in the same parks, blacks are less likely to own their home outright (30 percent versus 59 percent of whites), are more recent mobile home owners (four years compared with whites' five and one-half years), and are younger (thirty-five years on average) compared with whites (forty-one years on average).

When asked to name three advantages of their neighborhood, park residents most often select location, affordability, and people. Generally, three-quarters of residents are pleased with their trailer home and park. An elderly white woman is representative: "We have good neighbors. I don't see any fights around here. Everybody seems to work well together. I haven't had any problems here." An African American father similarly voices satisfaction: "We have paved streets and the grass is cut. It's close to town. The lot rent and housing is affordable. If you are renting, you will pay $500 a month. I'm buying and I am just paying $360." In short, a trailer park is a good deal for most. Specific complaints about park life, however, are common. "It's not really private as far as outside privacy. You have people walking across your yard. If you have company, you don't have space for parking," said one woman. A few (8 percent) consider their park undesirable after experiencing a theft or personal property damage by, they assume, neighbors. Most such complaints were heard in Lakeside, the shabbiest park.

Jobs that pay well, Addington's amenities, or a higher standard of living pull blacks from the rural countryside. About half of the adults (ten of twenty-one) in the thirteen families were raised in small towns or rural places less than an hour's drive from Addington. They characterize themselves as rural people. Another seven were either born in or have lived in Addington since adulthood. The remaining four adults came from cities such as New York or from elsewhere in North Carolina and migrated to Addington for marriage, to be near relatives, or in one case to keep a son out of an urban gang.

We saw in chapter 2 that African American families in North Carolina typically work in the service industries, although they hold managerial jobs that pay better and have benefits. Two women from the thirteen families are underemployed in low or moderate-wage jobs in the trade or service sectors. Families may supplement their incomes with work in the informal economy. In particular, the men with less education work in the informal economy, which allows them to match the contribution of better-educated women to the family. Vehicle and home repairs figure most importantly in work men do in the informal economy, while child care and transportation predominate among women's involvement.[9]

Park blacks, especially those who strongly identify as rural people, speak proudly of family history and of parents or kin still working the land they own.[10]

Their homeownership priority was learned from parents whose life in an agrarian society made landownership of paramount importance. One park woman proudly told about her grandfather, a rare black rural business owner: "When his family was liberated by the [slave-owning] family, the owner helped them to buy their own house and the store next door." Other park adults were also knowledgeable about their family history. They would tell of when their ancestors were liberated from slavery and became farmers and landowners.

Like much of rural America, park African Americans no longer follow parents into farming. But those who migrate to Addington are challenged to replicate the financial achievements of their parents, although they earn equivalent incomes. Eventual landownership—under a conventional home—looms large in their dream of a better life, although realization of the dream is financially daunting. If park families are unable to achieve conventional home and landownership, it will be a major difference between the two generations. That black park adults are from large families militates against their inheriting much land or money from parents, who in all likelihood will divide assets evenly among their many children (table 4.3). But African American park adults, unlike their parents, have the option of buying a starter home—a trailer without land, sited in an Addington mobile home park, although this bottom rung on the housing-tenure ladder clearly represents a dream compromised. One father, living in a new doublewide, expressed his goals: "I like my home. It's roomy, comfortable, well insulated—holds good air and heat. In the future, I would like to put it on some land out in the country. I think it loses value, sitting out here."

The Rogerses, a couple in their early forties with two children—the most well-off financially of the thirteen families with their two incomes—live in a doublewide purchased new seven years ago. Cora Rogers owns her own business, a successful beauty shop. Her early working in a hair salon that closed "helped me to get where I wanted to go." It motivated Cora to start her own salon, which now has five stylists who rent chairs from her. The Rogerses were the first from either of their families to move to Shady Grove park. They were followed, through chain migration from their place of origin out of state, by her mother and his mother and sister. Cora Rogers explains her future goals: "We have land in [the countryside] but I don't want to be in the boondocks. I'm looking for land and a possible move to a triplewide. I want to be financially stable and enjoy life. I have dreams to build a new salon with a school added, and even a franchise." She has already priced a triplewide plus land package ($92,000) and thinks they can manage it soon, as a result of her business's success and their investments. Land ownership remains central to Cora's vision of financial stability and the good life.

TABLE 4.3 Two generations of North Carolina black park families compared

HOUSEHOLD GENERATION	PARK FAMILIES (N = 13 HOUSEHOLDS N = 21 ADULTS)	PARENTAL GENERATION (PARK ADULTS' PARENTS) (N = 20)[a]
Homeownership (n = 13)		
Owns house only	13 (100%)	1 (5%)
Owns house and land	—	12 (60%)
Missing information	—	7 (35%)
Educational attainment (n = 21)		
Less than high school	5 (24%)	5 (25%)
High school graduate only	6 (28%)	6 (30%)
Some college only	8 (38%)	1 (5%)
College graduate	2 (10%)	2 (10%)
Missing information	—	6 (30%)
Occupation (n = 21)		
Professional, technician, administrative support	8 (38%)	6 (30%)
Service, craft, operative, sales	11 (52%)	12 (60%)
Disability and homemaker	2 (10%)	2 (10%)
Number of children (n = 13)		
4 or fewer	12 (92%)	10 (50%)
5 to 8	1 (8%)	4 (20%)
9 to 16	—	6 (30%)
Same church as Parents (n = 13)		
Yes	7 (54%)	*****
No	4 (30%)	
Missing information	2 (15%)	
Distance from trailer park (or Addington) to origin community (n = 13)		
In town	4 (30%)	
Less than 30 minutes	3 (24%)	*****
Between 30 and 45 minutes	4 (30%)	
More than one hour	2 (15%)	

Source: Intensive sample of 13 park families, including 21 adults.

[a]N = 20 because information was lacking for one male who did not complete the genealogical instrument.

Kinship Connections

African American park families are deeply embedded in their extended kin net-works.[11] Because the park parental generation possesses large sibling sets living nearby, they have access to rich support and resources. Those lacking such support struggle financially but in some cases create kinship-like ties with friends and church networks as an alternative.

> *Brenda Roberts is a certified nursing assistant, and her husband, Calvin, works in construction. They are in their thirties and have been married for fourteen years. They have two children, a girl fifteen years old and a boy eleven years old. Calvin is their stepfather. After renting for eight years the Robertses moved into Cedar Brook trailer park six years ago. Calvin said where they previously rented "was noisy. . . . I was tired of renting. We wanted something better." They bought a year-old singlewide and have only two years left on the loan for their neatly kept home. When the home is paid for "I would like to move back to Thomasville, where my parents live," says Brenda. "My grandparents' house, my daddy and his brothers and sisters all live there in a row." She likes the rural place because it is quiet and "you can leave the door unlocked. Everybody is related, and it's like a neighborhood there."*
>
> *Brenda talks with her mother daily and sees her three brothers about three times a week. "I am the baby. . . . They are always looking out for me. They give me money or anything I call for . . . they bring me food if I'm hungry. . . . All my relatives. . . . there are none that I don't talk to. I talk to my aunts. I talk to my daddy's sister and her daughter about four or five times a week. . . . My aunts and my mother will get my kids when I don't want to get them. . . . My parents do everything for me. . . . My daddy came around 6:00 a.m. to bring me breakfast before I left for work. My coworker told me I was too spoiled." Her family knows that Calvin and Brenda eat out a lot, because she is not much of a cook. When Brenda does cook, the dinner starts with a prayer. Calvin tells their teenage daughter, "Give the phone a break," making clear the family has mealtime rules.*
>
> *Calvin's mother also lives in the country, but his father recently was moved to a nursing home. He comes from a family of ten and is close to two brothers and two sisters, who live in Addington. He sees them weekly. "We sit around Mama's house, share a cold drink, have cookouts, visit, and play cards. I loan them money, cars, and babysit their kids." His older sister fishes with him, and will "babysit my kids." Calvin's mother "calls me early Saturday and Sunday morning to bring her some breakfast. I take her to*

see my father. It is whatever she needs for me to do." They like to play horseshoes when relatives come to visit.

Brenda attends church with her parents in their country Baptist church, although she is not heavily involved. Other than one friend who attended grade school with her, Brenda has no other friends. "I don't deal with people," she explains about those not in her kin network.

A rapid decline in family size, exemplified by Calvin and Brenda's large sibling sets in contrast to their own two children, characterizes the thirteen African American families. (Table 4.3 compares the two generations.) Rural parents of the twenty-one park parents (from the family sample of thirteen) in particular all produced larger families than have their many offspring. Sizes of families of origin of trailer-park parents range from as high as sixteen siblings in two cases to ten siblings in three cases and five siblings in two cases. Of the twenty adult siblings (data for one adult are missing), sixteen come from families of three or more siblings, while a minority of four adults have only one or two siblings. The average household size of the thirteen trailer-park families, however, is approximately four persons—typically with two children under the age of eighteen. This dramatic decline in family size reflects a trend among rural American families more generally but is an especially strong trend among rural African Americans.[12]

Park adults in the family sample we knew best explain that they consciously chose to have a smaller family than their parents had. A mother, one of eleven siblings, provided an explanation for the present smaller black families: "Well, birth control was not fully introduced into society until the 1960s, so there wasn't anything available for parents to use to prevent pregnancy." Their rural parents, park adults also say, had large families because of a need for farm labor. A married park couple, each of whom was raised in a large family, decided two children was what they could afford, given their educational aspirations. And she explained, "I saw how [my parents] came up and struggled. . . . I didn't want a big family, although my parents took care of us and we never wanted for anything. . . . I want my kids to continue on in school and go to college."

Kin network embeddedness—defined by proximity to kin, frequency of contact, and strength of bonds—is prioritized by black park families. Underlying the trailer-park residence choice of blacks is careful strategizing to live and work near kin. Kinship, for example, acts both to push and to pull them toward a mobile home purchase and to site it in an Addington trailer park. Over half of adults' extended kin networks (thirteen of twenty-one adults) live either in Addington or in half a dozen small towns scattered within a twenty-five-mile radius of the city. An adult regularly "stays in touch" with parents and siblings. For most (eleven of thirteen), to stay in touch means almost daily contact or at least a weekly visit. If a park family sees a particular relative just a few times a year, it is usually explained by the distance between them.

A highlight of weekly social life for black park families and kin is the Sunday dinner get-together. Several households prepare the meal, or one family member cooks the dinner for all. Special occasions, such as holidays and Father's or Mother's Day, are also opportunities for the kin network of parents, grandparents, parents' siblings, and their families to gather for a meal. For example, Brenda Roberts regularly gets together with her three brothers who live in Addington: "We are a close-knit family. Sundays are our family day. I may cook one Sunday and everyone will come over. And my brothers will cook the next Sunday. Sometimes we get together, on Fridays, and take our kids to Chuck E. Cheese.... We'll keep each other's kids. We'd do anything for each other."

African American kin networks also engage in extensive and substantive exchanges. Parents provide generous financial assistance to their park sons and daughters. Babysitting, errand running, visiting, and giving emotional support are common sibling exchanges. Large sibling groups and grandparents, who share child-rearing burdens, are another example of black kin network resilience.[13] A married mother of three describes the resources that circulate in her kin network: "My parents basically take care of me by babysitting, cooking dinner, and running errands for me. My sisters and I do the same thing for each other— we help raise each other's children; we also babysit and run errands for one another.... I have friends, but my sisters are my girlfriends. We go out dancing, take vacations, eat, and go to the movies together."

Although her three sisters live at some distance, Georgia Walker, the single park mother of two, describes how rich exchanges bind them: "We enjoy each other's kids.... We all have children. We help each other financially. We give each other emotional support. My sisters give me advice on parenting my children, given that they've been mothers longer than I have." Ms. T. describes the close bonds among her five sisters: "We always get together. I love them. We go to church together every Sunday. Somebody is always fixing dinner. Everything I do involves my sisters and without them, I would be lost. My mother died four years ago, but she left us bonded.... I run errands.... I babysit. I cook for them. Anything within my means, I try to do it. If they need for me to do something, I'm there."

Black families who remain strongly connected to a rural place—for their community identity, social networks, church, and ties to land—do not engage socially in their Addington trailer park. Their strong kin ties leave little time or need for more social relationships. These families view their trailer park simply as a place to live. Typically, such park men describe themselves as profoundly rural—nine of the thirteen families self-identify as rural or small-town people. For example, a married father of two children with a large extended kin group commented, "I like the country. . . . I am looking for a doublewide [in a nearby rural place] . . . and I want to be on my own property. It's country and it's a better place for my kids. There's a lot of things I want to do in the country that I can't do here." In contrast, park women report they like living in Addington and enjoy its city amenities.

Embeddedness in a web of kinship tends to keep black park families stable residentially. They are unwilling to uproot and move far from kin. Although park families feel supported by their relatives, it is support that cuts both ways. Network demands may overtax a family at times.[14] And because of the dramatic decline in black family size in a single generation (table 4.3), park-family children raised among a small sibling set might not experience the same rich kin resources their parents draw on.

Alberta Matthews, a forty-seven-year-old single mother with a son, views their park residence as a temporary way station: "Our grandfather passed and we have land down in the country. My aunts and uncles have a piece of it and it is shared between all of the children. . . . We would like to move there and live on the land." In her case, underemployment is the trade-off required to maintain kin proximity. Alberta has a college degree in journalism. She decided against relocation for better job opportunities when she settled for underemployment in Addington to remain near family. Alberta started as a salesclerk but rose to a managerial position before being laid off when the national chain went through restructuring and closed its Addington store. Despite losing her job, Alberta did not despair, although forced to live off her 401K plan and monthly child support payments. While she seeks a new job, Alberta remains on her husband's medical insurance. Because they are only separated, the plan still covers her and their son. She stretches her limited income as far as possible by drawing deeply on her large, extended kin network. Alberta explains how the kin network and her husband, who is a constant presence, sustain the household during this crisis: "I have been very blessed. If there are minor money emergencies, I go to my husband. If I need my car repaired . . . he does it. I just purchased tires and he paid for half and I paid for half. For major or minor emergencies I go to somebody in the family. . . . If they can't do it, somebody knows someone who can do it most of the time." Despite being stretched thin financially (chapter 2), African American park families maintain more stability than their modest incomes would suggest because of their kin networks that provide both informal economic exchanges and rich resources of social support.

African American park adults feel a moral obligation to help kin in need. Kin are counted on, and they deliver, when trauma or tragedy occurs. Several park adults were raised by a relative—a grandmother or aunt—when a parent(s) could not care for them because of youth, divorce, or death. A woman whose mother had eleven children but died when the daughter was fifteen years old recalls that she "stayed with my grandmother after my mother passed." Her grandmother died just after she reached eighteen. "It was almost like she was waiting for me to graduate." The Wilsons, the older park couple, though on the edge financially, are raising a troubled grandchild because their daughter cannot or will not. Another park household cares for the wife's young niece while her mother is stationed abroad with the military. Because of the strength of the African American kin network, children raised by a relative other than a parent appear to weather the upheaval without undue emotional trauma. Divorce or being raised by alternative "parents" apparently does not trigger emotional trauma as a sort of collateral damage, as it does in Illinois. Park-family histories do not have stories of those who hit bottom because of parental abdication, willingly or accidentally, nor do they relate tales of recovery from a youthful period of hard living with drugs or alcohol. Fictive kin is a cultural practice that defines a strength of African Americans that enhances family resilience.[15]

Three park households of the thirteen are headed by single mothers—a widow; Georgia Walker, who is divorced; and Ms. T., who never married. The three have a husband as part of their dream. The other ten households are headed by married couples, of which eight live together and two are separated. That is, marriage seems a valued, even a preferred, status. Marital fragility is, however, evident in family histories. Among the twenty-one park adults, there are seven divorces in their backgrounds before they remarried. While divorce occurred frequently, so did remarriage. (Several parents of park parents, for example, had divorced but then remarried.) Alberta Reynolds and another park woman divorced and then remarried, although both are separated from their second husbands. In each case the second husband stays in the picture and provides financial or other resources, as noted above. Separation without divorce seems a strategy to assure children's welfare, despite parents not living together.

Stepsiblings gained through parental marriages are typically folded into the kin network. Viola Bankston considers herself closer to her stepsiblings than to her own siblings. The Donner household includes a mother; her two children from a previous marriage, Shantal and Simon; and a second husband. However, this blended family showed signs of problems. The teenage boy and the new husband did not get along, and Simon was floundering. Shantal, the ten-year-old daughter, was thriving amid the same circumstances. Shantal and her stepfather were quite close and loving. Simon turned for support to his first cousins in The Projects, who were a bad influence. Sadly, Simon dropped out of high school soon after the study, reflecting the challenges for raising black youth even in rural places.[16]

Black parents' goal is to raise successful children whose lives improve on theirs. They see education as the logical pathway to upward mobility. A mother of two who first became pregnant at age nineteen was unable to earn a degree beyond high school. She describes what she wants for her daughters: "No matter what, I want them to go ahead and complete school. I don't want them to stop to have families or babies. Just go straight through." Another mother, a high school graduate, also hopes her daughters will do things differently. "I want them to stay in school and finish college. . . . I want to keep those grandbabies away. I hope they have a job with their college education and be able to support themselves before they get married and begin having children." Life has shown these two park mothers that marriage and family do not guarantee security, as it might have for their parents. They realize better futures involve careful planning for their children. Georgia Walker explains the well-considered dream she has for her two daughters: "I want my kids to have opportunities . . . a better education, be more independent, have their own life after they get married. I want them to be more self-sufficient and don't feel that they need to be married. I want them to have a better life than me. A lot of little girls feel that they need to get married and feel that they need a man to take care of them—you know what I'm trying to say."

Two park households headed by single mothers lack kin nearby. They seem disadvantaged despite active kin connections they maintain long-distance. African American cultural practices, however, furnish alternatives that involve replication of what a kin network provides. For example, Georgia Walker lives far from her sisters, with whom she is close. She also lacks access to her ex-husband's local kin network. As a response to this disadvantage, Georgia has developed a close bond with her female pastor, whom she reveres and who is "like a mother to me." She explains, "The members of the church are my family. I can't separate my personal life from the church. People who I socialize with are members of the church. My best friend goes to my church. . . . My relationship with the pastor goes beyond the church." Essentially Georgia formed a fictive-kin bond with her pastor and members of the congregation that compensates for her lack of kin nearby.

Aside from the Bankstons, who consider the park their permanent address and have built a fictive-kin social network there, African American families generally view the trailer park as only a temporary place to live. When park friendships are formed, it is with their own ethnic group. Only children of elementary school age play in small, integrated neighborhood or school groups. By the time they become youth, their peer groups are ethnically homogeneous, mirroring the homogenous black networks of their parents and reflecting their racial socialization.[17] Black park families also lack much engagement in the community of

Addington. Because the trailer parks (excepting Northwinds) are incorporated into the city, park residents are eligible to vote locally, but only 41 percent report voting in the previous election. Reading the local newspaper also indicates community engagement, but only 20 percent do this.

Black park families find community through their rich and robust ties to kin and church rather than in wider Addington. Black social networks thus more closely resemble those of the New Mexico Hispanic park families (see chapter 5) than the smaller white kin networks of Illinois park families—which seem mainly limited to parents and sometimes the adults' siblings.

Situating Community in the Black Church

Addington's telephone directory lists approximately one hundred churches, a large number given the city's population of just under twenty thousand. An overlap in church affiliation might be expected among the group of thirteen African American households from just three parks (none of them live in Northwinds). We found, however, that eleven of the families each attend a different church (churches for two families are not documented, although we know they are churchgoers). Eight attend Baptist churches, two attend nondenominational churches (not affiliated with a particular Protestant sect or denomination), and one attends an African Methodist Episcopal (AME) church. Church affiliation primarily reflects where a park family's kin attend, and most refer to their church as a "family church."[18] People explain their membership in a particular church as "I grew up in that church" or "It's my family's church." As a consequence, black churches provide families access to another network that, along with their kinship network, endures over a lifetime. Their churches also supply both formal programs and tangible assistance that support trailer-park families both socially and substantively.

Alberta Reynolds is a good storyteller, who says, "I love to talk." She and her sixteen-year-old son Stephen live in a ten-year-old singlewide in Shady Grove park. She traded up because the new home has three bedrooms. "My son is so happy because we have more room." Her parents approved of the trade-up. "My father helped me purchase the home. . . . It came with everything but the refrigerator. . . . He is paying the mortgage." Alberta explained this substantial financial support with two reasons. First, Stephen is the only grandson of her parents and is close to them. Second, she has rheumatoid arthritis, and her family is concerned about her frail health. Stephen likes going to his grandparents' home, where they have four TVs in the living room, each tuned to a different game. "That's what we's about is sports—football and basketball," Alberta explained.

Alberta and her second husband are technically separated, but he stays committed to the family. She and Stephen are still on her husband's medical plan. He is a mechanic, and she worked in management in a national chain store that closed during the study. "He helps me out financially sometimes." Although Stephen is from her first marriage, he "has a good relationship with his stepfather." He is also a "momma's boy" whom she picks up and drops off for school because she doesn't want him to ride the bus.

Alberta explains her daily routine as "If I'm not working, I'm at church." She belongs to the same Baptist church as her parents, grandparents, and her aunts. In fact, her parents "met at church," where they both sang in the choir. Her father is still in the choir and wanted Alberta to sing a solo with him during the study. "I don't know why he wants me to sing, but I guess I'll sing the song with him. . . . I am spoiled too because of my father." Her aunts and uncles "all go to the church. . . . It's a family church." Church brings them all together at least for weekly services.

Alberta, however, is at church more than twice a week. She is deeply enmeshed in church affairs. "I make sure my pastor meets his appointments and that the bills are paid. . . . My pastor is really forgetful. I am the Sunday School treasurer. . . . I am sometimes surprised at what I am able to do. . . . On Thursday nights (twice a month) I have choir rehearsal. I attend Bible study every Wednesday." Stephen is also in the church choir and in Bible study. "The pastor's wife has a premonition that he's going to be a preacher because he's so outspoken at Bible study."

Her heavy church involvement strained Alberta's second marriage. Between the church and her strong family ties, "he felt overwhelmed. . . . He wasn't used to my lifestyle." He spent a lot of time working. "We never saw one another. . . . Also, he wasn't too engaged in the church."

Among the sample families, two-thirds of the twenty-one adults attend the church of their parents or grandparents. Only four households belong to a church not attended by other relatives. Church membership is characteristically a multigenerational phenomenon (table 4.3). Whether their church is in the countryside (four of the families) or in Addington city proper, those who follow a kin tradition of church affiliation refer to their congregation as "small," "country," or "family-like." And multigenerational family churches often incorporate other extended kin network members—aunts and uncles, nieces and nephews or cousins. Churches thus replicate for park families the environment in which their parents were raised. Perhaps it is this family-like environment of black churches that explains why all park couples not only belong to a church but are married if they live together. In contrast, we found common-law relationships and couples just living together as fiancé and girlfriend in both Illinois and New Mexico. Marriage did not seem the norm that it is among blacks in North Carolina.

Black churches typically incorporate a distinctive fictive kinship-like structure that resembles the family writ large. Congregates commonly use kin terms such as "church mother" for female church elders or "brother" or "sister" for peer members. The concept of church family denotes a special fictive-kin relationship, and the long-term bonds that people often maintain with other congregants are like family ties. Given the fictive-kin basis of church networks, exchanges of informal social support are likely and even predictable. Thus, a family church intimately represents an overlapping of the small worlds of kin and church that benefit the successful development of children.[19] Park parents describe ministers and congregation members as a source of emotional support, information, and substantial instrumental support—ranging from rides to financial assistance. The church provides youth mentors—like those that benefited Trevor Bankston.

People often turn to their church pastor or other church members as trusted intermediaries with the wider city of Addington. For example, Georgia Walker related how her church linked her with a legal adviser in Addington. "When I needed a lawyer, my pastor was the first person I spoke to. She gave me a name of a lawyer she trusted and one who will make legal decisions in my best interest." Georgia also gained information from church elders, who, like the pastor "know the right people and have the right contacts." Her church also holds forums about family matters. "If the children are not doing well in school, [pastor] has offered assistance in visiting the teachers [a conference] and finding help for the children."

For those four park families affiliated with "nonfamily" or nondenominational Addington churches, the pull of membership is to fill "a spiritual need." A single mother moved from New York to Addington as an adult and felt adrift. She joined a nonfamily church, where she is actively engaged. She explains her rationale for her choice: "I enjoy the fellowship and the teaching. . . . This church is different from the church I was attending at the time. [My former] church was a family-oriented church, but it was spiritually dead. . . . It was started by a certain family way back when . . . and the same family is still part of the church. It was difficult for them to adapt to change." Similarly, another woman lacking kin nearby joined a church after a work friend suggested she attend an evening service at her church: "I met a friend, an old acquaintance of mine, who invited me to come to revival one night at the church. When I went there, I met the pastor and I listened to her teaching. I liked the way she brought the Word. She brought a lot of things to light in terms of what I needed to change in my life.... I've learned a lot. I also enjoy the fellowship—the love and respect that members have for one another."

Blacks who attend a family church rely mainly on kinfolk for emotional support rather than the wider congregation. As one park mother who attends the same rural church as her parents explains, she avoids sharing intimacies with non-kin: "Most of the time, I depend on my family. I have a very close family. I can call on any of them for help." Another park woman is similarly reluctant to confess confidential matters with non-kin in her family-like church: "We are a quiet family so we like to keep things to ourselves. Since they are my family, they already know my needs. People tend to flood into your life. We try to keep to ourselves and when it comes to sickness, you don't want to be bothered. You need rest when you are sick. Our pastor is usually the last one to know. We don't want to bother the pastor with it."

But if a black park household lacks kinfolk living nearby, their church may become a main source of socioemotional support. Explains Georgia Walker about the relationships she has with people from her church, "The members of the church are my family. I can't separate my personal life from the church. People who I socialize with are members at the church. My best friend goes to my church. Some coworkers were my friends before we began going to church, but it just ended up that I invited them to church. Now that they are attending, it is an added plus.... My life is intertwined with my church's members."

Because attending church regularly presents opportunities for interaction among those with shared values, a church community easily substitutes for the absence of a nearby kin network. Church membership also serves as a way for obtaining needed resources.[20] For example, the Wilsons, the poorest couple of the thirteen families, belong to a large, integrated Addington church that recruited them. They lack substantive kin help but receive rich support from their church, explained Mr. Wilson: "They don't believe in the color barrier. Everybody is the same.... When we first got here, I was sick. [The church members] went out and bought us cooked meals. They went to the grocery store for me. They make sure I get to my doctor's appointment. They were there when I went to surgery last month. They are looking out for me."

Black park families who maintain membership in a rural church have their country roots regularly nourished by worshipping with kin. Their church sustains them during what they hope is only an interlude of nonrural residence. Park families who attend family-like churches in the city also worship in the context of a kin group but do not share the dream of eventual country living. Viola Bankston, for example, is embedded in an Addington church where her mother and grandmother both belong. Lacking rural kin, she does not visualize a future life that differs greatly from the satisfying life she has built in the Shady Grove trailer park.

No matter where North Carolina black park families move in Addington city or the township, their church remains a large and constant presence in their lives. As one woman explained, although she knows several park neighbors well, "I basically keep to myself and basically others can keep to themselves.... They're good neighbors . . . decent people." Her rich social life is rooted firmly in her family's Addington Baptist church.[21] She has no need for park neighbors to be close friends.

Their church represents a vibrant form of community for African American trailer-park families. It is a stable community that gives their lives continuity even if they move, for example, from the rural hinterland into Addington city. Their church involvement combined with their kinship network means that families have multiple sources for obtaining social, financial, and moral support. The black adults almost all have divorce—theirs or their parents—in their background. Yet in contrast to the adults we interviewed at the Illinois and New Mexico sites, they are all married, and there are no common-in-law arrangements or "fiancés" in the picture. African American park families' uniform church engagement, through which they experience values related to marriage in biblical doctrine and the close supervision of members, is a likely factor supporting their marital practices. Maintaining respectability is part of the church membership package.[22]

The American housing dream of blacks living in a trailer park is one shared with other trailer park families—to own a conventional home on owned land. It is a dream, however, that must accommodate easy access to the extended kin network and, for most, their family church—which both make life fulfilling. Parents make it a priority for children to be in frequent contact with kin, especially grandparents, siblings, aunts, and uncles. Grandparents, even when parents are separated, continue to be involved in children's lives. Alberta Reynolds, a separated mother says, "I make sure [son] sees his [paternal grandparents] often."

Although Hispanics in New Mexico uniformly belong to the local Catholic church, it is a loose affiliation, and they do not receive resources from the church to the extent that North Carolina families do from their churches. Among the white Illinois families, few are involved in a church to the degree that North Carolina blacks are, except for two involved Illinois families who distinctively also had youth with the most successful outcomes.[23] Similarly, North Carolina and New Mexico families are more embedded in a larger kin network than are Illinois families, whose reliance on kin, if any, is generally confined to parents.

The exception is one family whose large sibling set resembles those of North Carolina families. Illinois families are more mobile than those in North Carolina, and some are alienated from kin, at least at specific points of their life history. Thus the black families in North Carolina do well socially and financially in part because of the strength of their kin and church networks.

Finally, for African Americans who live in trailer parks the trailer-trash slur lacks power to tarnish either the family's identity or its achievement of home-ownership. In fact, these racially integrated parks informed our understanding that the stigma has a particular sting for white families but not for blacks or Hispanics. Eley heard three white park residents in North Carolina talk about their being thought of as trailer trash. But the idea of stigma was never raised by African Americans living in the same park.

THE NEW MEXICO PARKS

Rooted in Place

Life among park families in Mesa Vista, New Mexico, is a life rooted in place. Trailer-park families here know there is no real shame in a park address. Owning a home in a trailer park is a means to the end of staying close to kin in a town that is home. One father explained, "We've just always been here. As far back as anyone knows this has been our home." Proximity to kin extending across generations and a deep sense of belonging to place provide critical supports in a region where finding work, earning a living, and even coping with poverty present real challenges.

Mesa Vista with a population of 8,500 lies along the Rio Grande as it winds south from Albuquerque. As in many sites along that river, Pueblo Indians and later Spanish occupied the place that is now Mesa Vista. The original plaza and mission tied to the single Catholic church remain the heart of downtown and date back to the end of the sixteenth century. A small technical university anchors the west side of town. Clusters of mobile homes and student apartments along with old Victorians and sprawling adobes from a wealthier nineteenth-century era line streets named for early local families who continue to dominate the political scene: Baca, Garcia, and Roybal. Such a mix of housing is typical in rural New Mexico, where zoning regulations are lax.[1]

Close to one thousand mobile homes together make up one-quarter of the local housing stock. According to one zoning official, "If you know anything at all about the area, you know that there are pockets of trailers that together just buckshot the town. No one here is going to say anything against it. Chances are, everyone knows someone that lives in a trailer." That everyone knows someone who lives in a trailer speaks to the extensive and enduring nature of ties to place in a region long classified as minority-majority.[2] Poverty maps published by the USDA reinforce the economic need behind the ubiquitous presence of trailers. With the local poverty rate hovering above 20 percent across the last four decades, Mesa Vista is shaded in on these maps to indicate not just poverty but a classification as a "persistently poor place."[3] That kind of economic backdrop, and the deep generational ties of families to community, means that daily life among Mesa Vista trailer park-households unfolds in regionally distinctive ways.

> *It's after 10:00 p.m. when Darlene Vega crosses the acequia and pulls up to her parents' house. She dims the headlights but leaves the engine running. Quietly she enters the back door. Her father has been sitting up, waiting, knowing she would be here to pick up the kids. Her shifts at a local fast food restaurant are staggered. "I open, close, open, close, open, close and then have Sunday off," she explains. Today was a "close" shift. She had seen the kids off for school at 7:00 a.m.: "They get to the bus stop by themselves." She watches from the kitchen window of their trailer while she does the morning dishes. Ordinarily Darlene would return to bed in an effort to catch up on some much-needed sleep. Today, though, her off-work hours were spent trying to get her car running. Yesterday she had to call into work when her car wouldn't start. She can't afford to miss another shift. First one and then the other of her two older brothers came by to help. Between the two of them, her car is working again. That kind of assistance is critical, particularly when her husband, Ron, is on the road trucking. She's tired. She gathers her small daughter in her arms and moves toward the door. Her father follows, carrying her son. She had dropped the kids off here on her way into work, as she does each day she has a closing shift. That her parents provide child care helps stretch her $7.50 an hour wage. Kids loaded in the car, Darlene nods a good-bye and heads home, already anticipating the early start of an "open" workday.*

Mesa Vista Trailer Parks

Darlene and her family live in one of a dozen or so trailer parks scattered throughout Mesa Vista. Local trailer-park development spans the last three decades of the twentieth century and typically began as a local family developed, lived in, and managed a park. Only two of the seven parks studied remain under original mom-and-pop ownership. Two local investment corporations, two absentee investor owners, and a large real estate investment trust now round out ownership of the other five parks. Despite the loose zoning restrictions in Mesa Vista, trailer parks are most often located on the periphery of town, invariably adjacent to one of its less desirable features, including a major drainage ditch, railroad tracks, an interstate highway, and the municipal water treatment facility. The seven trailer parks included in the study ranged from decent to shabby.

Tumbleweed, where Darlene lives, is reputed to be the best local park. It sits alongside a major highway just north of town on a frontage road. Pampas grass adorns the entrance, and mature cottonwood trees provide shade for homes and a modest play area. The park includes sixty trailers snuggly tucked hitch end out along a main loop and two cross streets. Lots measure twenty by fifty feet, leaving little space around a typical twelve-by-forty-eight-foot singlewide. No lots are large enough to accommodate a doublewide, but an absence of these larger units is not unique to Tumbleweed. One of two resident park managers observed about Mesa Vista, "If you can buy a doublewide, you can usually afford a piece of land to put it on." Tumbleweed's tiny yards, each bordered by a low chain-link fence, are fastidiously kept.

Originally owned by a local family, Tumbleweed changed hands several times in the last decade, most recently when a California investor who calls himself the "Mick-ster" purchased it five years ago. For Mick, buying this park and others was purely an economic decision. He formerly owned rental properties but found mobile home parks a better investment. With a measure of pride and arrogance he explained his concept of investment park ownership:

> Put it this way, if you have sixty rentals, you have sixty air conditioners that can break down, sixty stoves, sixty roofs that can leak . . . you get the picture. I don't have the immediate local headaches of just starting to carve the Thanksgiving turkey and the phone rings and it's somebody wanting you to come over and unclog their toilet. I don't want to hear about it and I don't have to. . . . I decided to own a park without owning any of the homes. The other part is that by living there the people are essentially buying the park for me. Eventually I'll own the land. Then I can turn it around and sell it for two times what I paid for it or trade it for another one. . . . Then there is the fact that I can sit here and say, 'The sun is shining, let me see. I think I'll raise the rent $10 a month.' What I'm doing is giving myself a $2,000/ month raise just because the sun is shining and I feel like it. Now I'm being a little facetious here. But I can do that and I'm not really making a big difference in anyone's life.

Tumbleweed lots, at the time of the study, cost tenants $138 a month with water, sewer, and trash disposal included. For those who own their home in full, about one-third of the park residents we spoke with, lot rent constitutes the bulk of their housing expense, besides their heating and cooling bills.

FIGURE 6. A modest playground, typical of New Mexican parks, is surrounded by dirt roads and tightly clustered singlewide homes. Source: K. MacTavish.

Although Tumbleweed residents related occasional problems with a noisy neighborhood, most often tied to suspected drug and alcohol use, they spoke appreciatively about the park's generally safe, quiet atmosphere. Slightly over half report the neighborhood as a "somewhat" to "very desirable" place to live. Despite the park's quaint size and the common presence of relatives down the street (almost one out of three households has kin living in the park), there is little talk of close-knit ties in Tumbleweed. Rather, as one resident of just a year said, "Quite honestly, I don't think the word 'neighborhood' enters my mind at all." An ethnic divide, evenly split between Hispanics and Anglos, explains some of the estrangement residents feel from each other.[4] One Anglo resident offered a theory on ethnic differences: "Some [Hispanics] are nice and some are . . . aloof and cool and keep to themselves. . . . A lot of it depends on religion and ethnicity, it seems to me. I mean you try to get to know everyone. You don't want to seem, you know, prejudiced, but it seems to me that the Hispanics here keep to themselves. They're so involved with their family they don't care much about interacting with others." Life stage also plays a part in detachment as half the households include children, while the other half is older and adult-only.

Longtime residents report stories of efforts at collective action like a petition to have the road paved or another initiative to stop a landlord's practice of rentals. The roads remain unpaved, but the efforts to limit rentals appear to have worked as we only encountered two renters. Despite its reputation, vacancies are still common in Tumbleweed, a phenomenon that Mick saw as less related to park quality and more to community size: "Keeping the peace is not a problem in that park. The challenge is in keeping the place full. Knowing what I know now I wouldn't buy another park in a place like Mesa Vista. The town's just too small. The vacancy rates are just too high in a town that small. From now on I won't touch a park in a town of less than a hundred thousand."

At the extreme of shabby parks is Sandia Estates, which occupies three city blocks a short distance off the town plaza. The park sits adjacent to the city's sewage treatment plant, earning it the unenviable nickname "Stinky Acres." Technically, Sandia Estates is not a trailer park at all. Rather it is, or originally was supposed to be, a subdivision for manufactured homes. Several local businesspeople, including a banker, developed the park in the mid-1980s. The development began as a single street followed by the addition of another and then another over time. Sandia Estates now consists of three unpaved streets, each a block long. Plans, if realized, aim to expand to two more blocks to the south.

Lots are larger than in Tumbleweed but still make for a tight fit for a doublewide. Sixty lots hold approximately fifty-eight older singlewides. Gossip related that when sales were slow, the developers brought in their own units and began renting these out. Rentals were also generated internally. According to city zoning enforcement official, "A lot of times someone might buy a place [in there] and then move out and rent it to someone else. It's no different than you having a second home and renting it out." Approximately one in ten park households is renting. With the price of the land bundled with a trailer, housing costs range from $175 to $350 a month. The price and the model of land and homeownership seemed appealing to families as two-thirds of the households we spoke with included children, a proportion higher than in Tumbleweed but lower than in some other Mesa Vista parks. A city official estimates that for the majority (90 percent), the pathway to homeownership in Sandia Estates went through a contract sale rather than a mortgage loan.

Visual impressions of Sandia Estates' street life validate every negative, stereotypical image associated with trailer parks. A dirty young child dressed only in a diaper wanders unsupervised, a shirtless man works beneath the hood of a truck with no wheels, a mangy stray dog roams the streets in search of scraps, and a toothless woman sits on her back steps smoking an afternoon cigarette. Residents in fact identify appearance as what is worst about the park neighborhood, explaining, "You drove through it! It's like they don't care what the place looks like." The city zoning official winced at the mention of this neighborhood. Referring to it as "one big eyesore" he added, "We continue to have problems with that development and there's nothing we can do about it. It was built as a subdivision so it doesn't have to comply with the regulations for parks. It was grandfathered in like everything else when the zoning codes were enacted [about ten years previously]." Older homes of twenty years on average add to the park's unsavory appearance. Yet Sandia Estates is residentially more stable than other Mesa Vista parks. Just under half of those we spoke with had lived in their current home for five years or more, many claiming "first on the block" status.

As a subdivision, Sandia Estates is unique in other ways. With no management per se, residents take governance into their own hands. While there are no apparent shared norms about appearance, old-timers reported past episodes of collective neighborhood action and a sense of community norms focused on protecting the neighborhood. One resident explained, "We talk to each other. Sometimes we do call the police but mostly we work it out between us. Everyone here works and so if you're going to have a party it can't be too late. We tell each other 'I'm having a party' and we know it can't go any later than twelve because people have to get to work the next day."

Another indicator of collective action in Sandia Estates is a strategy developed for keeping drug dealers out of the neighborhood. A longtime resident

FIGURE 7. As home- and landowners, residents of trailer-park subdivisions are free to fence their yards and otherwise customize their home sites. Source: K. MacTavish.

explained, "We've had a problem with drug dealers and partiers up on the other end of the street. As soon as that starts, we call the cops on them. Over and over if we have to until we get rid of them." More often, however, people act alone. One longtime resident known locally as "Grandma" keeps a BB gun near the front door to ward off stray dogs. Another resident bangs on the neighbor's fence before calling the police when a party goes on too long. Perhaps this sense of control adds to residents' satisfaction here as three-fourths of them rate their neighborhood as somewhat to very desirable, a rate higher than in other local parks. That same proportion of residents identify Sandia Estates as a permanent rather than temporary home, despite its ramshackle appearance and shabby reputation.

In between these two extremes of shabby and decent lie the other five Mesa Vista parks. With dirt roads ubiquitous and amenities lacking, no park approximates the ideal of a manufactured home community that the industry promotes or even resembles the Illinois Prairieview Manor or the North Carolina Addington parks. Rather, these parks fit more the notion of "trailer courts," a term from a bygone era but one casually used here by locals. Park management ranges from a heavy, hands-on approach, at least for renters, to no management. Some trailer parks are close to the center of town and others more remote. All but one is incorporated in the Mesa Vista town limits, potentially subject to its zoning regulations, and provided with city water, sewage hookup, and trash service—which most often means strategically placed dumpsters rather than individual bins.

Demographic comparisons between the park and town populations show a match on ethnicity but differences by social class (table 5.1). Although the class gap is not as great as that between Prairieview and the Illinois park, Mesa Vista trailer park residents are younger, poorer, and less well educated than their town counterparts. The households comprising each separate park are somewhat distinctive (see appendix B). Hispanics hold more than a two-thirds majority in three parks but constitute a much smaller fraction of the population in the others. Some parks like Tumbleweed include more adult-only households, while children fill the homes in other parks. Educational levels and employment patterns are likewise stratified between parks. These population distinctions create a unique park ambience. Yet when combined, the seven parks provide a fair representation of residents and residential life among Mesa Vista trailer parks. Descriptions of daily life in the New Mexican parks draw on the seventy-nine randomly selected households in the park survey and the lives of ten families we came to know well over the year's study in Mesa Vista. All but two from the ten in the family sample were first interviewed for the park survey, but these two households were eventually included in the park sample, for a total of eighty-one park households interviewed.

TABLE 5.1 Population traits of New Mexico trailer parks and town

TRAIT	TRAILER PARKS	MESA VISTA
Ethnicity		
% households Hispanic	66	55
Age		
Median age	26 years	31 years
% householders 65 years and over	17	20
Household type		
% family households	60	63
(% female-headed, no husband present)	(30)	(14)
Average household size	2.96	2.44
Income		
Median household income	$17,355	$22,530
% below poverty	39	24
% reporting public assistance	27	10
Educational attainment, all adults[a]		
% less than high school	23	25
% high school graduate (including equivalency)	49	26
% some college or associate's degree	14	24
% bachelor's degree or higher	14	25
Occupancy and tenure		
% owner-occupied	80	60
% renter-occupied	18	40
% in home for 1 year or less	23	23
% same home 5 years prior	34	54

Source: Park data from the survey of a randomly sample of trailer park households (n = 79); town data from U.S. Census Bureau, "DP-1 Profile of General Demographic Characteristics: 2000"; "DP-2 Profile of Selected Social Characteristics: 2000"; "DP-3 Profile of Selected Economic Characteristics: 2000"; and "QT-P20 Educational Attainment by Sex: 2000."

[a]Educational attainment data for the park sample include all adults over 18 years of age, while U.S. Census data include adults 25 and over only.

Park Living as an Economic Necessity

Seated in a swivel office chair outside his 1973 singlewide in Sandia Estates, Joe Martinez props his feet on a plastic milk crate ottoman. He is wearing the blue coveralls from his part-time job at the recycling plant. "You want to know why people live in trailers? I'll tell you why—they're poor and that's all they can afford." While Joe's admission is true by formal definition for fewer than half of park residents in Mesa Vista, it is true by experience and meaning for most. By official federal poverty measures, two in five park households are poor.[5] With a median reported income at just over $17,000 a year (for comparison, $24,210 in 2016 dollars) for an average family size of three, people are hard-pressed financially. One in three park households gets by on less than $1,000 a month, and one in six reports less than $500 a month in income. The consequence of needing to get by on little in a place that is poor explains much about who lives in a trailer park and the nature of daily life there.

For trailer park residents in Mesa Vista, affordability ranks as the main draw to park living. "I needed some place to live I could afford," was an often-heard explanation for a move into a trailer in a park. With a mean monthly cost of $250 (house and lot rent) compared with a median rental cost of $421 and mortgage payment of $673, as reported by the Census for Mesa Vista, park residence seems an economical housing solution.[6]

Finding a "real deal" on a trailer serves as a point of pride. "I looked all over before I bought this one," one older single resident explained. "It was the last one on the lot and they weren't doing singlewides anymore. I didn't get to choose any of the features, but I got thousands off." More often a real deal is accomplished by buying a used, sometimes repossessed, unit through a lease-to-own or contract sale that requires little or no down payment (table 5.2). Half the family sample used a contract sale route to homeownership. Three-quarters of the park sample bought their home used. Frank Tafoya, for example, bought his 1979 singlewide in Sandia Estates five years earlier. The home was in "real poor" condition: "It was

TABLE 5.2 Residential status of New Mexico park households

RESIDENTIAL STATUS	PERCENTAGE
Ownership	
Own home in full	32
Own home, making mortgage payments	42
Buying on contract sales	6
Renting home	18
Tenure	
Previously lived in mobile home	59
Define home as a "permanent"	49
Prefer rural or small-town living	73
Structure	
Singlewide	92
Doublewide	5
RV	3
New	25

Source: Survey of randomly selected trailer-park households (n = 79)

a bank repo and the last owner walked through the place with a sledgehammer. I had to do a lot of repair." Recently he moved on to recondition the exterior by painting the trailer a uniform flat brown. The metal steps Frank added lean to one side, and a makeshift chicken coop is conspicuously empty except for a dusting of gray feathers.

A formal contract is not always required in a close-knit town where trust is assumed. Marie Martinez explained buying her singlewide through a casual contract sale arrangement with a stranger who soon became a friend:

> We didn't know each other at first but we're friends now. I had called her up wanting to rent the place and she wanted to sell it. A couple of months later she called and asked if I would be interested in buying it. I told her I didn't have enough for the down payment. She said she didn't care. She financed it herself. Now she comes by to visit when she's here and she calls me for advice. She's a first-time mom so she likes to call and tell me about her baby. She called the other day and I said— "Oh, I know I need to send the payment." She said, "That's not even what I'm calling about! I just wanted to tell you what the baby is doing!"

The financial pressure behind the need for affordable housing in Mesa Vista is tied to the challenge of earning a living here. Finding a job, much less a good job (one with decent pay and benefits) is tough in Mesa Vista. In 2000, Mesa Vista County, like most counties in central New Mexico, fell under classification of "low employment places," indicating that fewer than 65 percent of working-age residents are employed in the formal economy.[7] Forty-six-year-old Diego Montoya has been looking for work for since he was laid off from a machinist job at the local university seven months prior. "I've had no luck," he admits gesturing to the job applications that surround him on the couch. His unemployment benefits exhausted, Diego and his daughter subsist on food stamps, the federal cash assistance program called Temporary Assistance for Needy Families (TANF), and his modest VA benefits that together total $300 a month. Half of this ($158 a month, including a $20 late fee for making payment after the third of the month) goes for lot rent in Tumbleweed. He is clear about what it is like getting by on such a pittance. "Three hundred dollars a month is nothing! I'm living just above homeless!" In the Mesa Vista parks, one in three households shared Diego's status of having no income from work in the formal economy. While some are elderly, most are working-age adults out of work.

Finding work is no guarantee of financial security in Mesa Vista's marginal economy. Among half the families raising children, wages earned from full-time work do not lift the family above the poverty threshold. Mary and Mike Trujillo both work full-time—she as a medical assistant and he in construction. Together they bring in a combined $1,800 a month. With four young children, that income qualifies them for food stamps, Medicaid for the kids, and the designation of being a working-poor household. Single mother Susan Miller, an Anglo, lives four doors down from the Trujillos. Through her job at a local nursing home she earns $18,000 a year with another $2,000 a year in child support—enough to technically lift the family of three above the official poverty threshold, but as she explains, "Whatever I do make, I seem to spend it all." The payment on her 1964 singlewide and the lot rent consume a quarter of her income. She continues: "We bought this place to save up for a house. I never thought I would get stuck in it after a divorce."

Any quest for financial security among New Mexico families is complicated by life events. Early parenthood and divorce that first paved the way to park residence continues to economically challenge a park household. Teenage motherhood has been termed "the fastest ticket to poverty."[8] In more than a third of park households with children, the mother had her first child before reaching the age of twenty, a rate that mirrors the state rate.[9] For half our family sample (five of ten mothers), motherhood began young, with women giving birth before their eighteenth birthday. Park families headed by young unwed mothers, in particular, show signs of financial distress.

> Erlinda Lopez reported eight moves in the fifteen years since leaving her parents' home as an unwed sixteen-year-old mother. She cycled through rental units in four local trailer parks as well as a string of rental houses in town. Twice she returned to her parents' home. Describing her last move back to her parents' place at age twenty-five, now with four children, Erlinda asks rhetorically, "Is it easy to live with your parents when you're an adult?" Antonio, Erlinda's oldest, recalls periods when the family was technically homeless: "We did a lot of coming and going from my mom's parents and staying with friends."

This kind of mobility, typical among the Mesa Vista park family sample (an average of seven moves over an average of fifteen years since leaving their parents' home), is characteristic for young adults here in general.[10] A difference, however, is that these women move from place to place with young children in tow. At least three other park families reported a move back into a parent's home after early entry into parenthood. For all but one of the mothers among the ten families, their trailer in the park provides the first opportunity to own a home and live independently as a family, following long, complicated residential histories.

Divorce, another thread tied to economic hardship, also explains Mesa Vista park residence. Eight of the ten mothers in our family sample reported a first marriage ending in divorce. Seated in the living room of her white paneled singlewide Inez Martinez, a longtime case worker in social services, reflected on how her divorce brought downward housing mobility: "I lived in a house before this. I always lived in a house. I raised my children in a house. After the divorce I wanted to buy a house but I couldn't afford it. I could afford this."

Buying a trailer in a park is an economical solution for getting by on limited resources in this poor area of southern New Mexico. On average, housing constitutes a quarter of families' budgets—a figure designated by economists as reasonable. Modest choices help stretch families" limited resources. Factory-issued front steps and thin trailer doors provide entry to humble, used singlewide mobile homes. Inside furnishings, mostly obtained used or as hand-me-downs, are frugal aside from the typical large-screen TV for family recreation. In the most modest homes, a bed means a mattress set on the floor for a child sleeping in the living room area. Modest choices mean that debt levels for Mesa Vista park households are low. Only one of the ten families reported significant credit card debt, of a monthly balance nearing or exceeding annual incomes.

Finding Community in a Hometown

That one's family has "always been here" is grounds for bragging rights in Mesa Vista. In particular, claims to being a Hispanic family rooted in place for generations draw important distinctions from the relatively newly arrived Anglos or recent Mexican immigrants, termed "wetbacks" by some in reference to their assumed illegal or undocumented status. In tracing family histories, all but three of the fifty-two park survey households with Hispanic ties report local kin with family connections that span several generations and include "the entire family," meaning parents, siblings, aunts, uncles, cousins, and grandparents.

A few park parents relate moving away from the area, but connections to place and kin are a strong pull back. When their parents divorced, Ruby and Marie Martinez followed their mother to Albuquerque. But summers and holidays spent with grandparents in Mesa Vista forged enduring connections to place that facilitated both sisters' eventual return. A first marriage to a military man drew two other women away to a peripatetic life among military bases up and down the east coast. When these marriages ended, the women and their children returned home to Mesa Vista.

Mesa Vista park residents show their ties to town daily. Hispanic park households, in particular, vote, read the local paper, and engage in social, religious, and recreational activities at substantial rates. One park resident even made a serious bid for the office of mayor, finishing a close second behind the incumbent. Hispanic fathers report coaching their sons' Little League teams and reminisce about their own experiences playing on the same fields. Park mothers actively engage in their children's religious education through the local Catholic church, where parents attended parochial school themselves.

Given their embeddedness in community, Mesa Vista Hispanic park households share an aspiration of staying in place, purchasing land where they might move their current trailer, or perhaps buying a new home (often a mobile) to remain in a community that is by all measures home. A single father of two who describes his family ties to Mesa Vista as "since like my great-great-great-grandparents or something" represents this shared dream. While he anticipates moving into a "real" house in the next four years, he never contemplates severing ties with his hometown. He is adamant that "if I won the lottery—even then I would keep a house here. I might have a house in Hawaii and another in Alaska for variety, but I would always have one here." This strong attachment to place (and kin) typifies Hispanic trailer-park families.

Some Anglo park households too claim long-term ties to place. More often, however, these families relocated to the area from western states such as California, Oregon, or Idaho. A few are midwestern transplants drawn to central New Mexico by the milder weather. Some have a history of high mobility, having moved from place to place in search of work, more affordable housing, or the chance to mend family relationships. One mother of three has moved "too many" times in the last five years to count. Retracing, she recalls a move from Mesa Vista to Colorado with her first husband in search of work, a postdivorce move to the Midwest to be near kin, a move back to Mesa Vista, and several moves in town, including one in which the trailer moved with the family, a real option in rural New Mexico.

Overall, local kin are less common for Anglos, with half of the twenty-seven Anglo households having no relatives living in town. For the remainder, local kin represent shallow ties, one generation or one relative deep—a grown child who stayed on in town, an aging parent who moved here to be cared for, or one sibling following another by way of chain migration. Shallow kin networks and being more newly arrived put Anglos at a disadvantage for community inclusion. "Out where I live," explained one Anglo resident, "Anglos are like outcasts." Close to two-thirds of Anglos see their current home as only temporary. Like their Hispanic counterparts, they expect to stay another year or two or maybe five years in the park before moving to owned land. For several, such a move includes buying a stick-built house, but for most it is less specific.

Almost half of Anglo and Hispanic households alike anticipate that their offspring will leave Mesa Vista as young adults. One Hispanic father realistically lamented, "Job opportunities are real limited here. And they want to go to college so there's nothing for them here then." Anglo parents, too, emphasize the need to move to more urban areas for richer opportunities. When asked if her two children will stay in the community, one Anglo mother emphasizes, "God, I hope not. I hope they go to Albuquerque to college." Another responded, "I HOPE NOT! I hope she'll move on from this," leaving it unclear whether she means the park or the town. Park parents' belief in the next generation's exodus is clearly predicated on launching kids—giving them wings to leave rather than anchors to stay.

Family Life in the New Mexico Trailer Parks

For Mesa Vista park families, particularly those with Hispanic ties, life takes place in a kin-network context. They are like Addington park families in this way. Family ties are maintained through "visiting." Saturday and Sunday are devoted to time with kin. These weekend visits, as opposed to a daily "pop-in," invariably include a shared meal. Dinner at Mom's house on Sunday provides a chance for one Hispanic mother and her children to spend time with her mother, grandmother, sisters, and the children's cousins in addition to her stepfather and father. These visits may include a haircut, life advice (which may or may not be taken), community gossip, a car repair session, or at least the arrangement for one. Family time is an investment for park families who give as well as receive social and substantive support. Through these relationships, families stretched thin gain access to the skills and time or money resources that serve as vital social and economic buffers. Support given by kin at times is extensive and enduring.

> For Mike and Mary Trujillo, family help began when she became pregnant her sophomore year of high school. Mike moved into her parents' home, and the young couple lived with her family for five years through the birth of a second child. The couple married and moved out on their own only after both finished high school. Both attended alternative high school programs, gained some technical training, and were, as he says, "ready to move out financially." Now in their midtwenties, they continue to receive significant support from both his and her families. Maria's father bought the older-model, once-luxury sedan she drives to work. Mike's brother often provides the mechanical skills needed to keep that car and their older model pick-up truck running. They are buying their older singlewide trailer from his sister, having assumed the loan payments. They view the purchase of this trailer as a boost to advance them toward their aspiration of a home on owned land. Mike explains, "The trailer's almost paid off. Then we just have to look for land." In addition, Maria said her parents "help me with everything." Everything includes child care and money when needed. This

*level of support keeps the family afloat, given the daily reality of two par-
ents working at low-wage jobs to support four children.*

Compared with the Trujillos, other Mesa Vista park families receive less
extensive but still constant kin support. All but one park family (nine of ten)
receive help with child care, avoiding that substantial cost to already tight family
budgets. Overnight child care is available for nine of the ten families through
exchanges with a sister or from an always-willing grandmother. For the lone
remaining mother, Susan Miller, her own kin are too distant to help. For half of
the families, any real emergency or money crisis involves a turn to family before
friends for help. A thirty-year-old Anglo single mother of three emphasizes that
minor emergencies like an unexpected car repair are of little concern as "I have
enough friends that know how to work on cars that it's not a worry." For a major
crisis she says, "I'd have to go see Mom. Last time I had a major disaster she paid
for it." Hispanic families similarly depend on kin for major emergencies, but they
differ from Anglos in that even the day-to-day kinds of help—such as hauling an
old couch away, picking up an item from Walmart, or lending a tool—are the
types of support readily supplied by kin. Marie Martinez explained the taken-
for-granted nature of this help: "It's just like a family thing. . . . We have a saying
in our family—'We don't lend anything we just give it away.' It all circles back
anyways."[11]

In Hispanic park households, investments in family bonds are said to take
precedence over friendship bonds. In part, this prioritizing might be simply
a matter of time, as one mother emphasized: "I don't really have any friends
because I spend so much time with family." A young Hispanic father of four
said something similar: "[Wife] and the kids and my brothers and sisters were it.
They are my focus." Residential decisions reflect the importance of maintaining
local kin ties. With their trailer almost paid off, Mike and Mary Trujillo have
started looking for land in earnest. Mary explains, "We're looking at a piece of
property. I put the paperwork in for a loan and now we just have to see if we get
approved. . . . I even told my parents they could move a trailer down to our land
if we get it." That she is taking the maintenance of family ties into consideration
with such a move is clear.

Park parents with Hispanic ties socialize children to prioritize kin. Daily
contact with relatives who live nearby is a clear expectation. Marie Martinez's
nine-year-old son, Tomas, happily explained the mandatory visits with his
grandparents in the same park: "I have to go visit them every day or they get
mad!" Recreation in the park neighborhood involves time spent playing with siblings. Older siblings help care for younger siblings, a responsibility about which
they do not complain. Ruby Martinez's children are an example of close sibling
bonds. Even their mother, commenting on the photo task for the study, noted,

"You can see how close they are. All they have here is pictures of the two of them and no one else." Children and youth alike say they saw their "real friends" only at school—neighborhood acquaintances are just that. The small size of the New Mexico parks, which offer fewer options for friends, may explain the lack of park friends. But close sibling bonds seem the cultural expectation that trumps neighborhood friendships. The sleepovers or play dates common in middle-class white families are rare among Mesa Vista Hispanic park households.[12]

Expectations of kin support are reflected in the doubling-up arrangements or cohabitation among Hispanic families in the Mesa Vista parks. In two cases, a middle-aged mother took in an adult daughter with her young children to support them. One such mother, at fifty years of age, although still raising a teenage son, has a twenty-four-year-old daughter back home with a four-year-old and another on the way. Owning her trailer home allows this mother to provide her adult daughter and grandchildren with essential supports. In another home, a young couple allowed her sister and family to move in temporarily. Their hospitality means four adults and three children living crowded together in a small, fourteen-foot-wide trailer. Cohabitation as a kinship support strategy is not unique to trailer-park life, but it quickly creates overcrowding in the typically modest, older singlewide trailers in the Mesa Vista parks.[13]

Given the intimacy of a family living in the close quarters, park children both Anglo and Hispanic are privy to the full range of family matters. Children, even younger ones, seem up-to-date on family finances. They are also keenly aware of their parents' relationship status, successes, and troubles. In one particularly complicated household, a nine-year old reported, "You know what happened. My mom has kicked [stepfather] out of the house. They had a fight and he tore the transmission out of her car. She called the cops and had him sent to jail. My mom isn't sure if she wants him to come back. She kinda does and she kinda doesn't. I hope he stays gone." Days later, this knowledgeable young girl beseeched, "Please this time can you kick back and have a beer with my mom—she needs a friend to talk to." Drug and alcohol issues, a challenge in Prairieview Manor as well, ran through histories in several families. For example, two fathers are on work-release jail terms for repeat DWI convictions.

Parents' regrets are foundations for life lessons. Ruby Martinez reported, "I've told them both that having kids too early, before they finish school, doesn't mean they can't reach their goals. It just means it's gonna be a lot harder and take a lot longer." Kids seem to absorb these messages, and girls especially are quick to identify early parenthood or a bad relationship as an issue that might deter them from reaching life goals. At times parents' mistakes become grounds for family joking. Ruby's teenaged daughter teases her mom, recently engaged and now expecting a child, about getting "knocked up" in her thirties.

While kin reflect a collective means of support, women's second marriages and relationship choices constitute individual strategies intended to stabilize park-family life. Initiated with the best of intentions, partner choices sometimes work out but in other instances do not. Erlinda Lopez, who left home as a young single mother, spoke of her first marriage: "We got married six months after Antonio [oldest child] was born. We wanted to make sure it would work out before we got married. And then it didn't work out." Three more children and ten years later the couple eventually divorced. Half the eight women who divorced in the family sample tried for better luck the second time, with a remarriage. This hopeful strategy paid off for three of the four women, whose second husbands make significant financial and emotional contributions to the household. Darlene Vega was adamant about her two older children's fathers: "My kids don't have anything to do with their fathers. . . . As far as I'm concerned they aren't their fathers." Her current husband Ron's job as a trucker provides the kind of good pay and stable work that allows her to consider staying home for the year following the birth of her third and their first child together.

Park mothers depend on second marriages working out because only two of the five in the family sample received child support from an ex-husband. For one park mother, recouping back child support owed is tied to her aspiration of eventual homeownership:

> He hasn't paid a penny yet. He's back in [East coast state] and I just can't wait until they finally catch up with him and yank his driver's license. That's what they do with deadbeat dads back there—they take their driver's license. I filled out all the paperwork so it's coming and I can't wait! He owes over $5,000 by now. I mean even if he would have sent as little as a hundred and been honest with me . . . you know said this was all he had for now, I would have been satisfied but he's sent nothing. When we do get it, that's what we'll use to buy our own place.

Susan Miller described the partner of her dreams: "Someone to help me out—to help get me there. You know how it is—we all want to think we can do it financially by ourselves but it's hard." Women do not sour on marriage; rather, they regard it as a solution to their economic struggles.

Town and School as Community Supports

Beyond household-level strategies for survival and the substantive support kin offer, the local community helps buffer life for lower-income Mesa Vista park families in ways not seen in Illinois or North Carolina. As the county seat, Mesa

Vista offers a rich range of social service supports. These services are characteristic of low-income New Mexico, where during our study year the state Human Services Department declared, "Serving 1 in 3" on its website. A Mesa Vista school administrator acknowledges, "We do have a lot of programs aimed at lower income families—particularly families transitioning off of welfare. . . . All over New Mexico you will find a lot of social service kinds of programs because we have a large poor population." Young children in five of ten park families started school in a Head Start classroom. Food stamps help families make ends meet. A respite program through the local mental health office provides one park child with a mentor and weekly family counseling to help overcome trauma from earlier life experiences. Virtually every one of the ten park families receives one or another of the above social services.

In Mesa Vista, social supports are typically integrated into public school activities. An after-school program serving grades K-3 opened at one local elementary school. Federal dollars funneled through the state provide funding for the program. Teachers who wish to work extra hours staff it. A snack, homework time, and a choice of activities such as cooking, cheerleading, sports, and computers round out the after-school program from 2:30–5:30 each weekday afternoon. An assistant to the superintendent with a long history in the district detailed the evolution of the program, "The original grant was to provide a program for TANF families, but we now have additional funding that will allow us to open the program up to all families in the district. We're also expanding to older kids." Apparently, the emphasis on universal access is basic to Mesa Vista programs. The same administrator explained, "This is a pretty tight-knit town and people like opportunities to be open to everyone. Otherwise you have one kid in a family eligible and his cousin is not and then you get bad feelings." The after-school program thus provides park children with the same kinds of structured opportunities—music, dance lessons, and after-school science enrichment—that middle-class children in town would enjoy. Open to everyone, these programs reflect a community ethos of equity that brings no stigma to participating park children and thus stands in stark contrast to the exclusion of trailer-park children from programs in Prairieview by mandated fees for them alone.

Generally, the Mesa Vista school district operates with similarly inclusive policies. All town children attend classes in the same grade-appropriate buildings, ranging from early childhood to upper elementary and then middle and high schools. It is an arrangement based on a conscious decision by community leaders. Again the school administrator explained, "That was decided by the school board and the main reasoning was that they wanted all the kids in town to go to the same school. They didn't want the town to be divided into two sides. This way it's more equitable for all the kids and I think the age groupings work better too. I like having all the younger kids in school together in one building and having the older elementary kids in a different building. It kind of shelters the young kids—keeps them more innocent." This inclusive policy means that park children ride the school bus alongside nonpark children of the same age. New Mexico trailer-park children thus do not feel set apart by segregation, as did children in Prairieview.

In the schools, comments about park children or the study that reflected any sort of generalized, underlying negative assumptions were rare. As the study was introduced, only one teacher asked exactly which kids would be included. She then identified one particularly problematic child she seemed sure would be of interest. When the list of names was read, she was quick to say, "Oh—I never have any trouble with those kids." A school principal, offering an opinion on the study said,

> Well you know I have a theory on that. It's not based on any scientific studies, just thirty years in the business. I really do believe the kids who live in trailer parks bring more problems to school. And you know what I think it is? I think it's an SES thing. Those kids are more likely to come from poor homes—one with a single parent or one that's less stable. I don't think it has anything to do with living in a trailer. It's economics. They're just poorer and that makes a difference.

Class rather than park residence marks trailer-park families as potentially distinct. As for stigmatization of parks, another school administrator explained, "We have staff that live in the parks so I feel like teachers would have a hard time discriminating against kids who live there. Besides there are so many people in Mesa Vista that live in trailers whether it's a park or not it's not much of an issue. Often trailers are nicer than the houses in town." There is a nicer side of town near the university, but neither park youth nor parents commented about that neighborhood as a higher-class enclave. In fact, friendships for park children and teens on occasion crossed over class boundaries to include the children of professors and university instructors.

As a college town, albeit one with a small institution, Mesa Vista has social and recreational offerings that rival more upscale suburban places. One father commented, "I like Mesa Vista. It being a university town adds a lot I think. We have things here that a town this size wouldn't have like parks and a library." The local library, started by faculty wives, is well used. The city parks provide space for vibrant Little League baseball and city-league soccer programs. Children in all but two park households take part in these and other enriching activities. For boys this means sports and for girls the dance team, cheerleading, and even private dance and piano lessons. Ample scholarship programs must be readily available as park families never mentioned cost as a hindrance. And engagement in such enrichment activities provides important avenues for positive development among children and teens (see chapter 6).

That few park parents speak of leaving Mesa Vista means that most recognize the value of the community to their families. While youth might not like everyone's knowing their business (something parents appreciate), they do seem to enjoy the sense of tolerance community adults have for adolescent behavior that comes when authority figures (e.g., principal or police) know them and their families. One park teen told about a recent prank in which she and a group of friends on lunch break from the high school managed to knock down all the orange cones set up for a highway project: "When we drove past the workmen, they were eating lunch. They all just laughed." Her mother remembered similar kinds of fun as a youth in Mesa Vista. Small-town tolerance is rooted in an ideology of shared responsibility for all the community's children that emerges when overlapping social networks connect the small worlds of home, school, church, and community. That the town's children are all put through catechism classes in the same church, play on the same Little League teams, and progress through the same school buildings ensures opportunities for park families to connect with each other across time and various community settings.

Living a Life Rooted in Place

In Mesa Vista, a marginal economy and compounding life circumstances translate into the necessity to get by on little. A home in a trailer park, as an economic strategy to keep a roof over one's head, brings no apparent shame. Park residents readily acknowledge their humble financial circumstances and freely identified as low-income and poor when asked. The topic of trailer trash was raised only a few times, and only strongly by an Anglo single mother, as she recalled her experience growing up in a trailer park back east. In a hushed tone, so her daughters at play in the next room could not hear, she said, "I guess what I really want to impress on you is, and my kids don't know anything about this yet as far as I can tell, but when I was eight or nine years old I didn't like to say I lived in a trailer park. I still don't like to tell people. I would never invite any of my friends from work here—I don't even tell them where I live. Not that it would matter to them but it matters to me."

Much more commonly, and especially among Hispanics, park residents are baffled by the concept that their park address carries baggage. One young mother, perplexed by the idea, furrowed her brow and commented, "I know that white people here feel a little weirdly discriminated against. My sister-in-law is white and she was telling me about trying to pretend she wasn't to fit in better when she was a kid. But I've never heard anything about trailers being bad. My brother-in-law brings his friends that live in big houses over here and they don't care."

Park residents take comfort that they are not at the bottom of Mesa Vista's social order, a position reserved for those newly arrived from Mexico who speak little English. However, in the town of Mesa Vista, where one in four families lives in poverty, there is little shame earned for just being poor. Clearly owning the land your home sits on, however, is considered a better way to be poor if you must live in a trailer. The casual integration of trailers and trailer parks into town illustrates that few social or geographical divisions by class exist in Mesa Vista. Rather, status is more about claims to community than about being a have or a have-not.

Strong integration in the community has important consequences for park family life. A trailer park, as just another place to live, is not considered a source of identity. Rather, park families, especially those of Hispanic heritage, share a town identity that overlaps with their ethnic identity. Trailer-park residence offers an affordable means for owning a home close to kin, in a town where they hold a strong sense of belonging. Older singlewide trailers cause Mesa Vista park families to sometimes cope with overcrowded conditions, but they have no need to cope with an identity soiled by a park address. Time spent worrying did not seem apparent among Mesa Vista families, who are confident of supports being available through kin and community. A lack of judgment by community professionals stood in stark contrast to park experiences in Prairieview. Teasing and laughter punctuate family conversations. Parents take considerable pride in their children's accomplishments. Half had the funds and energy for vacations, if only modest ones involving a weekend camping or staying overnight at a hotel with a pool in Albuquerque. All families harbor optimism that life chances will take them beyond their trailer park but at the same time allow them to remain a part of their hometown.

Part 3

IS THE HOUSING DREAM REALIZED BY TRAILER-PARK FAMILIES?

YOUTH AND TRAILER-PARK LIFE

When trailer-park parents talk about the future, what they want most for their children is for them to experience a middle-class life, better than what the parents have lived. A mother in Illinois's Prairieview Manor trailer park is emphatic about her daughter's future: "I hope she'll enjoy life more than I got to. I hope she has a career, a husband, and a family. I hope she's happy in her life. She's got to get an education—a good education, that's her main thing." A New Mexican mother whose own education ended with high school emphasizes, "I have tried to push my kids to do better—to get an education. My parents only saw working hard as the way. They didn't see education as making a difference, but I do. . . . I hope [daughter] doesn't get caught up in a relationship, or a marriage at as young an age as I did. I hope she waits and finishes her education first." While parents might be quick to point out the life events that first steered them on a pathway to trailer-park life, the dream shared among park parents of success in life for their children we define as (1) an education with high school completed and at least some college, (2) stability in a career and in relationships, and (3) avoidance of behaviors or choices that might endanger these achievements.[1]

Parents' strategy to secure a brighter future for their children in part involves mobile home ownership in a small town—a setting they value as a good one for raising children successfully. As parents, most agree that a trailer park is not necessarily an ideal environment for achieving success, but it was what was feasible for them. Yet parents hold out hope that park residence will somehow help secure their children a shot at broader life chances than they themselves experienced, or at the very least will not cost children those chances.

This chapter focuses on the outcomes of trailer-park life—the children and youth who call these neighborhoods home. Our fundamental question is whether growing up in a trailer park affects the life chances of these rural young people— that is, whether park residence is an *advantage* (because it is a better life than their parents experienced), something *neutral* with little perceivable effect, or something with a *negative community or neighborhood effect*. A negative community effect means that park residence somehow narrows the life chances for children and youth growing up there. Our question is important given that an estimated five million children under the age of eighteen currently reside in mobile home parks across the rural United States.[2]

The thirty-eight families we grew to know intimately among all those we interviewed living in the three park sites allow us to look closely at the development of twenty-five children in middle childhood (ages eight to nine) and twenty-four youth in middle adolescence (ages fifteen to sixteen). We chose these age groups intentionally as both represent periods when the physical and social worlds of young people expand so that neighborhood and community begin to play an increasingly important role in their development. By second or third grade, friendship networks grow, and children start taking part in sleepovers, and in organized sports or Scouts and begin navigating neighborhood spaces more independently. Successful experiences in a wide range of settings (e.g., home, school, church, or the neighborhood) ensure that a sense of competence develops during this period.[3] Failure to gain that sense of competence may have long-term negative developmental consequences—fostering tendencies to drop out of school or to turn toward delinquent behaviors. Positive interactions with non-kin adults like teachers and coaches, supportive peer friendships, and even repeated interactions with a friendly dog or identification of a favorite tree in the neighborhood are all recognized as developmental resources for a growing child.[4]

By middle adolescence (fifteen to sixteen years of age, or tenth and eleventh grade), the age of our park youth, young people go through the transition to high school, which brings expanded opportunities. Formal organized activities like sports teams or church youth groups—along with first jobs, first dates, and just hanging out with friends—take youth further from home and into settings that include more nonrelative peers and adults. Interactions with others in these small worlds have a powerful influence on how young people define themselves and the ways they think about their futures.[5] Cliques and crowds in high school serve as a social guide that determines the kinds of peers young people hang out with, how they spend their time, and even the pool of potential choices for romantic partners.[6] As youth make increasing bids for autonomy, the protective influence of supportive relationships with caring, non-kin adults is an asset criti-cal to healthy development.[7]

We employed a specific set of strategies toward understanding the lives of park children and youth. In interviews separate from their parents, we asked young people about school and family history, future goals, and about how they saw their lives as similar to or different from their parents' lives.[8] Park children were asked to draw pictures of the places and people important to their lives. Youth used cameras to capture a similar set of images. Both children and youth kept a detailed record of a week's worth of daily activities documenting what they did, where they were, and whom they were with. These images and diaries gave us a basis for talking with them about daily life. We also observed young people, spending time with them in their homes, at school, at church, and in the commu-nity. Each child led us on a tour of their trailer park.[9] During these tours, we talked about the park as a place to grow up and observed their routine interactions in the neighborhood. Their familiarity and ease in the park, or lack thereof, revealed much about neighborhood experiences. These interviews and observations were augmented by a review of school records, with permission granted by both a par-ent and a child or youth. Combined with the extensive interview data collected from parents (see appendix A), these strategies provided a richly detailed insight into the daily lives of park children and youth in their natural settings.

Using these data, we constructed a developmental profile for each young person that accounts for both current and historical patterns across their social and academic lives as well as behavioral aspects of their development.[10] These research strategies give us a way to consider whether trailer-park residence is instrumental in providing young people a pathway toward their own and their parents' goals of social mobility or a pathway that leads away from those dreams. We use these aspirations for social mobility as a metric for success.

As we did for the towns and parks, we gave children and youth fictional names to preserve their anonymity yet allow the reader to distinguish an individual from the larger group.

Developmental Realities

Even a superficial look at the twenty-five children and twenty-four youth across the three sites reveals that some young people are doing well while others are not. Ten-year-old Cheyenne is at the top of her Mesa Vista third-grade class, while Ricky, in a classroom just down the hall, struggles. In Addington, nine-year-old Shantal loves school, while her stepfather describes her fifteen-year-old brother Simon as "not trying to do anything in school." Sixteen-year-old Melanie ranks near the top of her Prairieview class with a GPA over 4.0. In contrast, fifteen-year-old Brad has dropped out of Mesa Vista high school and, according to his mother,

"He's in a lot of trouble now. He's up on two felonies and four misdemeanors." These vastly different outcomes indicate that despite sharing working-poor financial circumstances and a common residential context, trailer-park children and youth in all three regions seem headed either toward positive outcomes or alternatively toward compromised development and hard living.[11]

In looking systematically at the individual development of park children and youth, three distinct classifications emerged—pathways we label as "flourishing," "steady," and "floundering."[12] Academic failure, social marginalization, and persistent engagement in problem behaviors characterize a floundering pathway. For park children and youth, these patterns mean already narrowed life chances by the age of eight to nine and more so by fifteen to sixteen. In contrast, park children and youth on a flourishing pathway exhibit both social and academic success as well as a capacity for consistently staying out of trouble. For these young people, the future appears to offer a chance at broader life options. In between are park children and youth who travel a steady pathway. Adequate academic performance, stable friendships, and the general ability to stay out of serious trouble mark a steady pathway as satisfactory but not stellar or problematic. For young people on this pathway, the future is likely to lead to socially reproducing their parents' class status and its associated characteristics.

Brianna and Aaron, two children in Prairieview Manor, highlight the contrasts between flourishing and floundering. Nine-year-old Brianna sits tall in her desk at Prairieview Elementary and pays eager attention to the lessons her third-grade teacher offers. Each time the teacher asks a question, Brianna's hand shoots up enthusiastically. When Brianna is asked about her school performance, she is quick to say, "I'm a great student." Her tests scores, grades, and behavior back up her self-assessment. Brianna is a straight-A student even though her standardized test scores meet only average expectations. At the end of the year her teacher writes, "Brianna had a good year. She's got a lot of academic ability." Brianna stands out among her park peers.

Aaron is one of those peers. On an early visit, his mother hands MacTavish his report card. "I got almost all S's once," Aaron says bravely, indicating "satisfactory" achievement. This time there are C's in reading and math and a D in science. "You can see he's having trouble," says his mother. She continues saying, "He gets so frustrated with his homework sheets that he throws them and starts crying." Tears well up in Aaron's eyes as his mother says this. In class, Aaron hesitantly attempts to answer a question. Despite the teacher's efforts to draw a correct answer out of him, he does not seem to grasp the concept obvious to the other children. In the end, another child steps in and correctly responds. Aaron slides down in his seat, looking at his feet.

Such stark contrasts are similar when we compare Trinity and Miranda, two Prairieview Manor youth. "Trinity's not your typical trailer-park kid," Trinity's mother Ellen Adams declares proudly about her sixteen-year-old daughter during our recruitment call. Even before a full explanation of the project is provided, this single mother makes it clear that while they live in the trailer park, her teenage daughter does not represent what anyone might expect to find there. Later, in the cramped kitchen of the family's singlewide she explains, "Trinity's not like the other kids out here. . . . She's a straight-A student, a cheerleader, and on the dance team." Over the next six months of field study, Trinity shows herself to be just the kind of developmental success her mother describes. Among her park peers in Prairieview Manor, Trinity is indeed not typical. Rather, in the context of her trailer park, she shines like a "Superkid."[13]

Not half a block away, life for fifteen-year-old Miranda looks quite different. Miranda Harwood lives with her parents and her older brother Nick in a doublewide, her home for the previous six years. During our first meeting, Miranda's mother laments, "We're not real happy with the choices she's making right now." In a worried tone, she refers to Miranda's selection of friends, namely, a twenty-one-year-old young woman in the park whom her mom considers trouble. In the following months, Miranda misses seventy days of her sophomore year of high school, endures a miscarriage in the early months of an unintended pregnancy, and navigates a rocky relationship with a boyfriend. Throughout it all, mom wrings her hands, unsure of what she might do to alter the course of her daughter's development—a pathway she sees as headed toward misfortune.

A few children (five of the twenty-five) and youth (four of the twenty-four) in each study site flourish, like Brianna and Trinity. These young people stand out among their peers by exhibiting both social and academic success as well as the capacity for consistently staying out of trouble. For these young people, the future seems to offer a chance at broader life choices. We also find some children (four of the twenty-five) and an increasing number by middle adolescence (eight of the twenty-four) floundering, like Aaron and Miranda. Academic failure, social marginalization, and persistent engagement in problem behaviors mean already narrowed life chances. Most often, however, park children and youth lodge somewhere in between—that is, they seem headed neither toward a future filled with the opportunities their parents hope for nor toward one leading to the kind of compromised development their parents fear. Rather, the young people who make up almost two-thirds of the children (sixteen) and half of the youth (eleven) fall into the steady category—they travel a developmental course that appears headed toward reproducing their parents' working-poor class status and in all likelihood trailer-park residence.[14]

A close look at the everyday encounters of young people in their trailer-park neighborhoods and small-town schools reveals how these same places function very differently for children and youth on a flourishing as compared with a floundering pathway. Here we draw most heavily on our Illinois and New

Mexican study sites, which provide the richest child and youth data. MacTavish, who led data collection in both sites, focused her study on the community effect of trailer-park residence on child and youth development. Where possible we comment on how the patterns we identify play out in North Carolina among the African American children and youth. We look first at the daily lives of children and then turn to examine youth (see figure 8).

A Trailer-Park Childhood

Access to the park neighborhood seems a necessary ingredient to a flourishing pathway in childhood. At nine years of age, Brianna is a child who knows everyone in her immediate Prairieview park neighborhood. As her father describes her, "Little Brianna thinks she needs to be out every minute the sun is up." Standing on the deck of her family's dilapidated singlewide, she can name all her neighbors—providing both first and last names, along with rich details about each household. Walking around her neighborhood of four years, Brianna waves at children and adults who pass by. She readily stops to talk, and they expect her to chat. In drawing her favorite places, Brianna includes a detailed picture of the

FIGURE 8. A flourishing child depicts the Prairieview Manor playground as the "Fave Place" in her community. Source: Park child.

playground area in her trailer park. Each apparatus, from swing set to teeter-totter, appears in a rainbow of colors. In the center is a small, red structure she has labeled "My Club." In reality, Brianna's "club" is an abandoned utility shed near the rear of the recreation area that she and her network of friends claim as their own special hangout. Her bright colors, details, and composition show she feels secure in her neighborhood (see figure 8).[15]

Like Brianna, the four other flourishing children are actively engaged in their trailer-park neighborhood. During the summer, these children spend hours play-ing in the recreation area, riding their bikes back and forth to the pop machine near the park office, visiting friends, swimming in the park pool, or hanging out in the street. Like Brianna, they know their neighbors, can recognize a friend's vehicle, can report on which dogs are friendly and which are not, can tell whose yard to cut through and whose to avoid, and typically claim some small place of the trailer park as their own.

As Brianna and other flourishing children make their way through the neigh-borhood each day, they encounter familiar sights, sounds, spaces, and people. For Brianna, such daily encounters have led to her designating the park's rec-reation area as her "Fav Place in My Community" complete with the personal clubhouse. For other flourishing children, similar encounters lead to establishing neighborhood havens that include a special climbing tree, a fort, and even a large, child-dug hole intended to trap wayward adults. For flourishing children, then, the park neighborhood is a familiar, predictable, and safe place. Neighborhood is a place they feel mastery over. Acknowledging their sense of mastery over the neighborhood, a flourishing child proudly proclaims, "I know my way around this whole trailer park." Mastery means he or she belongs to a place and that place belongs to them.[16]

For Aaron, a floundering child, neighborhood life in the same trailer park is much gloomier. Despite living almost two years in the Prairieview trailer park, Aaron has little concrete knowledge about the people in his neighborhood. When he travels the park streets, usually on his bike, he worries about getting hit by a car or beaten up by trailer-park teens. His concerns are defensive relative to what he views as a hostile world. He says, "I might have to bring me a baseball or some rocks to throw at them [teens] if they bother me." Yet Aaron cannot provide a specific example of an altercation with park teens. When asked about places in the trailer park he would never go, Aaron talks about "a shed-thing" in the rec-reation area, "It has wires and outlets all over and vines growing on it. I would go there with you, but never alone!" This is the same shed that Brianna claims as her clubhouse.

As his least favorite place in his community, Aaron draws his school. There are no windows in Aaron's drawing of his school—only two closed doors and a stark roof line drawn in gray pencil. The lack of color and stark composition of the drawing show his insecurity and dislike for school.[17] Aaron exhibits a sense of defeat in the same contexts in which Brianna experiences mastery and achievement.

Flourishing children by definition report a wide circle of friends. Their friendship networks tend to overlap between the trailer park and school. The network of friends Brianna plays with in the neighborhood is the same crowd she is seen with on the school playground. Social exchanges begun in one setting are continued in the other. These are intimate friendships as children are able to reveal detailed knowledge of each other's lives. Exchanges often include private details about a mom's new boyfriend or a family's financial status. For the flourishing children in the trailer parks, friendships include largely neighborhood peers, whether these children are flourishing, steady, or floundering. Within such groups, a flourishing child holds a high social status as the one sought out by less successful peers.

Together, the daily encounters flourishing children have in the trailer park support success in this developmental period of their lives. In the opposite way, floundering children seem to miss out on similar resourceful encounters despite sharing residence in the same neighborhood. With limited engagement in the neighborhood, floundering children report few opportunities to independently encounter places and peers in their park surroundings. Home is the place central in the life of this group. Peer friendships are both less frequent and less intimate than among flourishing children. Likewise, their sphere of contact is less centered on the park and more often includes nonpark peers as a result of their parents' intervention. Interaction with nonpark friends outside school typically involves a formal play date, chosen by a parent, and a one-on-one rather than a group interaction. The park neighborhood, even as a place just outside their front door, is not a place floundering children find familiar, predictable, or safe, as do flourishing children. Floundering children construct no sense of mastery over neighborhood, and despite their being in third grade, these children lack the autonomy important to healthy development by this age.[18]

The importance of neighborhood in a child's development is made clear in contrasting the patterns of engagement for flourishing as compared with floundering children. On a flourishing pathway, children access resources embodied in people and places in their trailer-park neighborhood that enhance their development. A floundering pathway is devoid of similar resources. What, then, is it that defines whether children are able to engage in their trailer-park neighborhood in a way that offers access to resources? Family strategies provide part of the answer. We consider first the two extremes of flourishing and floundering and then turn to a steady pathway as a test case. Comparison of the steady pathway with those of flourishing and floundering allows us to "test" whether the developmental differences identified stem from a trailer-park neighborhood effect, from individual attributes, or from family processes.

Family Processes and Trailer-Park Engagement

How a park neighborhood is experienced by a child is broadly shaped by family processes. Parents adopt strategies intended to maximize benefits and minimize harm; they link their children to resourceful experiences while simultaneously limiting exposure to risks in the immediate neighborhood.[19] Thus, parents operate as a significant intermediary by defining the neighborhood for children and being strategic about what they deem to be an appropriate involvement. An underlying family strategy, particularly its rules for neighborhood engagement, shapes whether a child has access to resources and opportunities or limited exposure due to perceived risks in the trailer-park neighborhood.

Flourishing children are allowed ample access to encounters in the trailer-park neighborhood. Parents of flourishing children permit free roaming, with the condition that a child observe family rules for reporting home and moving around the park. Flourishing children explain a common family rule: "I can go anywhere in the trailer park but not out of it." Such a rule is based on a parent's positive perception of the park. One mother of a flourishing child explains, "It doesn't bother me one bit living here. We haven't had a bit of trouble with anyone and the landlord is great." Parents of flourishing children see the park as a safe enough place for children to wander freely.

Family rules similarly structure floundering children's access to the trailer-park neighborhood in an obvious manner. A floundering child, as shown above, is permitted limited engagement in the park neighborhood, according to family rules. Parents admit they intentionally restrict their floundering child's time out in the park neighborhood because they consider it a risky place. Aaron's mother explains, "There are a lot of kids that run around on their own out here—little kids in groups. The other day I was out front and there was a group of four-year-olds riding their bikes around. They're too young to be out on their own like that. I haven't let my boys do that. But Aaron is getting older. I'm hoping that he can get to know some of the kids from the neighborhood this year." Ironically, Aaron's mother grew up in Prairieview. She says, "I grew up hearing about 'Prairieview Manor kids.'" In a moment of reflection, she adds, "And now my kids are Prairieview Manor kids!" Her comments imply a negative view or at least a regret for her children's having a park childhood.

A similar strategy that restricts free neighborhood movement is found in Jennifer's home. She is also a floundering child. Her parents set clear boundaries that allow Jennifer and her younger sister access to only "our end of the street and the bus stop." Their limits are based on their negative perception of the park neighborhood. Jennifer's father recalls, "We used to live on the other side of the park. The trailer was falling down around us but the neighborhood was great." In their current setting, the family has trouble with all their immediate neighbors. Jennifer remarks, "My dad doesn't like them [next door]. They play loud music and smoke." Jennifer's mother shares these negative sentiments but includes more of the park in her evaluation. She says, "I would never take my kids to the pool—not with what goes on there."

For their part, both flourishing and floundering children seem compliant with parental rules. Flourishing children enjoy their sponsored access to the neighborhood. These children spend a good deal of each day out of the house and around the trailer park when not in school. Like their parents, they feel a sense of trust about the park setting. Though they enjoy the freedom of being outside and somewhat on their own, flourishing children abide by the parameters set by parents. They venture only as far from home as is permitted. In short, flourishing children are trustworthy and so deserving of their freedom.

Floundering children, on the surface, also abide by parental restrictions. Yet all five floundering children reveal they sometimes break parental rules to obtain greater access to the park. Aaron says, "I tell my mom that I'm just going to ride down the street, but then I ride real fast all the way to [my friend's] house." Jennifer and her sister pointed out a clearing near a drainage ditch behind their house that they frequent, although it is forbidden territory: "We really aren't supposed to play back here, but we do anyways. Our mom just doesn't know it."

Floundering children are hampered by the unreasonable restrictions set by their parents. At the same time, as seen in the earlier fearful comments by Aaron about travel in the trailer park, they absorb parents' definition of the park neighborhood as a risky place. Such impressions could eventually work to further restrict their engagement with neighborhood peers and even inhibit feelings of safety and predictability important to emotional security.[20] Essentially then, floundering park children are caught in a double bind in which they are damned if they do and damned if they don't.[21] When they attempt to make the expected transition to wider social arenas—in this case the neighborhood—doing so involves countering parental (or even personal) expectations about their trailer park.

Children and a Trailer-Park Neighborhood Effect

Is there, then, a trailer-park effect on child development? For children, the connection between daily neighborhood engagements and flourishing development hints of a positive community effect from trailer-park residence. A link between floundering children and the pattern of limited neighborhood engagement reinforces such a notion. Generally, however, it seems that a rural trailer park can function as a positive place for children in middle childhood.

Yet what about the other children—that group that makes up the bulk of the sample (sixteen of twenty-five, or 64 percent)? When we compare the steady child pathway with those of flourishing and floundering children, distinct features emerge that differentiate the middle pathway from the other two extremes. Such differences sharpen outlines of a trailer-park community effect. Like their flourishing park peers, steady children have access to places and people in their neighborhood. Family rules allow steady children free engagement in the park. Again, such rules derive from parents' generally positive perceptions of the park as a neighborhood good enough for raising children. A mother of a steady child relates, "I like living in [trailer park]. I like the home. I like the yard. We have a nice, peaceful little neighborhood." Yet despite seemingly equal access to the same resources and opportunities that flourishing children have, steady children do not embrace their access as robustly. Perhaps these children are learning to be content with their immediate surroundings and a social life that in all likelihood takes place among kin rather than friends. Perhaps the difference is in one's curiosity level about the environment and people. On a steady course, children accept what is there by default—no curiosity, no questioning, and probably no getting into trouble either. They just inhabit where they are—and make no waves.

Billy, a steady child, frequents the Prairie Manor park streets and the pool. When he is outside he speaks to neighbors, but more frequently he is inside watching television or playing Nintendo, a task at which he is an expert. He has only limited knowledge of his neighbors and is surprised to see MacTavish one day with another park child. Billy lives only two blocks from the other child, and they are in the same grade. He remarks, "I did know [name] lived here. He goes to my school." Such a pattern of only superficial engagement is typical for steady children. That is, rather than actively and deeply engaging in their neighborhood, steady children choose other, less social activities like television, video games, or computer games that keep them from more developmentally enhancing interactions outside, with the neighborhood. As the test case, then, steady children do not support a negative community effect from a trailer-park childhood.

Family rules do not explain differences in engagement between flourishing and steady children; individual personal traits do. As compared with static peers, flourishing children are especially skilled at navigating their park neighborhood in ways that gain them access to resources and opportunities that translate into a sense of mastery. Like Brianna, flourishing children, "have to be out every minute the sun is up." Steady children are not as driven to engage in the world around them. Flourishing children engage in their neighborhood in a qualitatively more

FIGURE 9. Park children were asked to draw their home. Many produced images that included a pitched roof idealized in children's drawings versus the flat roof more common to trailer homes. Source: Park child.

interactive manner than do steady children. Here are details of Brianna's active engagement taken from field notes dated June 21, at 5:00 p.m.:

> During our interview on the porch, Brianna looks over my shoulder— I think she is looking at someone, but no one is there. She gets up, not

saying anything, and appears to be hunting for something in the grass next to the shed. She says, "My tree?" I get up and walk to her. She has two small trees in the grass—she is standing over the dead one. She seems to want an answer about why one had died while the other one has not. She asks me some specific questions about roots and how they affect the life of a tree. As we sit there, Brianna picks up all the dead pine needles and gathers them into her hand. Before we leave, Brianna lays the pine needles in a pile next to the dead tree.

Brianna repeatedly demonstrates a deep curiosity and caring about the world around her. Further along on the walk, for example, she stops, entranced by a large ant colony. She crouches, sitting on her heels, watching the ants for several minutes. Another incident during the neighborhood walk reveals personal traits of perseverance and pride in accomplishment that push her to achieve:

On the way to the playground, we discover a stainless dinner fork in the road in front of someone's driveway. I hit the end of the fork tines with my foot, launching it into the air. Brianna wants to imitate the action, but has trouble—I think a combination of her big platform shoes and her nine-year-old motor skills. She tries several times and either misses the fork completely or steps on it soundly. She tries over and over and over—there is no getting between her and the fork. She makes some progress but still misses. Finally, she hits it right on and it spins into the air. She looks up with a big smile and says, "I think my temper helped me out." She carries the fork home with her, saying she will practice the maneuver. She places the fork on the TV when we arrive home. As if remembering her accomplishment, she strokes the handle, sort of petting it, after she lays it down.

In similar encounters about her neighborhood, Brianna is curious, confident, and determined—characteristics that mark flourishing children as distinct, even when compared with steady peers. Access to the park is a necessary ingredient, but individual attributes provide the sufficient conditions to flourish.[22] Such personal characteristics shape the rich quality of developmental experiences shared by flourishing children in the parks across Mesa Vista, Prairieview, and Addington.

Trailer-Park Adolescence

Unlike the flourishing children, flourishing adolescents distance themselves from the trailer-park neighborhood. Fifteen-year-old Trinity explains this choice: "I don't like living in a trailer park, but really I don't feel like I'm a part of it.

I like Prairieview and that's where I feel I belong." Through her extracurricular activities—cheerleading, dance team, church, and a summer job—Trinity's life is centered on the town of Prairieview rather than her immediate park neighborhood, where she has lived for the past six years. Identifying favorite places, she includes only places in town such as her church, the local Dairy Queen, and the city park in the heart of Prairieview. Commenting on her photo of her favorite places she says, "This is just a park in town. We [she and her network of town friends] always go there after we go to Dairy Queen. We go there and swing and play and sometimes just sit." Trinity includes a picture of her school chorus room as well saying, "Music is really important in my life. I have a lot of good memories in this room." Trinity has broadened her network and engagement to include many middle-class people, places, and activities. Her performance as a straight-A student ensures that she fits in at Prairieview High School, where over 80 percent of her classmates will go on to college, most to four-year institutions.

Daily life for Miranda and other floundering youth in Prairieview, Mesa Vista, and Addington contrasts with that of flourishing Trinity. Miranda is forthright about her negative school experience, "It's lousy. I don't ever go to school. I get in trouble for the littlest things at school. I've been kicked out of class fourteen times. I got suspended last year." Miranda's performance in school is characterized by poor grades and frequent absences. Daily life for Miranda is centered on the Prairieview Manor trailer park, her home for the past six years. Miranda is up-to-date on the latest trailer-park gossip. As she drives her mother's new truck around the park, she frequently stops and talks with friends. She is almost always seen in the company of trailer-park adolescents ranging from thirteen to twenty-one years old. Still, she complains about the trailer park saying, "It sucks. There's nothing out here anymore, like there used to be. We used to have fun but now everyone's moved." Miranda includes photographs of the town schools to represent places she would never go. As her favorite place in her community she includes a picture of her boyfriend's car on a "No Motor Vehicles Permitted" bike path near her park. Miranda has narrowed her network and daily life to a small set of social ties. Essentially, she and other floundering youth are alienated from community life other than that defined by the park's circumscribed boundaries.

Youths' Engagement in the Park

Trinity's and Miranda's lives cast light on how a rural trailer-park environment functions for youth growing up there. When we compare the daily lives of flourishing and floundering youth, patterns emerge for how social interactions in the trailer parks and other social contexts shape these diverging pathways of development.[23]

Like the children, park youth display distinctive patterns of engagement in the park. For a flourishing youth, life centers on various structured activities that take place outside the park. Flourishing youth participate in school activities such as sports, drama, music, art, or other clubs. They are also involved in community activities, especially through church or by holding a paying job. Flourishing youth distinctively avoid engagement with other youth in the trailer park where they live. In the opposite way, floundering youth like Miranda report a different pattern of neighborhood engagement. Daily life for floundering youth centers on socializing with peers in or near the trailer park. Much like the flourishing children, floundering youth know their neighborhood well. They spend considerable time on the streets of the trailer park, cruising and hanging out with peers. Like Miranda, they express strong antipathy for the town and school and try to distance themselves from those contexts. At a time when flourishing youth widen their social worlds, floundering youth narrow theirs, limiting them to experiences in the trailer park and with their peer group there.

The engagement patterns of flourishing and floundering trailer park youth described above offer access to contrasting kinds of developmental experiences. The link between flourishing youth development and strong participation in the adjacent small town suggests a supportive small-town community effect. The association of floundering development with a pattern of social engagement restricted to the trailer park reinforces the presence of a community effect from this neighborhood form—an effect that works to narrow life chances. Examining the relative resources and risks of different patterns of engagement highlights the strength of these assertions. Again, we focus first on those flourishing and floundering and then use steady examples as a test case.

Youth Pathways, Small-Town Resources, and Trailer-Park Risks

We definitively know more about the pathways of adolescent development than about those of middle-childhood development. Resourceful pathways are distinguished by the presence of conventional or rule-abiding peers and adult role models who provide guidance and by opportunities to engage in activities that enhance a sense of efficacy and achievement.[24] In contrast, a nonresourceful or risky developmental pathway isolates youth from such resources and opportunities and effectively ensures their exposure to risks from nonconventional peers and nonproductive activities. For flourishing and floundering park youth, such resources and risks are meaningful to developmental outcomes.

Through strong links to the social networks of town and school, daily life for flourishing youth is structured by opportunities to engage with mainstream town peers and adults and to take part in activities that enhance their developmental experiences. When asked to identify three people important to them, all flourishing youth designated adults from the adjacent town. Teachers, ministers, the parents of friends, or their employers are identified. The value of these varied adult relationships for expanding their social horizons and networks is clear to flourishing youth. Referring to her photo of one adult she identifies as important to her life, Trinity says, "This is [my friend's] mom. She's always been there for me. She's a really good role model. She's always treated me like a member of the family." Pointing out a high school teacher important to her Trinity explains, "This is my chorus teacher. She's awesome! She knows everything about life. She gives me the best advice. I can go to her with any problem and she has the right answer. She's such a good person—she truly makes it her mission in life to care about and help others."

For flourishing youth, such relationships mean that they are embedded in overlapping networks of peers and adults across the contexts of church, school, and town. Correspondingly, their knowledge of park residents and other park youth is limited, despite the robust neighborhood knowledge shown by flourishing children. Being incorporated in the overlapping social networks of the small-town adjacent to their trailer park marks flourishing youth as belonging to the town. In this way flourishing trailer-park youth purposely make their trailer-park neighborhood irrelevant to their social world and simultaneously assure their access to rich small-town resources documented as supportive of successful development.[25]

Participation in sports, music, arts, or productive work instills the discipline needed for accomplishment.[26] Opportunities for such activities are available to youth in Prairieview, Mesa Vista, and Addington. Flourishing youth access such opportunities through their links to town residents and school professionals. The benefits are acknowledged by flourishing youth and their parents. For the past four years Antonio, a flourishing teen in Mesa Vista, has worked weekends at a local farm. Of his boss Antonio remarks, "He's a hard worker. He's taught me what it means to work hard." Speaking of her daughter's involvement in the church, Trinity's mother explains, "She's doing so well right now. She has so much self-confidence. Last Sunday she said the prayer in front of the whole church. That takes a lot to get up there and do that. Next month she's going to sing a solo." Flourishing youth, observed at length, repeatedly display a well-defined sense of discipline, responsibility, and accomplishment gleaned from their growth through jobs and activities. Flourishing youth fulfill responsibilities at home and in school. They keep research appointments, competently complete assignments, and are confident when they share personal information.

In contrast, floundering youth, who focus their social life in the trailer park, perceive barriers to accessing nonpark opportunities. For these teens, peers and pop culture figures whom they don't know are central to their lives. Brian, a floundering Mesa Vista teen, names his mother, his thirteen-year-old live-in girlfriend, his Chihuahua, and Snoop Dog as important to his life. Speaking of Snoop Dog, a "gangsta"-style rapper whose recordings garner a parental advisory rating, Brian remarks, "He is just it. I want to pattern my life after his." The peers and adults floundering youth associate with are typically nonconventional. Combined with isolation from community resources, such associations present significant risks to youth. All floundering youth engage in perilous activities such as unprotected sex, petty theft, vandalism, and alcohol and drug use. Every incident involves peers from the trailer park. Speaking of his floundering teenage son's friends, one Illinois father comments, "If he's hanging out with them you can be sure they're trouble." Although several of these youth obtained employment during the study, in each instance the job was temporary, for the youth either quit or was laid off. Scheduling appointments and completing various study protocols were difficult. Floundering youth exhibited few markers of self-discipline or accomplishment, characteristics of flourishing youth. Rather, truancy from school, unexplained absences from home including overnights, and incomplete research assignments were the norm for floundering youth.

The importance of neighborhood is made clear in contrasting the patterns of engagement for flourishing versus floundering children in middle childhood. Similarly, the developmental importance of the wider community for youth is shown in the contrasting flourishing versus floundering pathways in middle adolescence. Floundering and flourishing park youth pathways share little beyond a common geography. On a flourishing pathway, youth access resources embodied by individuals and opportunities in the adjacent community that enhance their development. A floundering pathway is devoid of involvement with resourceful individuals and rich opportunities and focuses exclusively on park peers.

What does it take to construct a flourishing pathway in adolescence for youth living in a rural trailer park?

Family Processes and Youth Pathways

Family perceptions about the trailer park and town also shape the parenting strategies used with park youth. While the busy activity schedules of flourishing youth keep them out of the trailer park for a considerable portion of the day, when they are around the neighborhood, negative perceptions curtail their engagement. Interestingly, these perceptions are expressed mainly by the youth themselves rather than parents. Trinity's mother explains, "Trinity hated riding the bus. You could see it—she would stand off away from the other kids. Here's Trinity and here's all the other kids fighting and cussing. She told me, 'Mom, I'm not like those other kids.' After that, I never put her on the bus again." Other flourishing youth report a similar personal decision to avoid interaction with park peers. Melanie, another flourishing teen explains, "We used to be friends back in junior high. She and I and this other [park] girl were friends. But then I stopped hanging out with them. It seemed one of them was always telling the other one something I said about her that I didn't, and then there would be these arguments. I got tired of it. So I stopped hanging out with them."

Antonio, a flourishing New Mexican youth, made a similar decision when his park peers became what he calls "gang wannabes." Like Trinity, other flourishing youth avoid riding the school bus or are not seen hanging out on park streets.

A decision by flourishing youth to disengage from the trailer park coincides with greater opportunities emerging to link with the adjacent town. For Trinity, the shift toward town-centered social ties came in seventh grade. Through school, she formed a friendship with a town girl who asked Trinity to attend church with her family one Sunday. Ever since, Trinity has been active in the church and in its youth group as a popular leader. Trinity spends a great deal of time with her friend's middle-class family. She vacations with them and works summers in the family business.

For other flourishing youth, the story of transition similarly involves a key peer or adult contact who helps the park youth forge ties with the wider community. Melanie began her move toward stronger community ties in fifth grade with a park friend's invitation to attend her city church. Over time, Melanie's social world became centered on this church community. Ultimately, she chose to leave the Prairieview high school to attend the private high school run by this church. Antonio's links outside the park were first strengthened through the job at a local farm and later through involvement in a teacher-run after-school stage production program, along with his participation in the high school wrestling and football programs. Flourishing youth are characterized by strong contacts made through specific middle-class adults in town such as a teacher, coach, minister, or employer with whom they are open to learning and being taught.

Parents of flourishing youth tend to support their community attachment by investing time, energy, and even money to promote it. Trinity's mother relates how she has actively facilitated her daughter's links to town over the years:

> After we moved here, one night we were sitting around talking about what we wanted more than anything. Trinity said she wanted to be popular. I said, "Okay, if you want popular, we'll get you popular!" Then

I thought—Oh my gosh! I'm a single mom in a trailer park! How am I going to get her popular? . . . I thought how do you get popular? You have kids over to your house! So I told Trinity to invite all the kids over. I bought pizzas and pop and candy. I would pick them up and take them home. It was great.

Apparently this strategy worked. Trinity became popular. According to her mother, however, Trinity soon realized that few of the popular kids were actually her true friends. "She came to me and said, 'Mom I don't want to be popular anymore.' I thought okay, how can we undo this?" Trinity's older brother (a flourishing youth in college) encouraged the shift by telling his mother that being in with the popular crowd was not always a good choice. Trinity's mom explains, "He went to school in [the city] and he was different than Trinity. He was always on the outside. He didn't care about being in with the in-crowd. When we started having the parties he said, 'Mom what are you doing?' I said, 'I'm trying to make Trinity popular.' 'Popular!' he said. 'Why do you want her to be popular! Don't you know those are the kids that drink and smoke and get in trouble!"

The problem was eventually solved when Trinity had a disagreement with a leader of the popular group, as her mother relates:

> This one girl decided who was in and who was out. Trinity was really worried about it when [the girl] got mad at her. She said, "Mom, she'll ruin me!" I told her this might be good. "You said you didn't want to be popular anymore. Maybe this will fix things." I told her, "Those kids aren't your friends. They've been coming to our parties and eating our pizza and drinking our pop, that we've paid for and not one has had you over to their house." I told her, "That's not a true friend—a true friend gives things back to you."

Hosting these teen parties proved to be expensive for Trinity's mother but indicates her willingness to invest their limited funds on Trinity's behalf. Trinity and her mother live modestly in a cramped, older singlewide with sparse furnishings. Trinity's bed is a simple mattress on the floor. Yet she is always dressed in the latest fashion, wearing only new-looking, name-brand clothing. When the pizza parties came to an end, Trinity's mother expressed a bit of relief: "We were spending our whole week's grocery money in one night. The rest of the week we either had to eat leftover pizza or cold cereal." When Trinity stopped wanting to be popular, her mother followed her lead, giving Trinity direction:

> Trinity asked me how she could find a real friend and I told her. . . . Look for someone that looks like they want a friend and then talk to them—say something nice. So the next day she met [someone who became

her friend]. [The friend] was just so excited that Trinity—one of the popular kids—had talked to her she was like, "Oh my gosh, it's Trinity talking to me!" [The friend] asked her over that weekend. Ever since then they've been best friends. They were even baptized in the church together.

Trinity's mother's active efforts to forge her daughter's links to town are ongoing. She selflessly sacrifices personal time during the day to support Trinity's engagement in town. Fortunately, Trinity's mother has a work situation that allows some flexibility. She describes her daily schedules in the summer months:

> On Tuesday and Thursday I have to wake Trinity early for cheerleading practice. Practice starts at 6:00 a.m. On those days, I drive her to practice at the high school. Then I pick her up at 7:30 a.m. and take her over to [her friend's] house so they can ride to work. Then I go into work. At noon I pick Trinity up from work and take her home and fix her a sandwich, and sit with her while she eats. If I have time I do that during my lunch hour. Then I go back to work until 5:00 p.m. In the evening we sit down to dinner as a family when we can. That's our intention—what we strive for—but sometimes with all the things Trinity does she isn't here. After dinner, [she and her new husband] usually run errands while we wait to pick up Trinity from her activities.

The parents of other flourishing youth report similar investments of time and effort to support a park youth's successful development. Melanie's mother is on disability from an injury received on a past job, and her father works as a janitor. Their combined incomes allow Melanie's mother to stay at home full-time. Melanie's mother, then, in addition to her great commitment, has ample time to invest in her daughter. For example, during an interview session her mother says, "I hope it's all right if I fold these newspapers while we talk. Melanie has a paper route and I like to have the papers ready when she gets home." Such parental devotion is typical in Melanie's home. Melanie tells the story of how her father helped obtain her car—a small, very yellow two-door economy model:

> Dad bought it for me. It was really his but it was mine to use when I needed it. But then he needed to trade it in for mom's Grand Am. Well, one day I was eating at a pizza place. I looked out the window and there it was! It was my car! When we got home I said, "Daddy, please can you trade the truck in and get my car back for me?" The next day he did. I think he got it back because he was tired of having to hurry home from work so I could use the Grand Am. This way he could take his time with getting home, and I would still have a car to go places in. . . . Originally

I was supposed to pay for it from my paper money, but Dad helps out a little. He gives me money for gas a lot too.

Antonio's stepfather, in particular, invests great time and energy in facilitating Antonio's ties to the Mesa View community. Such investment has meant a developmental turnaround for Antonio, who was at one period sliding into a floundering trajectory. His stepfather explains,

> It was the year that Antonio's parents got divorced [fifth grade] that things started slipping for him. I think that hit him very hard. When I met [his mother] she was a single mother raising two sons. Antonio was running with the wrong crowd. I brought a lot of discipline into the situation. I stepped in and got Antonio the job at the farm. [The farm owner] is a friend of mine. Antonio being out of the house reduced a lot of tension between him and his mother. Working on a farm taught him a lot.

Antonio, as seen above, readily credits the farm job with helping him learn responsibility and gain a sense of achievement. His stepfather connects such lessons to Antonio's recent return to behavior that indicates the pathway to his flourishing: "He certainly has settled down. Grades were never important to him before, but he's beginning to understand they will be to his future—to what college he ends up attending. Now Antonio hangs out primarily with kids who are somehow connected with [the university]—professors' and instructors' kids."

Floundering youth do not make a successful transition appropriate to their age beyond family to wider social contexts. Rather, for these teens and their parents, particularly in Illinois, a perception that townspeople stigmatize them deters any desire to form bridges. Referring to town, Miranda's mother says, "They think we're all trailer trash here. [But] it's not that bad out here." Repeatedly Illinois parents of floundering youth voice that "they treat us like trailer trash in town." Perceptions of stigma make floundering youth reluctant to participate in town-based activities. Jason, a floundering teen, was once a high achiever academically and in sports. He wanted to continue his football career when he moved to the Prairieview park four years ago. His father recalls, "He wanted to play. But he just didn't feel welcome." Since then, Jason has slipped socially and academically. He was arrested for vandalizing a Prairieview village police car. Other floundering youth talk about prior participation in town activities. Miranda recalls attending the town's Boys and Girls Club in earlier years: "I loved it there. Sometime I still go back even though I'm too old now." Miranda has found no replacement for this middle-childhood community resource.

Floundering youth, greatly deterred by bad experiences and failures, eventually decide to avoid school and town activities. Thus, rather than making connections with key individuals in town, like those that flourishing youth cultivate, floundering youth link with those who accelerate their downward developmental trajectory. Miranda's closest relationship is with a twenty-one-year old single mother and former Prairieview Manor trailer-park resident. During the study Miranda spent the night at the woman's house, neglecting to inform her parents of her whereabouts. Miranda was grounded over the incident. Her mother worries: "[Miranda's friend] is a touchy subject around here right now. Let's just say we don't particularly like Miranda hanging out with her." She is unhappy with where Miranda's older friend is leading her, a direction reinforced in Miranda's park-peer relationships. Miranda and a Prairieview park peer both became pregnant in the past year. Miranda at fifteen years old miscarried, while her fifteen-year-old friend opted for an abortion. Thus Miranda represents a female floundering trajectory that incorporates a teenaged pregnancy and becoming a high school dropout.

Jason began hanging out with what his father terms "the wrong crowd" in Illinois. Brian was running with the youth that Antonio, who lives in the same New Mexico park, identifies as being in a "gang wannabe" group. These youths were involved in an incident that led to Brian's being arrested. Brian and his friends now face the same felony and misdemeanor charges. Jeremy, another Illinois floundering youth, was repeatedly observed in the company of young park adults his father identifies as drug dealers. Jeremy's father reports just living through a three-day period when he had no idea where his son was, whom he was with, or what he was doing. These boys represent a pathway characteristic of floundering male youth—whose involvement with delinquent friends and illegal activities narrows their life chances and endangers developmental outcomes.[27]

Parents of each floundering youth express concerns over his or her involvement with problematic companions. Yet parents' strategies prove ineffectual in protecting youth from such risky influences. Miranda, for example, carries a pager so her mother can monitor her, but Miranda ignores the pages. On one occasion, her mother shouted into the phone, "Miranda Sue, I know you're picking up your pages. You better get home right now because the lady from the university is here and you have an appointment with her." Miranda never returned the call, nor did she keep the appointment. Miranda's mother often resorts to calling around the neighborhood to locate her but is seldom successful. Jason's father used an intervention strategy of placing him under the care of a relative in town. He explained, "I have him staying at my brother's when I can't watch him. He just seems to get in trouble every time he's out here [in the trailer park]." Thus, rather than investing time and energy in fostering their youth's positive links to town, the parents of floundering youth must focus on buffering the strong negative influences of the associations each youth forges in the trailer park. If a youth wants to find risky friends or activities, the potential for both exists in the park. Engaging consistently in such behaviors, floundering youth make it more likely that they will lodge at a lower status than their parents, who are trailer home owners, job holders, and responsible adults.

Thus far, the analysis of community effect on child and youth development has focused on contrasting flourishing and floundering pathways. Understanding that a neighborhood may function to either mitigate or exacerbate the effects of class status underlies this perspective.[28] That is, a community or neighborhood effect has the potential to override or mitigate the tendency for social reproduction and the persistence of lower-class-status behaviors among the rural poor. As a residential context, a rural trailer park appears to have such an effect. A minority of trailer-park children and youth in the three distinct rural regions travel a pathway toward life chances that differ from those predicted by their parents' working-poor/working-class status. For a small group, the tendency toward social reproduction is mitigated by the rural trailer park's location near a small town. Proximity for these park youth presents a small-town community effect with broader opportunities and a chance for social mobility absent in the trailer park itself. For others who do not form bridges to the resources of the adjacent town, the trailer park shapes a community effect that compromises development and narrows life chances. But what of the *steady* park children and youth who appear headed toward socially reproducing the working-poor/working-class status of their parents? Does the argument for a trailer-park neighborhood effect account for the developmental outcomes of these children and youth whose developmental trajectory is not as dramatic as that for the other opposing outcomes?

Youth and a Trailer-Park Neighborhood Effect

Like flourishing youth, steady youth forge ties with the adjacent community. They play on school sports teams, participate in school clubs, and attend local-church youth groups much as do flourishing youth. Steady youth therefore have access to the same resources and opportunities as flourishing youth. In addition, parents of steady youth do their part to support such engagement by providing transportation, paying fees, and encouraging their youth. Yet on close inspection, differences are evident between the patterns of engagement and the quality of resources experienced by steady as compared with flourishing youth.

While steady youth successfully navigate ties to the local small town, at the same time they retain strong ties to the trailer park. Flourishing youth, in contrast, abandon any ties in the trailer park. Steady youth thus divide their time between town and the park, whereas flourishing youth focus exclusively on their ties to town. Qualitatively different resources derive from these patterns of engagement that distinguish a steady from a flourishing pathway.

Consider Mike, a steady youth. Mike is on both the football and wrestling teams at Prairieview High School. He enjoys taking part in these sports and was convinced by the football coach to take a summer farm-labor job intended to instill discipline in the team members. Mike attends a church youth group as well, though mostly at his mother's insistence. He willingly participates in these activities, but more than anything he enjoys riding BMX bikes with his friends in the park. It is these friends who form the center of Mike's social world. This pattern of partial engagement in the town along with extensive involvement in the trailer park is typical of steady youth.

Steady youth thus have contact with potentially important community role models or mentors such as teachers, coaches, and clergy. But they do not develop the intense ties to these community adults that flourishing youth forge. Flourishing youth, as we heard in their own words, identify such adults as individuals important to their lives. In each case, flourishing youth relate stories that define the strength of their relationships to nonpark adults who in turn structure their social worlds.

It is clear that for Melanie, a flourishing youth, life centers on her church. When she shows several photos of people from church she comments that each has a great influence on her. The first picture shows an older woman holding a young boy on her lap. Melanie relates, "This is [name]. She's a lady from church that teaches the fifth- and sixth-grade Sunday school. I was in the fifth- and sixth-grade class for like five years. She didn't care that I stayed. She's always been there for me and she always knows just what to say." Melanie's affection for this woman is clear in her sweet conversational tone. Next is a photo of a young man in a suit, standing in a sanctuary. Melanie explains, "This is Pastor [name]. He's twenty-four, but he acts more like one of us. Whenever we go out and want to do stuff, he's the one we take with us because he lets us have so much fun. He's a good, strong Christian example for us all." Finally, Melanie shows a photo of a beautiful young woman holding a baby girl. She explains, "This is [name]. She used to drive the church bus route out here. She would give me all her clothes that were too small for her so I would have something nice to wear to church."

The relationships each flourishing youth has with a community mentor—a teacher, a town friend's parent, a minister, or a boss—are intense. Melanie visits the family of a former minister in another city during her spring break. Trinity has traveled the past four summers with her best friend's family on their annual vacation. Antonio refers to his farm boss as "kind of a second father for me. And his boys are like brothers." Steady youth also have access to adults as resources and activities as opportunities in the small towns of Prairieview and Mesa Vista.

For steady youth, however, such participation does not yield the rich, life-shaping experiences treasured by flourishing youth. Steady youth relate no stories of how specific community individuals changed their lives.

The links formed through participation in town prove qualitatively more meaningful for flourishing youth than they do for their steady trailer-park peers. A supportive small-town community effect is transmitted through the strong relationships flourishing youth form with middle-class town adults. As described above, Melanie's life centers on her church. When we ask Melanie what her life would be like without involvement in the church, she emphatically says, "Bad! Horrible! With all the druggies right down the street I'm sure I would have been into that. I wouldn't be who I am without the church in my life." Interestingly, Melanie's prediction is what happened to her floundering peers. The relationships such youth maintain with park peers have led to narrowed life chances through involvement in drugs, unprotected sex, and delinquency.

Rural Trailer Parks as a Place to Grow Up

Sadly, misconceptions and missed opportunities largely serve to separate flourishing, steady, and floundering pathways. Parents' perceptions, particularly in Illinois, of the trailer park as a risky social context—as, for example, in Aaron's case—lead them to limit a child's engagement with what seem to be easily accessible social resources in the neighborhood. Yet, as we saw in the developmental outcomes of steady children, access to the neighborhood does not ensure optimal development that promotes social mobility. It is the personal entrepreneurial characteristics of flourishing youth that distinguish their neighborhood experiences and their forging of a successful developmental pathway. For floundering teens, the adult support and investment needed to help a youth effectively build bridges between the trailer park and town is lacking. The resources and opportunities that Illinois and New Mexico flourishing youth gain by proximity to middle-class townsfolk are not embraced by floundering teens in the same setting. But again, accessibility does not provide a full counterexample to a park community effect. Steady youth have access to similar small-town resources, yet their developmental pathways differ from those of flourishing youth. To flourishing children, the personal qualities of the youth or a parent make for distinctly richer developmental experiences in the same small-town context.

Though emerging from the same neighborhood, some trailer-park children and youth access the resources important to fostering their flourishing development, while others do not. The entrepreneurial qualities that flourishing children and youth possess allow them to mine the mobility-enhancing resources available from every small world—school, church, or work—in their social environment. What they glean from these contexts outside their trailer-park home positions them on a pathway toward a bright future. Such a future is available only to those children and youth who mine the trailer park and community environments for resources rather than accept by default what is casually available, as do steady children and youth. Floundering children and youth, who do not access any resources supportive of social mobility, are destined to struggle with compromised development and narrowed life chances. Those park ties steady youth forge are not as deleterious to their development as are those chosen by floundering youth. They choose ties with other steady youth who perhaps are more dedicated to a good time than to entrepreneurial activities. And if they all remain in the park as adults, these networks may prove useful in sustaining them. Thus, misconceptions and missed opportunities appear to have dire ramifications for the trajectory of child and youth development among those floundering. But a park peer group is not necessarily ominous for those who are on a steady pathway of development.

We did not find a clear trailer-park neighborhood effect because a single developmental outcome is not produced by growing up there. In fact, the majority of children—the flourishing and steady groups combined—do not display unsuccessful outcomes. But growing up in a park for potentially floundering youth appears to exacerbate family deficiencies. And maintenance of a flourishing pathway requires self-selection through entrepreneurial efforts, along with community middle-class "ladders" to achieve success.

REFORMING THE MOBILE HOME INDUSTRIAL COMPLEX

Across the three sites included in our study, all trailer-park residents experience direct and indirect effects from the players that operate as the mobile home industrial complex (MHIC) we described in chapter 1. Set within this complex, land-lease trailer parks function as a private and problematic solution to the public need for affordable homeownership opportunities for lower-income rural families. That solution, as we have illustrated, leads some entrepreneurial players to make hefty profits, but it leaves families largely let down by trailer-park life and motivated to move on. Yet making that move out of the park into conventional housing—an aspiration that our families share—is realized by only a few. Here we suggest a robust group of strategies intended to bring about reforms to the MHIC. The strategies we suggest seek to curb or balance financial and social aspects of homeownership and park life with the structure and profitability of the mobile home industrial complex to achieve a more equitable and quality product that would improve homeowners' financial bottom line and their lives more generally.

Mobile Home Manufacturers

Ellen Adams had modest expectations for the mobile home she purchased used. What she needed was affordable shelter where, as a single mother working a low-wage job, she could house herself and her two children. While her "first cost"—that is, her home purchase price—seemed appealing, "operating costs" associated with construction of her home—the cost of heating and cooling an all-electric home and the repairs needed to maintain it—were surprising to Ellen and other park families we met.[1] Ellen tried to address the high energy costs incurred during Illinois's intemperate summers and winters by hanging an unzipped sleeping bag across the picture window in her living room as insulation. Another family, as a more extreme effort, used actual fiberglass insulation as window coverings. These measures, and the litany of often costly and always persistent repairs families reported, along with those identified by sources such as the Centers for Disease Control and Prevention, suggest that the National Manufactured Housing Construction and Safety Standards Act of 1974, known as the HUD Code, and the Manufactured Housing Improvement Act of 2000, which ensured updates to those codes, had not gone far enough in ensuring low-income families a quality home product.[2]

The technology exists to produce "high-performing" manufactured homes. Clayton's "Energy Smart Homes," for example, include top-of- the-line features that ensure low operating costs and address safety issues (air quality, wind damage, and fire hazards) linked to manufactured housing.[3] Yet these newly designed high-end models are not the homes our study families live in. Nor are they the typical manufactured homes rolling off the factory floor. Analysts estimate that with existing innovations in design and construction, standard models of manufactured homes could be at least 60 percent more energy efficient.[4] The challenge, of course, is to produce these best-possible homes within a budget that would fit the market of low-income families.

There is a role for government and nonprofits in pressuring the industry for advancements in the performance of manufactured housing. Without policy regulations, adequate incentives, and oversight, manufacturers remain motivated by keeping costs down and profits high. They use the least expensive materials and technologies allowed—even if that means producing a home that performs poorly in energy efficiency and durability and diminishes the potential for low-income homeowners to benefit from these lower-end homes over the long term.

There are strategic moments that make advances in providing high-performing manufactured housing to families on a budget seem feasible. Motivated by the post-Katrina embarrassments of housing poor families in recreational trailers, the Federal Emergency Management Agency (FEMA), under the Alternative Housing Pilot Program, developed the "Mississippi Cottage"—an aesthetically pleasing small home that exceeded ENERGY STAR manufactured home requirements, could withstands 150 mph winds, provided good air quality, offered accessibility upgrades, featured metal roofs and other upgrades, and started at $50,000.[5] Several industry leaders in modular construction have moved into building green and affordable housing. Terradime Modular out of Pittsburgh, Pennsylvania, produced the Ecoplex modular home starting at $30,000.[6] These homes have the advantage of cost-saving, factory-built components, but their site assembly eliminates some of the concerns and limitations surrounding the transportation of a manufactured home. At present such measures, like the "tiny home movement," mainly have middle-class aesthetic appeal, and they require considerable knowledge to deal with designers and architects, but there seems potential for developers to think about their use on a more industrial scale.[7] Expanding the competition for producing affordable ownership alternatives seems a useful direction for dealing with issues tied to the current MHIC.

Legislative tools are available to push the manufactured home industry toward investing in technologies and innovation that would improve quality performance in all newly manufactured housing. The Energy Independence and Security Act 2007, signed into law under President George W. Bush, required the Department of Energy to develop energy efficiency standards for manufactured housing that take into account technical feasibility and cost-effectiveness. There would be benefits to regularly updating those standards to ensure buyers have access the best product possible within a budget feasible for modest incomes.[8]

Policy tools are needed to help move families like those in our study out of their often twenty-year-old singlewides and into newly produced, better-quality homes. While we have identified concerns about pressuring homeowners to upgrade to a new home—a process that in the end proves an expensive trap for study families—equitable mechanisms already exist for the replacement of substandard homes. The Energy Efficient Manufactured Housing Act of 2009 was legislation introduced in 2011.[9] Based on a successful state-level program, this measure would have worked to assist low-income owners of older mobile homes with financing the purchase of new ENERGY STAR manufactured homes. The bill passed in the House but stalled in the Senate. It is doubtful that it will be raised again. The nonprofit Frontier Housing in Kentucky, however, has forged ahead in developing a "Manufactured Housing Done Right" campaign that supports replacement of substandard units for low-income owners (defined as those making less than 50 percent of the local median income) in ways that safeguard homeowners from incurring added financial vulnerabilities.[10] Next Steps, a subsidiary of Frontier Housing dedicated to sustainable, affordable homeownership and to transforming the manufactured housing industry, is also making headway addressing issues of quality through the replacements of aging homes.[11] Significant cost savings from a more energy efficient home theoretically make an upgrade more affordable.[12] Park owners, of course, must be amenable if such an intervention is to help families in land-lease parks.

The high prevalence of structural defects documented for manufactured housing and seen among our study families is a result of manufacturing short-cuts but also damage incurred during transportation and installation.[13] The challenge for homeowners occurs in seeking a remedy as blame gets passed among players with none taking responsibility. The manufacturer points the finger at the transporter or the installer, while they in turn point back at the manufacturer. As a result, trailer homeowners are left to begin residence in a damaged home without finding any restitution.[14]

The Manufactured Housing Institute Act of 2000 was an attempt to help homeowners deal with such notoriously hard-to-deal-with concerns.[15] Implementation of the MHI Act, at least in states where it was adopted, established dispute resolution processes and instituted standards for licensure and training of installers as well as mandatory postinstallation inspections. Expanding such measures should ensure that more mobile homeowners start out with the quality of home they expected.

Mobile Home Dealers and Financers

The sales pitch from friendly dealer Craig Warrington felt welcoming to an unsophisticated first-time home buyer like Ellen Adams. For Ellen and so many of our study families, the financial considerations of buying a used singlewide centered on fitting the monthly payment into her budget, not on the long-term costs accrued from the accumulated interest on that transaction. Yet those long-term costs from a high-interest thirty-year mortgage on a used singlewide, as detailed in chapter 1, are considerable. That kind of profiting from low-income home buyers is common within a system of sales and finance that structures opportunities for exploitation.

Within the realm of manufactured housing sales and finance, as noted in chapter 1, the market is dominated by three large, vertically integrated operations. Dealing and finance can be predatory.[16] A recent investigative series by the *Seattle Times* and the Center for Policy Integrity concluded that Clayton Homes, a subsidiary of Berkshire Hathaway and one of the big three, uses "a pattern of deception to extract billions from poor customers around the country."[17] Deceptions included incentivizing dealers to steer borrowers toward Berkshire Hathaway's lending products, which carried interest rates as high as 19 percent, rather than helping customers find the most competitive loan. Efforts to shop around are often thwarted for a buyer, as Berkshire Hathaway controls lending companies under eighteen different names. Twenty-First Mortgage and Vanderbilt Mortgage, two leading high-interest lenders are, for example, both owned by Berkshire Hathaway. In other instances, rural minority borrowers (including Navajos)—a growing sector of mobile home buyers—were falsely told that Vanderbilt Mortgage, which offers the highest proportion of high-interest loans to minority buyers, was the only lender that would finance in their community.

Buyers also reported being lowballed on the quoted interest rate only to find a higher rate when it came time for them to sign the contract. Berkshire Hathaway, by a factor of seven, finances more mobile home purchases than any other lender. Clayton generated half a billion dollars in profits during the first nine months of 2015. According to the *Seattle Times*, that figure was up 28 percent from that same period during the previous year.

Even within the broader home mortgage system, built-in rural disadvantages mean that small-town mobile home buyers lack access to competitive home financing. The movement toward bank consolidation in an effort to become "too big to fail" has reduced lending options in rural areas that were already slimmer than those in urban areas.[18] And of course, these limited options are for lower-income families, like those in our study, further exacerbated by loan denial rates higher than those for suburban and urban mortgages. Roughly one in five rural home mortgage loan applications was denied in 2013; among manufactured home buyers that rate reached 38 percent.[19] Both rates are significantly higher than the 13 percent reported that year for urban and suburban applicants. Bad credit histories and high debt-to-income ratios explain many of these denials. But poor economic conditions and limited good job opportunities in many rural places, as we illustrated, pave the road to debt and credit problems.[20] Together these factors create what is essentially a poverty trap for families because a high-cost loan becomes the only available option. Roughly half of mobile homes purchased in 2013 were financed with high-costs loans, indicating that the problems we identify persist.[21]

Federal-level policy efforts intended to disrupt the most exploitive aspects of mobile home sales and finance are in place. The Housing and Economic Recovery Act of 2008 mandated a "Duty to Serve" three underserved markets including (1) rural, (2) manufactured, and (3) affordable housing.[22] That mandate, however, is still working slowly toward implementation. Comment on the proposed rule, which continued through March of 2016, generated a wealth of critical feedback, including much from the manufactured housing industry and mobile home dealers. That final "Duty to Serve Rule" issued in December 2016 by the Federal Housing and Finance Agency, which has the authority to oversee implementation, stipulates that Fannie Mae and Freddie Mac (federal lending enterprises) provide a secondary market for mortgages on residential properties in these three markets. For rural areas the focus of the proposed rule was on high-needs regions and populations such as middle Appalachia, the lower Mississippi Delta, border colonias, Native American lands and tribal members, and migrant and seasonal agricultural workers. That focus broadened to include more rural areas in the final rule. For the manufactured housing market, the original proposal was to focus on activities related to homes financed as real property. In the final ruling, chattel loans will count for Duty to Serve Credit, with the provision of adequate consumer protections. The FHFA did not, however, stipulate what constitutes adequate protections in that final rule. Blanket loans for certain categories of manufactured housing communities are also a part of the final ruling.[23] Listening sessions are scheduled for the early months of 2017. Fannie Mae and Freddie Mac will then start drafting their plans for implementation. Public review and comment on the plans will follow. While seemingly aimed at addressing real issues in manufactured housing finance, the wheels of government intervention turn slowly while families continue to suffer the costs of those delays and bear the consequences of policy efforts reshaped by lobby groups.

Passage of the Dodd-Frank Wall Street Reform and Consumer Protection Act in 2011 promised sweeping reforms to curtail questionable lending practices in the housing market.[24] The Manufactured Housing Institute (MHI), a leading organization for the industry, continues to voice significant concerns about these reforms.[25] While promising to address well-documented shady sales and lending practices, the MHI and others assert that the act imposes new standards on lending that will have the unintended consequence of limiting access to credit for low-income families.[26] There is no organization comparable to the MHI, however, that advocates the rights of borrowers—rural families in this case.

The closest approximation of consumer protections against predatory sales and lending seems to be educational guides for prospective mobile home buyers that provide information about consumer rights. Some states have developed and now require dealers to distribute these guides. Home buyer guides couple information developed by HUD or other supporting institutions with more state-specific guidelines on consumer rights, details about the trade-offs of manufactured homeownership, and information on how to choose a mobile home park.[27] The Public Policy Institute of the American Association of Retired Persons (AARP) and National Consumer Law Center are other sources for buyer information.[28] The United States Department of Agriculture Extension Service though land-grant universities has recently emerged as a provider of critical comparative information for rural first-time home buyers in particular.[29] Counseling home buyers on the advantage of a gently used trailer purchase as opposed to a new home might help families avoiding becoming financially ensnared by the MHIC.

Avoiding engagement with the more exploitive financial aspects of the MHIC is another strategy to improve family prospects. The reclassification of mobile homes as "real" property rather than "personal" property moves the borrower out of subprime loan markets and into more conventional mortgage financing.[30] Reclassification now typically requires that a mobile home be permanently affixed to the land.[31] Generally, removal of the wheels and axles and placement of the home on a permanent foundation are involved in making a home nonmobile, at considerable homeowner expense. The main homeowner attraction for reclassification is increased access to more favorable financing.[32] In 2015, some forty states set forth procedures for converting manufactured homes from personal to real property. Experts, however, assert that the legal complexity and onerous costs of adding a foundation required by many states keeps conversion out of reach for lower income families.[33]

Reclassification also brings the advantage of more favorable titling options, more equitable taxation, and better consumer protections, including safeguards against loan default.[34] Under reclassification, appraisal of manufactured homes would be transferred from the county tax commissioner to the county tax assessor's office, where "fair market values" rather than "blue book values" (values estimated based on age and condition, like those for a car) would be used.[35] Currently, reclassification must be initiated on an individual basis, making it questionable whether conversion to real property would be a meaningful option for the poorest of park residents or those who view a mobile home as only a temporary housing solution.

Park Operators: Trailer Parks as a Real Estate Commodity

When Ellen sited her trailer home in Joe's Prairieview Manor park, she learned some of the trade-offs involved in parking her home on someone else's land. She knew, for example, that she would be subject to a set of park rules regulating yard upkeep, the number of cars per home, and a curfew for kids. As a single mother, Ellen appreciated that there would be some oversight of neighborhood quality by park management. But her decision to site a home in a park was mainly a pragmatic one, based on the necessity of controlling costs, and as was the case for the families in our study, she owned no land. Ellen and the other families we spoke to were generally satisfied with park residence when a sense of equity or fairness prevailed. Lot rent increases without reason or egregious rules and extra costs for kids or pets left trailer-park families feeling disenfranchised, lacking a sense of control or empowerment in a system in which park owners who control the land inevitably control the fate of their tenant-homeowners.

That system of disempowerment grows more deplorable as investors move in to replace more benevolent mom-and-pop trailer-park operators. The Walmart model of park operation, which encourages stripping of amenities like pools and playgrounds, for example, also encourages owners to maintain distance from park tenants. Personal entanglement with park residents will, after all, make those regular lot rent increases and evictions needed to maintain attractive investor returns harder to enforce. Dissatisfaction with disenfranchisement from more democratic community rights provides a strong push factor for the desire to move on from park life. Yet as we have seen, few families likely realize that aspiration. What might make sense in the interim are policies that balance owner's rights to realize reasonable profits with efforts to make park life work better for families. We offer three specific, low-cost policy recommendations to support greater empowerment of homeowners in land-lease parks.

First, a tenant bill of rights with protections for eviction and other unreasonable practices is a low-cost means of ensuring park residents greater control of their lives and property. Such tenant protections are already in place in many states, which stipulate that park rules must be reasonable to be legal and enforceable. In New Hampshire, for example, extra rent charges for children or extra fees for pets are illegal unless extra services are provided. Furthermore, charges for maintenance and repair of park infrastructure such as electrical, septic, or water lines are not permitted.[36] We found that park residents are well aware of park rules; they are less aware, however, of whether these rules are actually legal. Legal assistance groups and housing nonprofits could play an important role in educating park tenants about their full rights. The USDA Extension Service, whose mission focuses on rural America, could again engage in such supports. In many states mobile home park resident associations exist, and they play a powerful role in bringing the voice of residents to the political table.[37]

Second, license requirements for park owners is highly recommended. Minimal requirements for owner and manager training might be part of the licensure process. A model exists in Oregon State Statute 90.734, which requires park managers to complete a four-hour continuing education training course every two years.[38] Of course, the state (or Extension Service) could be responsible for developing such a course—under their mandate to serve rural people.

Third, regulation of lot rent increases would address a central area of exploitation tied to land-lease mobile home parks. Vermont, for example, requires justification by the park owner for a lot rent increase and provisions for tenant action should there be a disagreement.[39] Tenants thus have a mechanism for protesting an unreasonable increase in the context of the accepted market-driven, unregulated situation. Even in the context of the national, housing-led recession, mobile home lot rents increased almost annually.[40]

Most radical in empowering park residents is a new model of mobile home "community" that holds the potential to alleviate the manifest circumstances trailer home owners face as a consequence of landlessness and disenfranchisement. Resident-owned communities (ROCs) hold great promise for essentially turning the investor-owned model on its head by creating a pathway to resident park ownership and a democratic community structure.[41] ROCs are land cooperatives in which residents own the housing community but not a specific land parcel. They emerged in the United States through the work of a nonprofit organization, the New Hampshire Community Loan Fund (NHCLF). In 1984 the NHCLF first provided legal and financial assistance to residents for the purchase of their park when it came up for sale.[42] By 2010, the NHCLF had assisted in residents' purchase of ninety-two mobile home communities and helped 5,200 households make the transition from an investor-owned park to a resident-owned community.[43] Other models for conversion to resident ownership exist nationally, with over one thousand ROC communities now in operation. Some have operated as cooperatives for over twenty years, a demonstration that the ROC model can stand the test of time. Regional differences exist, however, for whether local housing laws and policies make park conversation more or less likely. In a National Public Radio interview in May of 2012, Paul Bradley of the NHCLF identified "first right of refusal" protections as critical to give residents time to organize without the threat of being outmaneuvered by investors.[44]

Nonprofits help residents with what is typically the greatest challenge to their park ownership—the securing of financing to purchase their park's land.[45] Once mobile homes are tied to resident-owned land, the doors open to conventional mortgage financing, with lower interest rates than those offered on personal property or chattel loans. In fact, resident costs in a ROC average $40 a month less than in a land-lease park.[46] Furthermore, homes in a ROC sell more quickly, sell at higher prices, and hold their value better than those in an investor-owned community.[47] Landownership is the critical intervening factor.

ROCs' structure of democratic governance alleviates the disenfranchisement of residents' rights that we identified. Residents, who are tenants no more, elect a board and establish democratic procedures for the origination and enforcement of park rules, the prioritization and financing of infrastructure improvements, and the process for selection of new residents.[48] Nonprofit organizations like the NHCLF offer leadership development and training to support the transition.[49] There is emerging evidence of greater social acceptance of ROC park residents than of residents in an investor-owned trailer-park community.[50] ROC residents themselves report a greater sense of community.[51]

While rich with promise for more equitable mobile home ownership opportunities, the ROC movement is not expanding as quickly as some policy experts had hoped.[52] Conservative politics slowed the adoption of this model in the southeastern United States, which has the highest proportion of mobile home housing. In North Carolina, for example, where manufactured housing is common, only a single ROC exists. Furthermore, ROCs seem most common among parks for retirees fifty-five and older, suggesting that family parks, like those in our study, are less likely to realize the benefits of this new park-ownership model. Unfortunately, it is this group who would benefit the most, given our findings about the implications of typical trailer-park life for family well-being and developing children.

Finally, in a 2012 follow-up visit to the Illinois site, we saw a potential solution to the overcrowding issues. Prairieview Manor owner, Joe, now allows some long-term residents to permanently affix additions to their trailer for an aging mother no longer able to live on her own, an adult child needing to move back home, or additional storage space to alleviate visual clutter. Additions to a manufactured home are common for homes sited on owned land but not for mobile homes in a land-lease park. Additions as a policy would work only if the risk of financial loss on such an investment were addressed and the home lots were of sufficient size. Procedures to ensure the safety of an addition must also be addressed.

Small-Town Municipalities and Trailer-Park Market Scarcity

Ellen chose Joe's park partly on the basis of her understanding of the good schools and small-town atmosphere Prairieview would provide for her family. On many counts, Ellen was fortunate to find an available lot in Prairieview Manor. That the park had recently expanded, adding an adult-only section, likely eased the scarcity of mobile home park lots seen nationally. The shortage is in part the result of the closure of parks when investor owners sell off trailer-park land for a higher and better real estate use. Yet the demand-side balance of that scarcity, an equation that ensures that existing parks remain profitable for operators, is attributed to the ways in which small-town municipalities work to exclude parks. That exclusion is reinforced when social and physical marginalization of parks allows for the kind of stigmatization and ghettoization of parks and park residents so rampant in Prairieview. When a trailer park becomes the focus of an entire community's wrath, all pay some price. For families like those in our study, that price includes additional challenges to realizing the benefits of their hard-earned homeownership.

We suggest some policy strategies that would moderate or eliminate the processes whereby local municipalities, sometimes unintentionally, fuel the exploitation of low-income trailer-park families by other players in the MHIC. The strategies focus in a large part on changing or at least moderating local perceptions of parks. When parks are viewed as undesirable housing and the families who live there are stigmatized as freeloaders, it is difficult to engender much desire to include those folks in the community.

Change of exclusionary zoning is crucial to begin addressing segregation and ghettoization.[53] The common practice of locating trailer parks on the outskirts of town reinforces the social distance of residents from the mainstream community. As we saw, the inclusion of parks in New Mexico and the integration of park residents in the community fostered park families' engagement in their community in ways we did not see in the other sites.

Likewise, some *regulation of maximum park size* seems essential to reduce gheottoization tendencies for a park population. Nationally, mobile home parks average around two hundred lots in size. This provides a sufficient income stream for owners while making the park small enough to avoid negative perceptions of it as rural, ghetto-like, or threatening. The large six hundred-unit Illinois park seemed to threaten townspeople if the town were to annex the park. The smaller New Mexico and North Carolina parks seemed to pose no such threat to the wider community.

Communities could consider *implementation of models for inclusionary housing* when new development occurs.[54] Urban settings have long encouraged a mix of affordable and market-rate housing by giving tax incentives to developers. The incorporation of new manufactured housing in such developments seems logical as a strategy to normalize mobile home housing while increasing a community's affordable homeownership options. Santa Fe, New Mexico, for example, has a number of mobile home parks interwoven with modest conventional housing neighborhoods inside the city limits. Such practices minimize both ghettoization and segregation—the more pernicious effects of living in a trailer park.

Encouraging the development of new and model parks is another strategy. Parish Manor in North Carolina is representative of a more benevolent way to run a park for tenants that is highly successful.[55] Newer parks that more closely approximate industry ideals while still being affordable would not only change local perceptions of this housing and neighborhood form but would add an important alternative that might improve the quality of life for park families. It was not uncommon for us to hear that families had moved from shabbier parks into nicer ones, in a stepping-stone process that brought them closer to greater housing stability. Having options available is critical to moving up the housing-tenure ladder. Small-town governments, however, have to be savvy about the tactics of profit-minded developers. MacTavish witnessed one community in Oregon eagerly recruit a developer to open a new park. Local leaders saw this as a way to expand decent, affordable housing and perhaps drive the owners of several of the shabbier local parks to step up their game to remain competitive. In exchange for local zoning changes and a waiver of development fees, the town was promised a "model" park with paved streets, drainage, curbs, and driveways for off-street parking—amenities not present in any other aging local parks. Once the infrastructure was in place, however, the developer hauled in older, often dilapidated singlewides purchased cheaply from a dealer. The new park only added to the eyesore nature of perceptions of local trailer-park neighborhoods.[56]

An *amendment of tax codes* through the reclassification of mobile homes as real property, described above, would help modify the perception (seen in Illinois) that park residents are free riders who do not pay their fair share of local taxes. Small-town municipal budgets stretched thin could benefit from the additional tax revenue. The savings realized with a conventional mortgage might offset the additional costs in taxes for mobile home owners.

Finally, rural schools, as we learned, do not always function as the great equalizer for social opportunity as they should. Rather than opening doors for park youth, the Illinois schools reinforce the rigid class boundaries that exist between the town and the trailer park.[57] But people acting alone or collectively can shape *community institutions to be more inclusive*.[58] Elimination of language such as "trailer trash" and "broken homes" and the challenging of assumptions about trailer-park family life—such as those of teachers and school administrators in Illinois and New Mexico—are important. Coaches, teachers, and clergy are well positioned to act as positive liaisons between park parents, their children, and the wider community. Scholarship and transportation plans by administrators that expand rather than exclude community opportunities for park children are essential.

Our national debate about the utility of mobile homes and trailer parks as a housing solution for low-income families will no doubt continue. We have described a number of the ills associated with this housing and neighborhood form. Yet as a nation we cannot deny that this housing sector is critical for rural families on the economic margins. Our intent has been to focus on the reality of life in rural trailer parks rather than on harmful stereotypes. Given our portrayal, the dialogue needs to move beyond debate to focus on how we might preserve and improve this housing sector so essential for our nation's low-income families. It is a housing form that provides such families a chance to mount an entry-level rung on a housing-tenure ladder, rather than deny them a chance at all. A trailer sited in a rural trailer park has the potential to meet a need for accessible and affordable housing among rural households of modest means. In a situation in which there is a scarcity of affordable housing, rural American families feel fortunate to have a choice that allows them homeownership. But they make this choice when other options are rare or nonexistent. It is rarely a first choice, and it stands in stark contrast to the many housing options many middle-class families have.

FAMILY DREAMS AND TRAILER-PARK REALITIES

The American Dream of a better life—an optimism shared by young trailer-park families—is also a housing aspiration reached by only a few. This reality is the paradox for families living in a trailer park. A mobile home in a trailer park provides rural people of modest income their first opportunity for homeownership, but all want to or plan to move on. Their dream for social mobility, embodied by conventional homeownership, is inherently an optimistic perspective that for most becomes the poignancy of dashed hopes and gained pessimism about making do with life in a trailer park.

During the study, one family from each of the Illinois, North Carolina, and New Mexico sites realized their American Dream by moving out of the park and into a conventional home on owned land. Each family followed a pathway that drew on its particular ethnic group's strengths and resources, distinctive themes we documented in each case study. These three families also share some crucial features of resourcefulness that account for their achieving a pathway out of the trailer park. Their transition from a park to a stick house and the failure of others to make such a passage provide answers to the questions we raised at the outset about whether trailer-park living has effects for families who raise children there.

Families Who Realized Their Housing Dream
North Carolina

Odette and Monroe Henry's move out of the Addington trailer park to a stick home was approaching during the study. As a single mother of two, Odette had lived over a decade in the trailer park before marrying Monroe. This marriage is the second for both, in their late thirties at the time of the study. They live in a four-year-old fully owned singlewide, bought by Odette as a trade-up and paid for up front. Although this is Monroe's second home in a trailer park, he has nothing good to say about life there. And the singlewide is "too small" for their blended family of five with another on the way.

Both Henrys completed high school, and Odette also earned three years of college credit. Each holds a good job, although Odette is temporarily unemployed because of her pregnancy. Normally she and her sisters work with their father, who is a housekeeping supervisor for a coastal tourist facility. Although she is underemployed for someone with several years of college, Odette's job pays better than most other local jobs and has generous benefits.

Of Monroe's large sibling set of fifteen, six brothers work together in a construction business founded by their father thirty years ago. Monroe earns close to $60,000 annually, along with medical and dental insurance for the whole family, and a 401k. His salary alone positions them in the highest income group of the North Carolina thirteen-family sample. Within the year Monroe expects to move the family to their new home that he, his brothers, and his father built during their spare time. In a systematic way his father and brothers combine their individual skills in construction, mechanics, or masonry to assure that each brother in turn will have a new home eventually, built on owned land without the exchange of any cash. Several brothers already own homes built this way, and now it is Monroe's turn. Monroe's kin group's construction arrangement provides an elaborate exchange system of indirect reciprocity in the informal economy.[1] The new home stands in a neighboring county small town, which Monroe prefers because "I was raised rural."

Each of the Henrys is deeply embedded in their extended kin network, both socially and for work. Their siblings live nearby in Addington and are crucial to the park family's well-being. Odette says, "I have friends, but my sisters are my girlfriends." The three sisters exchange child care, run errands for each other, and socialize together. Odette and Monroe each belong to the multigenerational family church attended by their parents and siblings. Odette regularly attends her family's Baptist church, although her daughters attend more often. The older daughter is already an usher. Odette says, "It's the church I grew up in."

The Henrys treat the trailer-park neighborhood as a risky social context, which requires constant parental vigilance. Odette carefully monitors the activities of her two daughters. "I don't allow my kids to roam around the park or the community by themselves." She relies on a "buddy system" for the girls (nine and twelve years old) to look out for each other. And the Henrys have a regular routine that structures the children's lives. They sit down for the evening meal together, although Monroe's construction work sometimes keeps him away. Their routines and rules highlight the Henrys as an organized family that carefully manages a life that supports their family goals.

Social mobility for the Henry family is made possible through rich, complex exchanges among their two distinct kin groups, which supply complementary resources.[2] The strength of black kin ties and strong kin-group leadership provided by Odette's and Monroe's family patriarchs gives them each access to a good job. Their family-connected jobs supply the stability required to accumulate the savings needed to buy the land and materials for their new home. Odette also carefully manages their finances, and they carry no credit card debt. The Henry family shows how a culturally derived sense of obligation and reciprocity among rural black kin groups enhances the potential for social mobility through realization of their housing dream.

New Mexico

Ruby Martinez-Roberts, in her midthirties, is a divorced Hispanic mother of a young boy and teenage girl. The family is embedded in Ruby's three-generation, woman-centered Martinez kin network of four related households living in the same small trailer park. Her older sister Marie lives next door. "Every two minutes. If I don't see her she calls me. . . . We're always together. We eat lunch, go grocery shopping—our kids are back and forth every day," says Ruby. Each Martinez sister has a son of elementary-school age, and the boys are inseparable. Ruby completed high school and several years of college, which qualified her for a clerk position in a state agency, a good job with benefits.

Ruby's home, the first she has owned on her own, is a well-designed single-wide trailer with a large, cheerful kitchen. She bought the used trailer from a friend by assuming the loan, which meant she did not need to pay cash up front. After two years of paying on the loan, Ruby is close to owning the trailer in full. Before her divorce the family lived with Ruby's Anglo husband out of state, where they "were buying a house." After the divorce and before her trailer purchase, she and the kids were highly mobile as Ruby went in and out of several relationships, including a short reconciliation with her ex-husband. But even conventional homeownership did not made life worth staying in that unhappy marriage or being far from Ruby's Mesa Vista kin. Living near kin in an owned trailer brought the family of three real stability.

Ruby's park kin—Marie next door and her mother and grandmother down the street—are a source of support, even a safety net for this single-female–headed household. But it is clear that having kin so close by has its downside: "My family is nosy and dominating. My sister is particularly nosy." That is, kin support comes with costs to privacy and independence. Ruby wants a life of her own and to marry again. But Mesa Vista lacks a good pool of eligible men who could offer her family a better life. Ruby's brother, who works in a neighboring state, unexpectedly provided the family a pathway out of the trailer park. While on a visit Ruby got to know his Anglo roommate, Tom, and they hit it off. Ruby is now pregnant, and they are to marry. Tom holds a good, skilled job and promises a life the family has dreamed of having. After their marriage, and during the study, the family transitioned to a conventional home.

This marriage is not a love match, and even Ruby's children understand that. Her second marriage is based on Ruby's careful calculations rather than on romantic love.[3] She made a rational decision that Tom offered the best potential for achieving her housing dream. He wisely took her house hunting, and they bought a brand-new four-bedroom home. "We looked at doublewides, but with the land and everything else it was more than a house. A new doublewide costs $54,000 and then the land we looked at was $13,000. And you can figure a thousand for each of the utilities to be hooked up. And [all together] you have more than a house costs," Ruby explains. "A house is just so much more stable. It feels more permanent," she adds, perhaps reflecting on when the family lived in a conventional home during her previous six-year marriage.

A second marriage became a pathway out of the park and toward upward mobility for this single mother. Ruby describes how she sold the remarriage to her kids: "For the first time we're going to be living in a house with two parents and 2.3 kids, a dog and a cat—the whole thing. We've never had that before. . . . I tell the kids, 'This is it. This is for real. All the adventuring is over. Mom's finally gonna settle down.'" Her children are happy about the change. Remarked the daughter close to their moving date, "I'm gonna be so glad to get out of here, and out of this trailer. It'll be good to finally live in a house. . . . A house is roomier. It's not all cramped up like a trailer. And you don't have neighbors right on top of you."

So Ruby sold her trailer and extracted the family from the close-knit Martinez kin network in the Mesa Vista trailer park. Over the past two years Ruby's supportive network, the owned trailer, and the return to her hometown stabilized the family's life. At the same time it was to her kin group's advantage to keep Ruby tied there.[4] But she was ready to get on with her life. Because the new husband was introduced by Ruby's brother, the kin link validated his status. And the marriage will assure that her brother at least is nearby. Thus, this move will not take Ruby that far from her Martinez kin network.

Sisterly competition now motivates Marie, left behind in the trailer park to look for a conventional home in town. "I guess, since both Ruby and my brother have houses now, I'm the one left in a trailer. My brother keeps telling me, 'When are you going to stop being trailer trash?' He's teasing me, but I figure if they can do it so can I."

Illinois

The Smiths—Mike in his late thirties and Kathy in her late twenties—are a white family with two elementary-school-aged children. They moved from the Prairieview Manor trailer park soon after the study, when Mike completed his required five-year journeyman stint for his license as an electrician. During this time, after getting her GED, Kathy earned an associate degree at the local community college. Both the Smiths work full time, he as an apprentice electrician and she as a restaurant waitress/manager in the nearby city. Kathy's income varies according to the tips she earns on her minimum wage job. Together they make close to $50,000 a year, which Mike considers lower-middle-class income. "We're just living here until I finish my apprenticeship," Mike explains. They live in a fully owned ten-year-old singlewide mobile home that they bought used. "I didn't want to just pay rent and have it go nowhere," Mike said. It is the Smiths' first trailer and trailer-park living experience. Kathy says, "I don't mind living in a trailer, but I don't like living in a trailer park." Mike remarks that the best thing about the home is that "it's paid for," and the worst thing is "the neighbors."

Kathy Smith is a cheerful person who sees herself as the self-appointed "Welcome Wagon" of Prairieview Manor. "When someone moves in I'm the first one over there. That's just how I am." Kathy scored waitress jobs for four park girlfriends at the restaurant where she works: "I just keep getting my friends hired there. I figure, hell, we already hang out together all the time, so we might as well get paid for it."

The Smiths appreciate the good Prairieview schools and the affordability of their trailer, which is about all they find positive about where they live. They make efforts to distance themselves from other park families. Their kids are dressed in brand-name clothing, for example, to distinguish them from the less well-off park children. They participate in town activities that involve their children. And Mike volunteers his services to the Boys and Girls Club. But their community engagement, the Smiths believe, does not bring social acceptance by the people of Prairieview. Kathy emphasizes, "When I walk into that school, I know there's not a person in there any better than I am. So I just won't let them be prejudiced against me. I know that Mike's parents live in a house just as nice as those houses in town. And my mom lives in a house just as nice as them too. Who cares that we live in a trailer? That doesn't make us trailer trash . . . doesn't mean that just because our kids live in a trailer park they should be looked down on."

Each of the Smiths has a parent in poor health in the nearby city. Mike says his father "likely won't make it 'til Christmas, and her mother isn't going to be around for much longer than that either." They chose to remain close by to assure that their kids get to know their grandparents before they die. The Smiths consider the trailer park a temporary residence. Kathy offered, "We can't get relatives to come here. On either side of the family, we're the only ones who live in a trailer park." Thus, their kin networks will not hold them in the park. And their social network is with friends rather than relatives. Yet friends, while important, are not enough to keep them here. Their plan, as soon as Mike completes his training and their parents' die, is to move wherever they choose—for example, Denver, where much construction is going on.

Mike Smith has a theory, "his personal belief" about the park address carrying a stigma that park children absorb mentally: "I think that the kids—mainly the teenaged kids out here—when they go into town to school they get—they feel—rejection a little bit from the people of Prairieview proper. . . . A lot of them retaliate by fighting and a lot of them just keep it inside of them. They form bonds out here . . . so it's them against the world. They take out their anxiety, their feelings in . . . vandalism. It's kids acting out their frustrations." Kathy agrees. "Well, of course you aren't born prejudiced—you learn it from somebody!" Mike adds, "I think they hear it from the adults." The Smiths' belief is that town children assimilate the unfairness of the trailer-trash stigma's being uniformly applied to anyone who lives in the park. "People from town do look at you [park folk] differently," Mike says forcefully. "If I thought for one minute that my kids felt that they were being treated differently and that they understood . . . it was because they lived in a trailer park . . . I would do whatever I had to get them out of that situation." Mike and Kathy perceive a potential for their children to experience stigmatization by the trailer-trash label and fear that their identities might be damaged by that treatment.

Each of these families left the trailer park in a different way. Families who do not make it either retain some optimism or seem to make peace with the trailer park—seen when they trade up to obtain better housing, for example.

The Pathway Out of a Trailer Park

The Henrys in North Carolina, Martinez- Roberts in New Mexico, and the Smiths in Illinois hold in common a set of circumstances that account for their social mobility achievement. Individual resourcefulness also worked to position each family well to attain their housing goal and led to the social mobility central to their dream. These shared circumstances include the following:

- The young couples, in their thirties, are high school graduates and earned some higher education or special training in a marketable skill.
- At least one parent (or both) holds a good, stable, full-time job with benefits that situates them among the better-off households in their trailer park.
- They previously had lived or have relatives who live in conventional housing and provide models for what it takes to buy and maintain such a property.
- They are not hobbled by housing debt because their trailer is owned outright, or little is owed on it—a result of a home bought used or fully paid for up front.
- They avoid taking on other burdensome debt, such as on credit cards or to buy new furniture or appliances.
- Especially important, the parents nourish a specific plan, not just a dream, for how to move out of the trailer park and obtain their goal of conventional housing and land ownership.

Social mobility for the Henry, Martinez-Roberts, and Smith families was essentially based on avoidance of the expensive financial trap of housing debt by buying a used home, using a contract sale or another option to avoid taking on a chattel home loan, and not adding new furniture or appliances to their home loan. The three families understand James Baldwin's memorable observation about the struggle "with how extremely expensive it is to be poor" and especially "if one is a member of a captive population. . . . One is victimized, economically in a thousand ways—rent for example, or car insurance."[5] We would add to this list chattel loans for trailers and trailer-park rents that essentially make families, as Baldwin said, a captive population. Despite modest income, however, these three families avoided the debt that keeps other families in a trailer park, financially entrapped, and enduringly poor.

Each family was strongly motivated by their rejection of living permanently in a trailer park rather than by rejection of a trailer as housing per se. We know this because the families did not rule out putting a trailer on owned land when they left the park. Fundamentally they shared a view of themselves as somehow different or better than other families in their park. Though park residents, they considered themselves trailer home owners *in* the park but not *of* it.

In contrast to these three families, many park families are sucked into taking on debt for a mobile home, the addition of furniture or appliances on that loan, plus monthly trailer-park fees that rise annually. If these families work bad rural jobs, their finances make it unlikely that they will be able to overcome these financial challenges or ever attain their housing dream and the better life it represents.[6] Unlike the three families in our study, most young families do not have a plan to help reach their optimistic dreams of moving out of the trailer park. Avoiding debt and having a plan to achieve their American Dream are critical traits that divide families who move out from those who must continue living in a trailer park.

For the three families who made it out of their trailer park, the strongest push factor was their desire to own a conventional home, symbolic of their achievement of social mobility. "Owning a house remains central to Americans' sense of well-being. . . . Nearly nine in 10 Americans say homeownership is an important part of the American dream," according to a 2011 national poll.[7] Thus, the dream we uniformly found among young trailer-park families is one shared by most Americans. We turn now to the answers we learned to the questions posed in the introduction. Fundamentally, we explore whether and how trailer-park residence and mobile home ownership affect families' dreams of a better life or shape parents' and children's lives.

Questions We Raised and the Answers Learned

Our aim with this book was to describe life from the perspective of the young families who call a trailer park home. Our exploration of their stories was driven by the overall question of whether a trailer park is a good, or at least neutral, place to raise a family. We take in turn each of the four specific questions raised in the introduction, drawing our answers from our findings at the Illinois, North Carolina, and New Mexico trailer-park sites.

Question One: Are there lasting effects to family and child identity that come from living in a trailer park—a neighborhood form so widely mocked and assumed to be culturally uniform across the nation?

The popular media perpetuate the misconception that the twelve million people who live in trailer parks nationwide *all* represent a distinctive *trailer-trash* subculture. We found little actual evidence across the three sites, however, to support this negative stereotype about park residents. Park families across the nation do actually share some characteristics. But these traits do not constitute a distinct culture, nor do they justify the trailer-trash slur. In general, those living in rural parks are of lower income and less educated than local populations. They are proud of their hard-won homeownership, care about the upkeep of their home and yard, and hold middle-class concerns for their children's successful development. And trailer-park residents' complaints are the same that Salamon found voiced by property owners in midwestern small towns or rural neighbor-hoods.[8] Of course, the land-lease trailer park folk of our focus as homeown-ers differ distinctively from the occupants of rental trailer parks, where families rent both their homes and the home sites. Rental-park residents are poorer and more transient than the land-lease park homeowners we describe. Rental trailer parks tend to be the shabbiest of parks and have the worst-quality housing—conditions traceable to mobile home industrial complex entrepreneurs. And rental parks are in all likelihood the source of the trailer-trash negative stereo-types, with the MHIC complicit in the stigma's perpetuation.

When the trailer-trash slur is used in social interactions, all trailer-park resi-dents are implicitly denigrated.[9] The slur ignores the basic humanity of those on the margins, who work hard to establish stable lives through modest, entry-level homeownership in a rural trailer park. And it overlooks the complexity of regional, ethnic, and class variation in the nation's trailer-park populations.[10]

When does the trailer-trash slur tarnish people's identity? We found that segregation of a rural trailer park from the adjacent small town—for exam-ple, the Illinois site—physically and socially enhances seeing park folk as the "other."[11] In addition, segregation contributes to people's experiencing a lack of routine social interactions and promotes reliance on stigmas. When a dis-tinctive and rigid social hierarchy exists between town and park populations, as in Illinois, it reinforces the divide.[12] Illinois park residents, all white, almost uniformly volunteered being targeted by the slur. Neither North Carolina blacks nor New Mexico Hispanics recounted being affected by the slur, but the whites in these parks did. The consistency of white reports reinforces that the slur of trailer trash equates with white trash and is a variant of it.[13] The trailer-trash stigma tends to reinforce and perpetuate the inequality of park folk—the stain of stigma matters. The film director John Waters famously said, "White trash . . . . is the last racist thing you can say and get away with it."[14] The trailer-trash slur functions similarly.

There are lasting effects on families and children when stigma is a reality in their lives. But we know that the trailer-trash stigma is present only under certain conditions: where white ethnicity is dominant, where a rigid class hierarchy is in place, and where segregation of a park population is enforced. All these conditions describe the relationship of the trailer-park residents to the town in Illinois. Because these conditions are absent in North Carolina and New Mexico, there seems little consequence for trailer-park families of being seen as from a galvanized ghetto.

The North Carolina blacks, like the whites in the Illinois park, overestimate their class position relative to income because they are homeowners (table C.1). The New Mexican Hispanics are the most realistic of the park ethnic groups about their income and status—they acknowledge that they are poor. But they

TABLE C.1 Park household self-report of income status

INCOME STATUS	ILLINOIS (%)	NORTH CAROLINA (%)	NEW MEXICO (%)
Lower	20	23	43
Lower middle	26	37	13
Middle	45	34	24
Upper middle	4	5	3
Do not know/other	5	1	17
Actual median household income[a]	$28,650	$24,537	$17,355

Source: Survey of randomly selected sample of trailer-park households (Illinois, n = 82; North Carolina, n = 65; New Mexico, n = 79).

[a]Incomes adjusted to 2000 dollars. All-U.S. median income in 2000 was $41,994 (see table A.1).

do not feel stigmatized by their trailer park residence. Perhaps admitting they are poor is easier in a more marginal economy. For Illinois white trailer-park folk, however, denigration by the trailer-trash slur means they are denied the respect they believe they have earned as homeowners. Their identity is thus stained—it is a lasting effect, particularly among youth. Black youth in North Carolina and Hispanics in New Mexico, treated as equals by the wider community, are not subjected to the stain of this slur.

Occasionally, as we found when Marie Martinez's brother kidded her, the trailer-trash slur is employed as a joke by blacks and Hispanics toward others of their ethnic group who live in a trailer park. The joke slur allows those who have achieved the housing American dream to assert superiority over those who live landless in a trailer park. Therefore, we are led to understand that the trailer trash slur also signifies a middle-class put-down.[15] Because Illinois park people classify themselves as middle-class, it no doubt adds to their frustration of being stigmatized with a poor-white trash slur (table C.1).

Question Two: Does owning a trailer home sited in a trailer park pay off as the first rung on a housing-tenure ladder for rural families?

For the three families profiled, their living in a trailer park paid off because they were financially prudent and avoided the expensive trap that buying a home with a chattel loan involves. They bought used homes or took only short-term loans like a contract for deed. Holding good jobs is also basic to their moving on from a park. For other park families, the typical yearly increase in fees for a park site to site their mobile home, along with a high-interest chattel loan for a home that loses half its value in a short time, prevents most rural trailer-park families from saving sufficient funds to move up the housing-tenure ladder. Thus, for the young families we met, although they all are optimistic that their trailer-park residence is temporary, except for families like the three profiled, it becomes permanent. The exploitative financial system rooted in the mobile home industrial complex is responsible for, and gains from, the entrapment of poor homeowners that owning a mobile home in a trailer park involves.[16]

What factors make trailer-park residence for most families a permanent trap that erodes the possibility of attaining their dream? Trading up in the park to improve their housing quality entraps a family with a new chattel loan and because of the expense involved in moving a larger trailer, it means for most staying in the same trailer park. Being caught up by the highly profitable practices of the mobile home industrial complex—for an often-shoddy product, exploitative home financing, and being squeezed monthly by park operators—is a barrier too high for most families to mount. In fact, a Consumers Union report says the experience of buying a mobile home is "more akin to buying a used car than a site built home." In addition, local municipalities that create the trailer-park scarcity out of distaste for the housing form contribute to fueling excessive profits for the mobile home industrial complex.[17]

The three families that successfully moved out of a trailer park and into a conventional home are the exception rather than the rule. These families also achieved their landownership goal when they bought a conventional home. Landownership is central to park families' dreams. Controlling the land under one's home brings the ultimate payoff for park families because in rural American especially it carries status, empowerment, and pride—factors never assured in a land-lease trailer park.

Question Three: Does living in a rural trailer park affect a family's sense of belonging to their immediate neighborhood or the nearby community?

"We Build Communities" is a motto touted by the mobile home industrial complex. Our study casts light on why it is a mistake to equate the physical structure of a trailer park with an actual social community. A community, it is clear, is more than a grouping of homes, even if the homes are clustered close together. As underlined by the trailer-park case studies, those who live in a place because they are landless and where they lack basic rights or input to park governance find that disenfranchisement in particular undermines engagement with neighbors or attachment to place. A place to live, not a community, is what trailer-park developers actually build or manage. The lack of a sense of community may to a certain extent account for the behavior of a small group of residents in each site that helps bolster the trailer-trash stereotype for all housed in these land-lease parks. They do not feel community pressure to conform to park upkeep standards and incur no penalty for their resistance. Only one park manager in North Carolina, of all those parks we studied, reported doing a background check on prospective tenants—a process that weeds out potentially problem tenants—those with criminal backgrounds or without the financial resources to manage stable residence. Residents appreciate any effort to keep drugs, domestic violence, and real economic hardship cases out of the parks.

Civic engagement is widely seen as related to homeownership, and citizens' engagement in turn confers community and national benefits.[18] Do trailer home owners living in a trailer park deliver the anticipated benefits of homeownership to the nearby community? According to standard sociological measures of community engagement, among the three ethnic groups the New Mexico Hispanic park families are most connected to their community (table C.2). They are more likely to vote and to read the local newspaper, and all belong to the single Catholic church—although they are not particularly active. The Hispanic families in the New Mexico parks, although landless, own that community. Mesa Vista is theirs by virtue of descent from their generations of families tied to place. Their sense of community (of attachment and of support) is largely traced to kin ties rooted in the town. Their small trailer parks incorporated into the town minimize the barriers between a park and the wider community.

North Carolina blacks appear least engaged in the wider community by the same community measures (table C.2). But as we documented, rural North Carolina black families and youth find a rich sense of community rooted in their rich and dense networks of kin and church.[19] North Carolina park families are either the descendants of those who first moved from more remote rural places into the small city of Addington, or they made the move themselves Their roots, other than kinship, are not planted in the place but in a black church whose membership has many generations of kin and for some spans town and country. Together kin and church networks buffer blacks in the trailer parks from feeling that their address is a bad one. Both the African Americans of North Carolina and the Hispanics of New Mexico do not need, or perhaps do not want, their trailer park to be the community or neighborhood that supplies their identity or attachment to place. The cultural trait of strong kin and church ties was and is an adaptive strategy among poor rural minorities. Their trailer parks are also smaller than the Illinois site and fully incorporated in the wider community.

TABLE C.2 Community engagement of park households

LEVEL OF ENGAGEMENT	ILLINOIS (%)	NORTH CAROLINA (%)	NEW MEXICO (%)
Voted in last election	41	41	69
Subscribe to the local newspaper	37	20	68
Participate in or belong to a church	31	49	53
Children take part in youth activities	32	19	29

Source: Survey of randomly selected sample of trailer-park households (Illinois, n = 82; North Carolina, n = 65; New Mexico, n = 79).

Illinois white families appear least connected to the nearby community when compared with North Carolina and New Mexican families, although they are native to towns scattered across central Illinois. Fewer whites than the other ethnic groups belong to local churches (table C.2), and only one-third read the local newspaper. In contrast to the other two groups, more Illinois family histories show a certain instability in their personal histories of hard living, high mobility, and multiple problems. These families, in addition to being landless, are relatively rootless—seemingly a double wallop for stability and respect.[20] And the trailer-park population experiences segregation and ghettoization by being a stand-alone neighborhood, officially unincorporated in the town.

The Illinois families' negative opinion about where they live is a strategy to differentiate themselves from the park while positioning themselves closer to the middle class—to which they aspire. Because they want to avoid the trailer-trash stigma, they instead cut off neighborhood ties that are potentially useful and supportive. They all hope after all to make this home temporary. But in fact the Illinois segregated context for the trailer park perpetuates a class divide with negative effects on park residents.

Although we found multiple kin networks in the Illinois park during the study, alienation from the park and the nearby community takes its toll on families who lack any sense of community in the park or in the town, and many were gone twelve years later when MacTavish revisited the park.

Question Four: Does a rural trailer park have the power to define the life chances of the children and youth who grow up there?

Nick Harwood, the Illinois trailer-park youth whom we met in chapter 3, saw his life chances defined by living in the large park whose residents were segregated from and denigrated by those from the nearby upscale subdivisions. To achieve a better life he recognized he had to get out of what he referred to as a galvanized ghetto. Like the three families, he had a plan for how to leave and the goal he wanted.

Being poor is not denigrated in the North Carolina and New Mexico hometowns we studied; there trailer-park families look much like everyone else. Perhaps being a minority in rural America—as are both blacks and Hispanics—makes people more respectful of others' accomplishments. But if with the privilege of skin color, poor rural whites cannot manage greater success than a trailer in a trailer park, they are denigrated—especially by middle-class blacks as well as whites.[21]

Did we find a *neighborhood effect*—negative consequences—for families and children living in a rural trailer park? That is, is a trailer park a bad, good, or neutral setting in which to raise a family or develop as a child? A well-understood indicator of a neighborhood effect is whether a neighborhood fosters or hinders life chances.[22] In a trailer-park setting, does the neighborhood have an effect on a family's ability to achieve its housing and social mobility goals?

As the profile of the three park families who moved out shows, for a minority of park families well positioned for social mobility, a powerful park neighborhood effect essentially is their strong push factor out, one that potentially pays off with enhanced life chances. Membership in a strong extended kin network, as we saw, is a crucial support for working-poor trailer-park families. Among the African Americans of North Carolina and the Hispanics of New Mexico, kin are important to what keeps a family rooted locally. Kin, however, explain less about whether a white family stays or leaves the Illinois park or the community.

Successful development for their children among the rural trailer park families is defined as high school graduation, perhaps college or advanced training, a good job, and a successful relationship/marriage, as it is for middle-class families. Park parents say that they would like their children to settle nearby, although they expect they will move away for good jobs—hard to find in rural America. For children and youth across the Illinois, North Carolina, and New Mexico trailer parks, we found highly variable outcomes, or a park-neighborhood effect. Some youth flourish while others flounder, but the majority of park youth experience a steady life course—in all likelihood destined to reproduce the lives of their parents (chapter 6). MacTavish found a decade later that the floundering Illinois girl who was pregnant at fifteen and dropped out of school was married with three children and lived in a different, less nice rental park in the same area of the state. As a high school dropout, she struggles to find work, in contrast to her parents, who had owned their trailer and were employed full-time much of their adult lives. She has traveled a consistently declining trajectory. The steady developmental outcome for most youth raised in a trailer park fundamentally underlies why working-poor status and a trailer-park life are highly persistent across the three sites and multiple generations of the ethnic groups studied.

Starting with meager resources and their own narrowed life chances, park parents, like other low-income parents, are doing their best for the children they raise in a rural trailer park. The patterns of social mobility we observed among park youth and families in fact resemble those predicted for the US population as a whole.[23] While the majority (57 percent) of those raised in the bottom quintile will experience some social mobility, fewer than one in three (30 percent) of those who do are expected to reach the middle.[24] Thus, we expect that even among our youth who flourished and seem poised for social and financial upward mobility, most will remain below the middle according to income and wealth. In reality, the steady children of working-poor park parents are likely to eventually look like them—resembling the two-thirds of Americans who live paycheck to paycheck and for whom upward mobility has vanished in recent decades.[25] Overall social mobility seems beyond reach for most trailer park youth, especially those without access to the crucial help of a middle-class mentor. In all probability, however, with greater access to health care benefits (via the federal Affordable Care Act, or ACA, of 2010) and with higher incomes (due to a higher minimum wage), more trailer-park families may achieve their American Dream of a better life than did those we interviewed. With the new presidential administration of 2017, however, the future of the ACA and the minimum wage is unclear.

Finally, we return to Nick Harwood in Illinois. We first met him as a senior in high school, bitter about being stigmatized by his trailer-park address. MacTavish contacted his sister a decade later and asked about him. With the education Nick received in the good Prairieview schools, he was the first in his family to graduate from high school, and he also did some college work. He married and lives with his family in the town of Prairieview as he planned, and he commutes to his good job in the nearby city.

Clearly, Nick recognized what was required to shed the stigma of being a trailer-park kid in the adjacent town of Prairieview, which looked down on the poor whites from the park. He crafted a plan of his own for social mobility. By his deliberate choice to live in the town, he rejected how both the trailer park and the town defined him. His adult choices, according to everything we learned, mean he should not be bothered by the trailer-trash stigma, nor should his children. But Nick's pathway has a downside if his transition is viewed in the context of the family and friends he left behind in the trailer park. If all those like Nick who are able to leave do so, the trailer park, much like an inner city, loses its more capable individuals, and those left behind in Illinois are exposed to the consequences of its neighborhood effect of being trailer trash.

In accepting her Academy Award, the actress Hilary Swank said she was just "a girl from a trailer park who had a dream." In not letting a slur define him, Nick was similarly able to be a guy who achieved his own American dream.

Acknowledgments

Sonya Salamon first started thinking about studying trailer parks while in residence at the United States Department of Agriculture (USDA), Economic Research Service (ERS). During that time, she talked over the topic with Calvin Beale (a beloved colleague who died in 2008), John Cromartie, and Mark Nord. Critical to the approach of studying poor people who live in rural trailer parks across the nation was Salamon's membership between 1987 and 1997 on the W. K. Kellogg National Rural Studies Committee (NRSC), chaired by Emery Castle. The work on the NRSC led to her realization that aside from one community study (called "Splitville" in her book *Newcomers to Old Towns*), her research had focused on the rural middle class, and she had largely overlooked poor people living in rural places. Gene F. Summers, vice chair of the NRSC and president of the Rural Sociological Society (RSS), led the society's Task Force on Persistent Rural Poverty, which resulted in an influential 1993 book that also shaped her thinking about the rural poor. David L. Brown on the NRSC and through the many years of our joint presidencies and membership in the RSS was important to developing the arguments the authors make in this book. Bruce Weber at Oregon State University, another NRSC member, was supportive of Katherine MacTavish's research among very poor rural trailer parks in Oregon.

Children raised in rural trailer parks as a research focus was developed with Christine M. Todd, an Illinois colleague who together with Salamon worked on a potential project to follow children in the middle childhood period over a school year. Todd's move to the University of Georgia ended that potential collaboration. But tracking children over time meshed well with both Salamon's art education B.F.A, and MacTavish's art education B.A. and M.A. in early childhood special education. For this reason, children became central to the original proposal for the trailer-park project. In addition, Salamon had long held an interest in a rural community or neighborhood effect—it was the subject of her Rural Sociological Society presidential address in 2002. A 2005 graduate seminar Salamon jointly taught with Christy Lleras helped refine her ideas about how a rural trailer park functions as a neighborhood with the potential to affect developing children who live there.

When MacTavish visited Urbana as a prospective graduate student, interested in studying with Salamon, it was the mention of a trailer-park study that captured her imagination. And so began our twenty-year saga leading to this book. It must be noted that the writing of this book was stretched out by Salamon's weathering lymphoma twice and moving four times and by MacTavish's move to Oregon State University and earning tenure.

MacTavish was a member of a qualitative methods workshop Salamon taught in which four graduate students (MacTavish, Jeff Stueves, Ani Yazidjian, and Carmen Vergara) developed a survey instrument. Each carried out about a dozen interviews in the Illinois trailer park, which constituted the project's pilot study. Michelle Eley arrived several years later than MacTavish, highly interested in studying rural eastern North Carolina, where she was raised.

All the data were gathered in the three field sites while Salamon was a faculty member at the University of Illinois, Urbana-Champaign. The Illinois and New Mexico field studies were supported by a major grant through the USDA National Research Initiative (NRI) Competitive Grants Program. Support for the data collection in the third North Carolina site came from the University of Illinois Campus Research Board and the Pampered Chef Family Resiliency Program. MacTavish was also supported during her graduate studies by a University of Illinois College of Agricultural Consumer and Environmental Sciences (ACES) Jonathon Baldwin Turner Fellowship, and a fellowship from the Department of Human and Community Development (now the Department of Human Development and Family Studies), at the University of Illinois at Urbana-Champaign. Eley's research on the North Carolina park was supported by a national competitive fellowship from the Rural Poverty Research Center (RUPRI). She received additional financial support from the University of Illinois Department of Human and Community Development's Emily Schroeder Fellowship.

After a presentation by Salamon and MacTavish to the Illinois Manufactured Housing Association (IMHA), the organization embraced the study by supplying in-kind support of an office unit in the Illinois park. The park owner (who must remain nameless here) provided an in-kind contribution of a park site for the IMHA unit and electricity for our "office." He also generously gave his time for multiple interviews and verified the legitimacy of the study for any park resident who inquired. Park owners and managers in New Mexico and North Carolina likewise allowed us access to ten additional trailer-park neighborhoods. Marni (Margaret Mary) Basic managed the original NRI grant and contributed excellent qualitative data collection with park families in both Illinois and New Mexico.

Writing of the book began at the University of Texas at Dallas (UTD), where Salamon was a research professor in the School of Economic, Political and Policy Sciences, 2007–2012, after retiring from the University of Illinois in 2006. She especially acknowledges the generous support of the then UTD president David Daniel for discretionary research funds for five years that provided crucial support as the book took form. She also acknowledges her colleagues at UTD Sheryl Skaggs, Richard K. Scott, and Brian J. L. Berry (then the school dean) for valuable discussions. Sheryl Skaggs, in particular, was the source for the job classification system used in the book.

Many colleagues' discussions contributed to sharpening our arguments and refining the book. We owe a great debt to RSS colleagues who study rural housing—Ann Ziebarth and Lance George. Charles Geisler's early work on rural trailer parks was inspirational. Linda Lobao and Ann Tickamyer contributed to our understanding of rural inequality. Mildred Warner provided insight into rural zoning. Michael Bell gave us a valuable critique of an early manuscript in our numerous revisions. Salamon's sister, Carla Blank, edited a previous version of the book that aided in its evolution. For MacTavish at Oregon State, Bruce Weber was an excellent sounding board for economic issues uncovered in our research, while John Bliss was a constant source of support and an intellectual provocateur. Devora Shamah, Megan Notter, and Brenda Barrett-Rivera made contributions to the intellectual work represented here during their time as graduate students. Alan Calvert at Oregon State provided great assistance with editing the photos. Myron Salamon jokingly came up with the term "mobile home industrial complex," which we quickly adopted. Finally, we are grateful to Michael J. McGandy, our editor at Cornell University Press, who guided this book through two years of many revisions.

MacTavish considers that working with Salamon on the trailer-park project provided a chance of a lifetime. Years of working with low-income families in rural New Mexico motivated her return to graduate school at the University of New Mexico in 1997. Her thinking then was that an advanced degree would allow her to make a social difference on a grander scale. The trailer-park study was a perfect intellectual fit and led to her life's work.

MacTavish's oldest daughter, Amanda, then the same age as the younger cohort of study children, played an important role in the research process. She often accompanied MacTavish into the field in both Illinois and New Mexico. With Amanda along, the study families saw MacTavish as a mother as well as a researcher. Several families generously and repeatedly took Amanda in for a day or an evening, much as they would do for a friend, while MacTavish was out interviewing. Amanda's insights, through the wise eyes of nine-year old, enriched MacTavish's understanding of park and family life. Her younger daughter, Camilla, played a similar role on subsequent field research in Oregon, although it is not the focus of this book. Over the many years that writing the book entailed, Salamon's husband, Myron, and MacTavish's husband, Drew, read countless versions of chapters from this book. Their insights were always spot-on and their constant support greatly appreciated.

We wish to acknowledge the important contribution of Michelle Eley to the book. Eley is a Community and Economic Development Specialist at North Carolina A&T State University. Her fieldwork and dissertation provided crucial data about African Americans in North Carolina, which represents a region of the country with the highest proportion of housing in mobile homes. Her focus on household finances helped round out the picture of family trailer park life. In addition, Eley's insight that only whites in the parks reported the trailer trash slur helped us to understand a basic finding for the book.

We are grateful for permission to utilize here, in somewhat different form, portions of the following articles that appeared previously and are used here with the permission of the publishers and journals noted: Katherine MacTavish and Sonya Salamon, "Pathways of Youth Development in a Rural Trailer Park," *Family Relations* 55 (2006): 163–74, permission from John Wiley and Sons; Katherine MacTavish, Michelle L. Eley, and Sonya Salamon, "Housing Vulnerability among Rural Trailer Park Households," *Georgetown Journal of Poverty Law & Policy* 13, no. 1 (2006): 95–117, used with permission from the publisher, Georgetown Journal of Poverty Law and Policy © 2006; and Sonya Salamon and Katherine MacTavish, "Quasi-Homelessness among Rural Trailer Park Households in the United States," in *International Perspectives on Rural Homelessness*, ed. Paul Milbourne and Paul Cloke, 45–62 (London: Routledge, 2006), used with permission from Taylor & Francis, U.K.

Finally, we owe a great debt to the more than two hundred trailer-park households surveyed and the almost three dozen families who intimately shared their lives with us over much of a year's time. In addition, we are grateful for the interviews provided by the owners and managers of the study trailer parks and the approximately fifteen small-town public officials and about a dozen teachers, principals, and school officials who generously shared their observations about park children who were their students in Illinois, New Mexico, and North Carolina. We cannot thank them by name because we promised them confidentiality, but they know who they are. We are sure not everyone will agree with the picture drawn of them, their communities, or their trailer parks. Our intention was and is to describe their lives and their towns accurately to capture what it means for ordinary rural families to live in a trailer park and raise children there. To this end, we wrote this book in a manner we think will be accessible to all the park families and to others we interviewed or observed.

THE STUDY, METHODS, AND SAMPLE

To examine what is shared and what differs among trailer-park folk across rural America, we employed a controlled comparison study that incorporated ethnically and culturally diverse rural populations.[1] Our study describes families with school-aged children living in three distinctive rural US regions where trailer parks are common. We chose a representative state and county study site in each region: eastern North Carolina in the rural South, southern New Mexico in the rural Southwest, and central Illinois in the rural Midwest. Nationwide, the 2000 Census found the largest share of housing in mobile homes concentrated in the South and West. New Mexico ranks second-highest nationally in the proportion of housing made up of manufactured homes with 18.6 percent (South Carolina is the highest with over 20 percent). In North Carolina (along with Alabama, Mississippi, and West Virginia) around 15 percent of all housing is in mobile homes, or about twice the national percentage. North Carolina ranks third among all states in its actual number of mobile homes, at 577,000.[2] Illinois ranks about thirteenth nationally in proportion of housing in manufactured homes. We use the 2000 Census throughout because of its relevance for the years we conducted the three ethnographic field studies.

The three park sites were selected according to the same dimensions to achieve a controlled comparison design: (1) the mobile home park must be homeowner, land-lease (rather than rental) so that the families are neither the poorest nor the most mobile of trailer-park residents and therefore expected to be residentially stable for the year's study; (2) the target park population should include around five hundred households in a single park or an aggregate of several; (3) the park location must be adjacent to a town (population between five thousand and twenty thousand) with more upscale families and housing and with a population sharing the ethnicity of the mobile home park; (4) the park must be near an area experiencing rapid growth with construction and service-sector jobs available but affordable housing scarce. Thus, socioeconomic status, rather than ethnicity, should differentiate park families from town, middle-class families. Of the four criteria, the fourth proved to be unworkable in rural places. Sonya Salamon selected the Illinois park and accompanied both Katherine MacTavish and Michelle Eley during a reconnaissance process to select the targeted parks in New Mexico and North Carolina. A full-time project manager, Marni Basic, also assisted in collecting field data in Illinois and New Mexico.

At each site the ethnographic field study lasted about a year (the initial Illinois study extended over three years including two pilot studies). MacTavish helped craft our effort to target families with school-aged children as a way to find out whether children raised in a trailer park showed developmental effects from this distinctive neighborhood setting. The umbrella project design incorporated a first stage with a whole park survey of randomly selected households, which was followed by a second phase (over six to nine months), interviewing and observing about fifteen to twenty families, with theirs and the child's consent: ten with a child in third grade and ten with a tenth-grade youth. Several families at each site had a child in both age groups. Across the three sites the randomly chosen surveyed households, or park sample, presents a total of 226 households. The smaller, family sample of households with children (some drawn from the park sample at each site)—were followed over much of a year—through multiple and extensive observations and interviews. Incorporating all three sites, the total family sample is 38 families. All park names used, along with those of the adults, children and youth, are pseudonyms to protect the confidentiality of families and children as well as parks and park management, as we promised every participant. When survey percentages are cited, they are derived using SPSS Statistics Software to generate "valid percentages"—meaning they have taken into account missing data and the size of the full sample because not everyone responded to all survey questions.

Table A.1 provides basic demographic facts about the rural populations living in the three sites, drawn from the first phase single interview of approximately a 10–15 percent household sample, randomly selected from each park. It is evident in Table A.1 that by comparison with the nonmetro and all US demographics, mobile home parks cluster younger families and those less well educated and of low income. The demographic profiles reflect the three regions' economies, with the highest median household income earned by Illinois park folk, followed by North Carolina, and the lowest median income earned in New Mexico. These incomes, it should be noted, do not accurately reflect the education of earners, for

TABLE A.1 Cross-site comparison of trailer-park survey samples (n = 226)

STUDY SITE	MEDIAN HOUSEHOLD INCOME[a]	ALL ADULTS WITH LESS THAN HIGH SCHOOL EDUCATION (%)[b]	ALL ADULTS WITH B.A. DEGREE OR HIGHER (%)[b]	HOUSEHOLD ETHNICITY	MEDIAN AGE OF ALL	MEAN HOUSEHOLD SIZE
Illinois (n = 82)	$28,650	15.3	6.7	White (98%)	24.7	3.07
North Carolina (n = 65)	$24,537	18.3	4.3	African American (52%)	26.0	4.40
New Mexico (n = 79)	$17,355	22.9	13.7	Hispanic (66%)	25.5	2.96
Nonmetro U.S.[b]	$32,837	23.2	15.5	White (80.7%)	38.0	3.02
All U.S.[b]	$41,994	19.6	24.4	White (81.5%)	35.0	2.62

Source: Random surveys of park households.

[a]Incomes adjusted to 2000 dollars.

[b]Sources: Median all-U.S. income U.S. Census Bureau, "DP-3 Profile of Selected Economic Characteristics: 2000"; median nonmetro income from U.S. Department of Agriculture, Economic Research Service, "Report on Rural Poverty and Well Being"; nonmetro educational attainment from U.S. Department of Agriculture, Economic Research Service, "Rural Education at a Glance"; median age for nonmetro and all United States from Rogers, "Changes in the Older Population and Implications for Rural Areas."

the New Mexico park residents are better educated than are those in North Carolina, and those in Illinois have the least amount of education of the three groups.

The families in our study overwhelmingly own their mobile homes and rent a park home site, which is termed a land-lease park by the industry (see chapter 1 for more details). We chose to study mobile home owners because we considered such households more stable than trailer renters. Stability allowed us to follow a child over a school year, one of our research goals. Table A.2 shows ownership statuses across our sample and that 89 percent own their home. Although there are some renters (9 percent in the total sample), most were concentrated in the poorest site of New Mexico. As homeowners, rural trailer-park families view themselves as being on a rung higher on the housing-tenure ladder than families living in various forms of subsidized housing. Those living in a rental trailer park, in a rented apartment, or in publicly subsidized housing (Section 8) are considered by our mobile home owner families as beneath them in social status. Thus, although they live in a trailer park and are representative of the rural working poor, the study families understand that they are not the poorest of the poor despite what middle-class neighbors or the popular media might assume.

When housing poverty is the measure used for being poor, our minority mobile home owners from the South and the Southwest are financially better off, compared with about half of their respective ethnic groups in North Carolina and New Mexico, respectively. (See tables 4.1 and 5.1) As land-lease trailer-park residents who own their homes; they have adequate housing quality; most carry housing costs that do not exceed 30 percent of their household income; and their neighborhood conditions are *not* typified by crime, noise, litter, deteriorated housing, or poor social services, as is widely assumed. It is in *rental* trailer parks (where people rent both their home and its site)—not our study's focus—where families are more likely to fall into the category of experiencing housing poverty because so much of their income is absorbed by housing costs. This financial

TABLE A.2 Cross-site comparison of park household homeownership status

OWNERSHIP STATUS	ILLINOIS (%)	NORTH CAROLINA (%)	NEW MEXICO (%)	TOTAL (%)
Own home in full	38	26	32	32
Own home with a mortgage	48	42	42	44
Buying through contract sale	11	25	6	13
Renting	1	8	18	9
Other	2	0	2	2

Source: Survey of randomly selected sample of trailer-park households: Illinois = 82; New Mexico = 79; North Carolina = 65; total = 226.

situation is what causes high mobility. And they are more likely to face multiple problems associated with the trailer-trash stigma.[3]

We entered a mobile home park only after gaining the expressed permission of a park owner. On the whole, owners welcomed such a study and gave us full run of the parks, particularly because they felt park residents tend to be misunderstood and stigmatized. Only one owner in New Mexico refused. At one point during the study other (student) researchers showed up in the Illinois park. Salamon was quickly contacted by management about who these people were. Not being connected to our study, they were asked to leave. In the Illinois park MacTavish had access to an "office" to work from while in the park, generously provided by the Illinois Manufactured Housing Association after Salamon and MacTavish made a presentation to the board at their Springfield office. The park owner kindly provided a site in the park for the unit. Unfortunately, the office had no bathroom or running water, so MacTavish could not stay there overnight. In New Mexico she commuted about twenty-five miles to the targeted town. Her father's family home in the town was her home base. Eley lived during the entire field study in a mobile home rented from the owner (and mobile home dealer) of the largest park in the study.

The project research design was replicated in three phases in each site, according to procedures developed and tested initially with the Illinois site:

1. Collection of general community background data from local key informants, histories, and census archives done in conjunction with 2 and 3
2. A door-to-door random household survey of mobile home park households
3. An intensive phase that focused on a subsample of park households with children of two developmentally important age groups: eight to nine years old and fifteen to sixteen years old, third and tenth grades, respectively (see chapter 6 for a full explanation of why these ages were chosen)

The eventual park(s) targeted samples were constructed differently. In Illinois, the first site studied (1997–1999), the large park size—like a small town of 1,500—turned out to be unusual in rural America. In Illinois the single park had 600 sites (560 occupied) from which we obtained a survey sample of 82, or 15 percent of the park sampled. When we turned to New Mexico (1999–2000) and subsequently North Carolina (2002–2003), we found no park of comparable size. Thus we were forced to aggregate smaller parks to reach a similar-sized population from which to sample. We found no statistically significant differences among the small parks and so felt comfortable aggregating them and treating them as a single park. Our North Carolina random sample of 65 households was drawn from four parks with a total of 447 park sites, of which 410 were occupied, for about a 16 percent of the park units sampled. New Mexico had the smallest parks, requiring us to oversample in six small parks to obtain a comparable sample size of 79 from 252 possible sites, or a 31 percent sampling of park sites. Some slight differences in survey sample sizes exist between the original field studies and the book because we used more conservative criteria here. Because the Illinois park is as large as a small town, a diversity of household incomes exists within its population. In the New Mexico and North Carolina parks a similar income diversity is present but is represented across the range of multiple parks rather than internally within each park. (See appendix B for a detailed breakdown of the small park populations.)

Phase 1: Community Background Data Sources

Press releases providing an overview of the study were submitted to each local paper prior to beginning fieldwork. The news items published worked well in each site to legitimize the study for both town and park residents. Key community professionals were interviewed individually to gain a context in which to place what was later learned from park residents. Among those interviewed were village or city/county administrators, school administrators, police officers, park owners, and park managers. Absentee park owners in New Mexico and North Carolina were interviewed by phone or e-mail.

Participant observation was conducted throughout the field study so that we could gain familiarity with each site and become known by local residents.[4] We attended church activities, community festivals, and local sporting events and patronized local recreation areas, restaurants, and retail establishments. We subscribed to the weekly newspaper in each community for the study year. We recorded field notes as soon as possible after each observation, interview, or meeting.[5] The study team met weekly to discuss themes and issues that emerged as the first phases of field study progressed. Later in the survey and intensive study phases, these early themes and issues were refined as more time was spent with park residents. The Illinois team meetings could take place on the Urbana campus. New Mexico and North Carolina meetings were done via phone or e-mail. Salamon read all the field notes and made comments, which were the basis for these latter discussions.

In addition to the contextual data from interviews, additional context was generated from US Census materials obtained from the Census tracts archives for each trailer park. Census data were then, as a form of "triangulation," compared with that of the adjacent community to assess similarities and differences that might be downplayed or magnified by town or park residents.[6] The use of semi-standardized interview instruments ensured the collection of comparable data across sites but still permitted flexibility to adapt the questions as needed for understanding in differing regions and the opportunity to probe beyond the interview instrument. Combined, these research methods provided a general overview of each study community and park site.

Phase 2: Park Survey of Randomly Selected Households

Our goal was to obtain a random sample of 15–20% of park households surveyed. We obtained a park map from management in Illinois, in New Mexico MacTavish created park maps, and Eley obtained park maps from management or used aerial maps obtained from the county geographic information system (GIS) office. Each unit was assigned a number, and targeted units were selected using computer-generated random numbers. The same method was used for replacements if the first units selected were unable or unwilling to be interviewed or when a site proved to be vacant.

At the initial contact with a household, an informed consent form (approved by the University of Illinois Institutional Review Board, or IRB) was reviewed. Survey interviews were conducted only with park household members who verbally agreed to take part. As a means of introducing the study, park households were told, "Mobile home parks are often misunderstood by the general public. We want to learn what life is really like in a mobile home park by talking to you, the residents." Refusals varied by who the field worker was but generally had more to do with household time constraints than objections to the study. To a great degree, the difficulty in obtaining a higher sample goal was attributable to issues of residential mobility that frequently left units and lots vacant.

The survey instrument was designed to capture descriptive data to provide a broad overview of the park(s). Specifically, we obtained household demographics, residential experiences, neighborhood and community perceptions, and patterns of social engagement in the park and nearby community. Sections of the survey instrument focused on housing, the household, work and income sources, the neighborhood, the community, and future plans. Households' responses were hand recorded on the survey instrument and later coded and entered into a database. In addition, immediately after each typically forty-five-minute in-home interview, we recorded detailed field notes. These provided a contextual record for each interview, capturing information about the appearance of the home, household possessions and furnishings, household use of space, respondent demeanor and dress, and in some cases the presence of pets or smokers.[7] Distinctive comments were recorded in quotation form from memory as soon as possible after every interview or observation to achieve greater accuracy.

At the end of this phase in Illinois we used three focus groups in an effort to conduct "member checking"—a means of validating the perceptions that were emerging from the study.[8] Despite ample publicity, using park families as hosts, and offering food and prize incentives, each group was poorly attended. Much valuable information emerged, however, about the park neighborhood and perceptions of the park's management. This technique was not replicated in the other two sites.

Phase 3: Intensive Study of Park Families with Children and Youth

The second phase of data collection involved an in-depth study of a small sample of families with children. A focus on families is essential in neighborhood and child development research.[9] Ideally, a study of the contextual effects on children's development would employ a longitudinal approach by following children over a period of years. Because of time constraints, we used an alternative design. A sample of families with children at two critical developmental junctures (ages eight to nine and fifteen to sixteen) was identified in each study site. These ages represent developmental epochs during which neighborhood and community are increasingly important. Tracking how children fare during those developmentally appropriate transitions throws into sharp relief any community effects of park residence. These data are the basis for examining whether a community effect on child development and family well-being exists for rural trailer-park residence. Detailed information about the study and informed consent forms were reviewed during the first visit with the families and target child. Signatures were obtained from the parents after they received informed consent, and youth and children provided verbal consent for their participation. All procedures were reviewed and approved by the University of Illinois IRB.

The goal for the intensive sample was to obtain ten children and ten youth at each study site. Several study families at each site had more than one child that qualified for participation. An incentive of a $125 stipend (in Illinois and New Mexico) for each participating child in a household was offered (some parents gave the money to the child) because of the large amount of time involved. The stipend was given after all data were collected. We identified some families through the phase 1 survey. Using names provided by the families already enrolled or suggested by the park manager, we contacted other families. When this technique yielded fewer than the requisite number of children for each age category in Illinois, we used a Parent Teacher Organization (PTO) school roster of addresses and phone numbers obtained from a parent. Contacts made using this list brought the Prairieview Manor park intensive sample to eighteen families having ten children and ten youth. Early in the study process, two of the families with children in the younger group dropped out for personal reasons. Thus, the final Illinois sample included sixteen families representing eight children and ten youth. Within the younger group were six girls and two boys, and in the older group were four girls and six boys. This small sample, compounded by an uneven number of males and females in each are category, made gender comparisons unfeasible.

Recruitment for the intensive sample in New Mexico proved more challenging. Because the park sites in that state were dispersed, park families had less knowledge of one another. Thus the potential for personal referrals was limited. In addition, school rosters were not available in New Mexico. Four months of concentrated recruiting was carried out using a variety of methods to locate appropriate study participants. We posted flyers in the schools, grocery stores, and trailer parks and placed an advertisement in the local paper announcing opportunities for participation. High school guidance counselors and community organizations serving families, children, and youth were given recruitment information and asked to give it to potential participants. The parks in Mesa Vista were repeatedly canvassed on weekends and during after-school hours. The New Mexico intensive sample remained short of the target numbers. To increase the sample size, age requirements were loosened to include eight- to ten-year old children and fourteen- to sixteen-year old youth. Expanding the age of the study population is incidental to child development and therefore should not compromise the study.[10] These ages are still within the developmental epochs of middle childhood and middle adolescence. By expanding the age categories we brought the younger sample to the target count of ten, but the youth sample remained at only six participants. The gender division for the southwestern site included six boys and four girls in the younger group, with three boys and three girls in the older group. As in Illinois, the sample size and gender distribution preclude comparison of male and female trends. Ten families made up the New Mexico intensive sample, with six families having more than one participating child. We visited each household before the formal study took place. Detailed information about the study and informed consent procedures were reviewed during this first visit. Signatures were obtained from parents, but children and youth provided verbal consent for participation. We also obtained parental and child permissions to access children's school records.

Since the North Carolina parks were more racially integrated than we expected, there were not as many African American families to choose from with children of the appropriate ages. It thus took three months to recruit African American families for the intensive sample. Three households were participants in the park survey phase, but the remaining eleven households were found through personal referrals from the park managers or park residents. As an incentive, all eligible families received a $100 stipend for each participating child (different funding for this phase allowed for only this amount). By the end of the third month of recruitment, contacts were made with fourteen families having nine children (ages eight to nine) and eight youth (ages fifteen to sixteen). One parent with a child in the younger age group declined to participate in the intensive phase. One household with a teenage son, who consented to participate, dropped out for personal reasons. After several months, a decision was made to drop another household because of the challenges involved with scheduling a single interview with the parent and child after repeated attempts.

As in New Mexico, school rosters listing parents in the PTO were not available in North Carolina. Although Eley found two additional replacement families for those who dropped out, the Addington family sample remained short of the target numbers. We therefore extended the target ages for children and youth. A few participants are in the fourth and eleventh grades. A total of thirteen households with eight child participants and eight youth participants make up the North Carolina family sample. Three families have two children who qualified for participation. The gender division for the North Carolina site includes one boy and seven girls in the child sample and three girls and five boys in the youth sample. Again, the numbers were too small for any analysis of gender differences.

A series of instruments was used in the intensive phase. The four instruments included (1) background interviews (with a parent, child, and youth version of the interview), (2) the typical day interview, (3) the household economic strategies interview, and (4) exit interviews (similarly with a separate parent, child, and youth version of the interview).

Background interviews focused on family, residential, work, and educational histories and began formal data collection for the intensive phase. Participants were told, "These questions are supposed to tell me about the sorts of things your friends who have known you for years already know about you, but do so in a shorter period of time." This introduction seemed to put people at ease. We did not expect children and youth to necessarily report the same school experiences, family relations, social ties, or residential experiences as did their parents. Separate parent and child interviews assured that all family viewpoints were captured. Typically, the set of initial interviews took several sessions and on average about six hours to complete.

The *parent background interview* started by asking for a detailed description of each member of the immediate household. Each household member's first name, gender, relationship to the respondent, age, education, and occupation along with how he or she joined the household were requested. Next, similar information was obtained for extended kin and members of friendship networks. For kin and friendship ties, we asked about the length of association, the amount of current contact, and the types of supportive exchanges engaged in. People were then asked to rank order their personal relationships on a graph containing three concentric circles. The names of friends and family were placed according to an inner circle designating those closest to them and outer circles for those more socially distant.[11] A detailed residential, work, and school history was collected along with a parental report on the child's school history. Most often mothers were the primary respondents, but when possible and present, fathers were interviewed as well. The *child and youth interview* instruments followed a similar format but used language appropriate for each age group. Collectively, the household responses form a baseline for assessing household patterns such as socioeconomic class, residential mobility, employment solidity, marriage stability, kin relations, and social support systems.

Once the background interviews were completed, parents were asked to describe a typical household day. The *typical day interview* sought to document daily household routines and capture unique strategies for navigating family and work schedules. Specifically, the division of labor—such as child/youth monitoring, housework, meal preparation, and work schedules across the household—was the focus. These data provide the self-perceptions about typical family life against which observations made in the home over the six-month period of intensive study could be compared.

In the *exit interview* parents were also asked to document the overall household economic situation to obtain *economic strategies.* This interview was conducted late in the intensive phase, assuming that familiarity would facilitate a more open discussion about these sensitive matters. Surprisingly, people were not hesitant about revealing financial matters. Specifically, parents were asked to describe household expenses and the strategies for allocating typically limited incomes to cover such expenses.

Conducting this series of interviews had the added benefit of providing ample observation time in each home. Still, in an effort to observe the entire family in a focused activity we asked to observe a family meal. The immediate response to this request was to readily agree or to say, often with a chuckle, "We don't eat family meals." The latter response was far more common in the Illinois site, where an observation of a meal was completed with only one-quarter (four of the sixteen) families. In New Mexico, such observations were completed for half (five of the ten) families. The responses were a source of unexpected but useful data about family life. If participation in a family meal was possible, the data were rich. Witnessing each family in action revealed its unique interaction style, taken-for-granted routines, and household processes not otherwise obvious.[12] It quickly became apparent from child behaviors whether these mealtime interactions were routine or staged for the benefit of the researcher. Sharing a meal seemed to loosen any remaining barriers to observing the family in normal routines.

After these household-level approaches, interview and observation data-collection strategies aimed specifically at documenting the lives of study children and youth were carried out. Child and youth study instruments included (1) school record review and observations, (2) a drawing or camera activity, (3) a weekly activity log, and (4) a neighborhood walk. [13]

Review of school performance included a record review, classroom observation, and teacher interview to document academic and social competence in the school setting. Grade reports, standardized test results, behavioral reports, and general teacher comments were examined in an effort to construct an overall picture of each child's development. In general, a great deal of agreement was found between a family's self-reports about school performance and a student's formal school records. Two separate waves, one observation early in the intensive phase and another near the end, focused on each child in his or her classroom, at recess, and during lunch. These observations provided for the triangulation of data on each child's academic and behavioral performance. Teachers and school administrators were interviewed as well. The interviews focused on specific study children, as well as trailer-park children in general, to gain the official perspective on park children.

To obtain data about individual perceptions of home, neighborhood, community, and personal networks, each study child and youth was given an age-appropriate exercise to complete—drawings done by children, camera records by youth. Younger children were provided with a set of colored pencils and asked to draw pictures of their home, family, people important to them, and their favorite and least favorite community places. Each youth was provided with single-use camera and asked to document similar images. When the assignments were completed, images were discussed with each child or youth. Having pictures to talk about provided youth in particular with something that increased both the length and quality of verbal responses. Thus, greater insight was gained into the lives of these teens than otherwise provided by interview or observation data.

To capture a typical measure of daily time and social interaction, each child and youth were asked to complete a detailed log of a week's activities. This task required them to account for every hour awake each day by recording what they were doing, whom they were with, and where the activity took place. Activity logs, like drawings and pictures, provided another focal point that helped facilitate conversations with young participants.

Toward the end of the intensive phase each child and youth was asked to take the field worker on a walking tour of his or her neighborhood. The neighborhood walk interview instrument was designed to uncover familiarity with the park neighborhood, to document use of space and modes of transportation, and to reveal family and neighborhood rules for passage from the home and in the neighborhood. Children were first asked to talk about their immediate neighbors and identify peers, adults, and other elders with whom they had regular contact. Each child was then asked to follow his or her usual route of travel through the park and point out friends' houses, places they liked to go, and places they would never go within the park. Family, park, and informal community rules about children's travel were thus revealed. Rules for conduct, as reported by the younger children in particular, were routinely verified with parents. What parents reported as allowed and what children said was permitted frequently differed. Children in the younger study group sometimes reported being allowed to venture far from home, such as to the grocery store alone, but parents quickly denied these reports. Parents typically asserted that family rules restricted unsupervised travel to an area within park boundaries.

Each contact with children or youth provided opportunities to observe them in the home, neighborhood, or community context. Adding observation to interview data ensured that we captured not only what individuals said but what they did. Additional, general park observations were made during the six-month period of the field study's intensive phase. The Illinois Manufactured Housing Association, through an in-kind grant, provided MacTavish a small unit (trailer) in the Prairieview park, as mentioned above. This base permitted her to make less intrusive observations while tending the yard, taking an evening stroll, or just hanging out routinely. Invariably, she encountered study children (some much more frequently than others) going about normal daily activities. These observations provided rich insight into the daily ebb and flow of activity in the park, as well as the general experience of living in a trailer. Although no unit was available in the Mesa Vista study site, similar general observations during the course of the field study were made in the midst of regular visits.

Frequently, MacTavish's daughter—who was the age of the younger study children—accompanied her on visits to homes or for general observations. She proved invaluable as an icebreaker. With Amanda along, in the eyes of study families, MacTavish became a mom rather than just a researcher. On several occasions, one study family would watch Amanda while MacTavish was visiting with another household. Park families never accepted payment for child care but rather viewed it as an exchange of favors. Thus, obtaining a park definition of neighboring was an unintended consequence of Amanda's company.

Research during the intensive phase did not always flow smoothly with every study family, and these problems provided another source of data. It became clear that certain families chronically missed appointments either through forgetting or by reporting a conflict that arose at the last minute. Marked differences existed between the households that made an effort to change an appointment and those that were unlikely to do so. Some parents clearly monitored a child closely to make sure he or she kept appointments, while others made no such effort. Similarly, variations existed as to whether children and youth completed the drawing or camera activity or returned the activity logs. Some completed the assignments promptly and fully, while others lost the camera or drawing supplies, needed continual reminding before he or she made an effort, or just did not complete the assignment. Missing tasks thus became important data by commenting on households' taken-for-granted processes, scheduling, child monitoring, or socialization goals. We found households consistently organized or disorganized. Combined, these methods produced the rich, thick data necessary for a thorough qualitative study.[14]

As noted above, Eley's agricultural economics background and her interest in black churches as an African American shaped her research. Eley's living in one of the four North Carolina parks facilitated daily participant observation and getting to know the residents in her immediate neighborhood. She attended six churches to which some intensive phase families belonged for both Sunday worship and other activities. The church setting provided an opportunity for seeing the families outside the park. School visits provided another opportunity to observe children away from the mobile home park. Eley, like MacTavish, followed local news by subscribing to the Addington newspaper during the study year to document the local school system, community issues, and the real estate market.

To the above instruments used in Illinois and New Mexico we added questions highlighting church involvement and informal economy for the North Carolina site. We suspected that African American families would be deeply embedded in their local churches. We expected that such churches would deliver rich social and economic resources for low- and modest-income African American parents and children living in mobile home parks. The rationale for the additional documenting of the informal economy was partly based on renewed interest in the subject among other social scientists. But more important, we also expected the informal economy of rural African American park households to be shaped by cultural norms based on personal relations and networks embedded in family, community friendship, or ethnic group. We also considered the informal economy work activities as an example of a problem-solving strategy for provisioning the household by mobile home park families. The most challenges encountered were in meeting study goals for the phase 2 intensive sample of obtaining enough families to have ten children and ten youth at each study site. We wanted to follow these children for as much time as possible during the study year to observe them in their family, park, and school lives.[15]

Two instruments were added to the North Carolina intensive phase. Parents were asked to describe their values, feelings, and experience concerning their church involvement. The church involvement interview focused on whether church participation enhances a park household's access to social and economic resources. It was also important to document how household members' experiences and meanings behind church-based support influenced their overall well-being. Specifically, membership and church attendance, types of supportive exchanges, nature of communal relationships with the church, and the extent of the church's community involvement and outreach were the focus. Eley regularly attended Sunday services, alternating among six churches. She also observed activities at the church such as meetings and services. Participant observation at various churches was helpful for documenting support to park families, through relationships with friends or acquaintances as well as kin church members. In addition, she wanted to learn to what extent mobile home park parents and children are involved with church activities and whether these activities enhance self-esteem, promote prosocial behavior, and generally facilitate a sense of meaning and purpose.

North Carolina parents were asked more detailed questions about how they manage household money. The family *economics interview* was generally conducted at the same time as the mealtime observation, but on occasion this interview was done separately. It was done late in the intensive phase because of the sensitivity of the subject matter. On the whole, parents were not reluctant to reveal financial matters and their method for meeting household expenses. First, we asked what proportions of the household's monthly income were spent on housing, utilities, food, clothing, transportation, child care, savings or debt payments, and entertainment. Some questions covered household budget decisions made for daily purchases, major purchases, savings or investment plans, children allowance, entertainment, and buying on credit or loans. We also asked about how and when parents acquired their possessions, such as the home, furniture, appliances, computer, and vehicles. These data gave us information about family financial management and kin network support. We also inquired about whether they had household, medical, and other insurance; methods for handling money emergencies; their retirement; and goals for their children's future.

Data Analysis

In analyzing data from the three park ethnographic field studies, we used a "vacuum cleaner" approach to taking field notes. Sweep up anything and everything you see and hear and write it down. We never know until the full analysis what may be important as a clue or theme that unlocks or explains how things work. The ethnographic methods we used are based on the assumption that behavior is best understood by extensive observation of people going about their ordinary affairs in the settings where they normally live and work. Hence, the year-long time frame of each field study. Our intention was to derive an emic understanding of what it means for a family to live in a rural trailer park. We constructed the description of each trailer park and how it worked from the household or bottom level up. The park households we interviewed and observed provided a view of how their park functioned and the relationship of the household (or not) to the larger park. The comparative design, using the geographic and ethnic contrasts of Illinois, New Mexico, and North Carolina, allowed us to understand what is shared or not culturally and what is unique among the populations living in trailer parks.

We used an inductive process that aimed to combine analysis of data simultaneously with data collection. Salamon read the field notes that were recorded as soon as possible after the interviews and observation, and we regularly met, used e-mail, or talked by phone to discuss the data being generated and ideas forming with it. From these conversations, emergent hypotheses were formed about how things worked. MacTavish and Eley could then return to the field and ask the families if a particular behavior was typical or unusual, or test whether our hypotheses made sense to verify or dispel these early ideas. When we identified some pattern or theme as distinctive, we often counted how many times it occurred in the recorded data or we turned to people's comments to learn their thinking about the particular issue. We attempted to interview all adults in a household and to observe all family members and a cross-section of the park population, which allowed us to compare their perspectives.

When the study began and during the analysis, we tried, as ethnographers, not to make assumptions about trailer parks and park families, based on the taken-for-granted stereotypes common to them. Therefore, we strove to find the park families' meaning for their homes as a possession and shelter, their trailer park, park management, other park families, and the larger community nearby.[16]

What we looked for in the analysis process were patterns and themes we had identified during the actual fieldwork. We were particularly concerned with whether families found community in their trailer park, how they felt about their neighbors, how they felt about the park's relationship to the community beyond its borders, and their beliefs about the park as their permanent place to live or merely a way station. In addition, the extensive data we obtained allowed us to distinguish between what people said and did and what was left unsaid or undone.

When a theme emerged in the inductive analysis process, it tended not to be subtle. Once we identified a theme—if accurately captured—it suddenly appeared consistently to us in the data. The basis for this occurrence is the principle that everyday behavior in families is not random. If we had used only a single survey interview of park households, the variation among park families might have been masked.

Our thinking about chasing the housing dream grew out of our analysis for the book. Going back to the data again and again, in the process of many revisions the book involved, we began to see and hear the strength of families' optimism about an eventual pathway out of the park that sparked the focus we came to have for the book. The process of our thorough comparison across the three site studies reshaped our big-picture understanding of mobile home parks as a residential context for families. Those comparisons, and newly emerging information on changes in park ownership and affordable housing, became evident after the field studies were completed.

NORTH CAROLINA AND NEW MEXICO PARK POPULATION DETAILS

TABLE B.1 Population traits of North Carolina park households

TRAIT	SHADY GROVE (N = 35)	CEDAR BROOK (N = 21)	NORTHWINDS (N = 6)	LAKESIDE (N = 3)	TOTAL ADDINGTON PARKS (N = 65)
Ethnicity					
% white households	40	48	83	none	45
% black households	54	52	17	100	52
% Hispanic households	3				3
Household type					
% with children	63	57	50	100	62
(# single parent)	(6 of 22)	(4 of 12)	(1 of 3)	(1 of 3)	(12 of 40)
(# cohabiting)	(none)	(1 of 12)	(1 of 3)	(none)	(2 of 40)
% older adult (65+	11	10	none	none	12.3
years)	4 of 35	4 of 21	none	none	8 of 65
# extended kin					
Income					
Median household					
income	$23,900	$23,400	$34,100	$47,800	$24,537
% below poverty	19	19	none	none	16.4
% reporting public					
assistance	none	14	none	none	4.6

(continued)

TABLE B.1 (continued)

TRAIT	SHADY GROVE (N = 35)	CEDAR BROOK (N = 21)	NORTHWINDS (N = 6)	LAKESIDE (N = 3)	TOTAL ADDINGTON PARKS (N = 65)
Highest educational attainment in household					
% less than high school	9	19	none	none	10.9
% high school or GED	37	48	17	100	35.9
% some college but no degree	56	29	17	none	45.3
% 4-year college degree or higher	9	17	17	none	7.8
Homeownership status					
% own home in full	26	38	none	none	26.2
% own home, make mortgage payments	37	33	83	67	41.5
% buying on contract sales	37	33	19	33	24.6
% renting	6	14	none	none	7.8
Residential status					
Median time in current home	3 years	3.5 years	1.5 years	2 years	3 years
% who have previously lived in mobile home	43	57	83	none	49.2
% define home as "permanent"	29	29	67	33	32.3

Source: Survey of randomly selected sample of trailer-park households.

TABLE B.2 North Carolina park characteristics

CHARACTERISTIC	SHADY GROVE (N = 35)	CEDAR BROOK (N = 21)	NORTHWINDS (N = 6)	LAKESIDE (N = 3)	ALL ADDINGTON PARKS (N = 65)
Lots					
Total number of lots	204	165	101	34	504
Monthly lot rent & services included	$140 water, sewer, and trash included	$110 water, sewer, and trash included	$165 all utilities included	$125 water, sewer, and trash included	$133[a] water, sewer, and trash included
Homes					
Median cost/ month	$390	$318	$553	$524	$383
Median age	5.5 years	12 years	2.5 years	2.5 years	5.5 years
Park ownership	Local owner/ cooperation	Out-of-state investors	Local investor	Local investor	Varies

Source: Survey of randomly selected sample of trailer-park households.

[a]Median lot rent.

TABLE B.3 Detailed population traits of New Mexico park households

TRAIT	TUMBLEWEED (N = 20)	SANDIA ESTATES (N = 21)	LOS ALTOS (N = 6)	LOMA LINDA (N = 12)	CHAPARRAL (N = 9)	BACA'S (N = 11)	TOTAL MESA VISTA (N = 79)
Ethnicity							
% with Hispanic ties	50	71	67	83	100	36	65.8
(# ethnically mixed)	(2 of 10)	none	(4 of 4)	(1 of 10)	(2 of 9)	(1 of 4)	(10 of 79)
Household type							
% with children	50	70	67	58	100	36	59.5
(# single parent)	5 of 10	3 of 15	none	1 of 7	2 of 9	2 of 4	13 of 49
(# cohabiting)	2 of 10	none	none	1 of 7	2 of 9	3 of 4	8 of 49
% older adult (65+ years)	25	10	17	17	none	27	16.5
# extended kin	3 of 20	1 of 21	none	2 of 12	2 of 9	none	8 of 79
Income							
Median household income	$19,834	$15,074	$6,818	$13,636	$25,826	$20,000	$17,355
% below poverty	35	29	100	33	25	11	39.1
% reporting public assistance	28	24	83	33	11	9	27.3

(continued)

TABLE B.3 (continued)

TRAIT	TUMBLEWEED (N = 20)	SANDIA ESTATES (N = 21)	LOS ALTOS (N = 6)	LOMA LINDA (N = 12)	CHAPARRAL (N = 9)	BACA'S (N = 11)	TOTAL MESA VISTA (N = 79)
Highest educational attainment in household							
% less than HS	17	37	20	42	11	none	20.3
% high school or GED	28	90	60	33	78	27	43.2
% some college but no degree	17	11	none	33	none	27	16.2
% 4-year college degree or higher	39	none	20	8	11	46	20.3
Homeownership status							
% own home in full	45	10	33	50	none	55	31.6
% own home, make mortgage payments	35	71	33	8	44	36	41.6
% buying on contract sales	5	none	17	25	none	none	6.3
% renting	10	19	17	17	44	9	17.7
Residential status							
Median time in current home	3 years	4 year	< 1 year	2 years	< 1 year	6 years	3 years
% previously lived in mobile home	55	67	100	58	44	36	58.2
% define home as "permanent"	40	71	50	33	56	36	49.4

Source: Survey of randomly selected sample of trailer-park households.

TABLE B.4 Detailed New Mexico park characteristics

CHARACTERISTIC	TUMBLE-WEED (N = 20)	SANDIA ESTATES (N = 21)	LOS ALTOS (N = 6)	LOMA LINDA (N = 12)	CHAPARRAL (N = 9)	BACA'S (N = 11)	ALL PARKS, MESA VISTA (N = 79)
Lots							
Total number of lots	58	60	50	21	38	25	252
Monthly lot rent	$138	Subdivision with no lot rent	$185	$110–$130	Subdivision with no lot rent	$80	$130[a]
Utilities included	water, sewer, and trash included		all utilities included	water, sewer, and trash included		water, sewer, and trash included	water, sewer, and trash included
Homes							
Median cost/month	$291	$259	$265	$190	$350	$120	$250
Median age	10 years	20 years	13 years	21 years	12 years	18 years	16 years
Park ownership	Out-of-state investor	Local dev. corporation	Nonlocal investor	Local dev. corporation	In-state investor	In-park owner	Various

Source: Survey of randomly selected sample of trailer-park households.

[a]Median lot rent.

Notes

INTRODUCTION

1. See Schafft, "Poverty, Residential Mobility and Student Transiency"; Adam and Chase-Lansdale, "Home Sweet Home(s)."

2. Hart, Rhodes, and Morgan, *The Unknown World of Mobile Homes*; Hurley, *Diners, Bowling Alleys, and Trailer Parks*; and Wallis, *Wheel Estate.*

3. Hurley, *Diners, Bowling Alleys and Trailer Parks*, 211.

4. Ibid., 214–15.

5. Rohe and Watson, *Chasing the American Dream.*

6. Hurley, *Diners, Bowling Alleys, and Trailer Parks*, 214.

7. Ibid.

8. See Geoghegan, "Why Do So Many Americans Live in Mobile Homes?," for details about who lives in mobile homes.

9. Various definitions of "rural" exist. For our purposes, we employ the USDA-ERS definition that uses counties as a basis for metropolitan/nonmetropolitan (rural) classification. Nonmetropolitan counties include some combination of open countryside, rural towns (places with fewer than 2,500 people), and urban areas with populations ranging from 2,500 to 49,999 that are not part of a larger labor market area. See Cromartie and Bucholtz, "Defining the 'Rural.'"

10. The Housing Assistance Council (HAC) estimates that nationally, 2.3 million households reside in rural mobile home parks. This number represents our best approximation of the total number of children under the age of eighteen living in forty-five thousand rural mobile home parks.

11. Quoted in Cullen, *American Dream*, 4.

12. Rohe and Watson, *Chasing the American Dream*; Shlay, "Low-Income Homeownership."

13. Cullen, *American Dream*, cites the optimism observed by Alexis de Tocqueville as a central part of the American Dream. Cullen argues that the kind of optimism about the potential for social mobility even among the poor and immigrant populations that defined our national identity two hundred years ago continues today.

14. Several scholars, including MacLeod in, *Ain't No Makin' It*, warn of the implications for youth when notions of an achievement ideology are associated with the American Dream.

15. Pew Charitable Trusts, *Pursuing the American Dream*, reports that among those raised in the bottom quintile, 43 percent remain in the bottom as adults and fully 70 percent fail to reach the middle.

16. Duncan, *Worlds Apart*, makes a clear case for the resources essential to social mobility and the implications of their unequal distribution.

17. Smith and Tickamyer, introduction to Smith and Tickamyer, *Economic Restructuring and Family Well-Being*, provides a compelling look at the effects of rural economic restructuring on rural wages. While blue-collar jobs have diminished and service and white-collar jobs have expanded, the real story lies in the decline in wages. They document the persistence of an urban advantage in maintaining wages. In contrast, rural wages have significantly declined since the late 1970s. Also see Sherman, *Those Who Work*, which

looks in particular at implications for rural families and communities around the loss of traditionally male-dominated jobs.

18. Marre, "Rural Areas Lag."

19. See, for example, Putnam, *Our Kids.*

20. Rampell, "Americans Think Owning a Home Is Better," for example, reports in the *Washington Post* on survey data collected by Fannie Mae and Gallup indicating Americans' confidence in homeownership as a key investment strategy even postrecession.

21. Shlay, "Low-Income Homeownership."

22. Wray, *Not Quite White;* Wray and Newitz, *White Trash;* and Hartigan, *Odd Tribes.*

23. Edelstein, *Contaminated Communities.*

24. MacTavish and Salamon, "Mobile Home Park on the Prairie"; MacTavish, "Wrong Side of the Tracks"; Benson, "Good Neighbors"; Huss-Ashmore and Behrman, "Transitional Environments"; Miller and Evko, "An Ethnographic Study"; Wray, *Not Quite White.*

25. Boehm and Schlottmann, "Is Manufactured Housing a Good Alternative?"

26. MacTavish, Eley, and Salamon, "Housing Vulnerability"; Mitchell, "I'm In over My Head."

27. Desmond, *Evicted;* and MacTavish, Eley, and Salamon, "Housing Vulnerability."

28. For characteristics of rural and small-town community attachment see Elder and Conger, *Children of the Land;* Salamon, *Newcomers to Old Towns;* Bell, *Childerley;* Fitchen, *Endangered Spaces;* Duncan, *Worlds Apart.*

29. Boehm and Schlottmann, "Is Manufactured Housing a Good Alternative?," 159.

30. Gladwell, "Starting Over."

31. Wilson, *The Truly Disadvantaged;* Furstenberg et al., *Managing to Make It;* MacLeod, *Ain't No Makin' It;* Sampson, *Great American City;* Putnam, *Our Kids.*

32. See Elder and Conger, *Children of the Land,* for a full discussion of small-town traits beneficial to developing youth.

33. Carr and Kefalas, *Hollowing Out.*

34. Salamon, *From Hometown to Non-Town;* Elder and Conger, *Children of the Land.*

35. See Geoghegan, "Why Do So Many Americans Live in Mobile Homes?"

1. THE MOBILE HOME INDUSTRIAL COMPLEX

1. Gibson, "America, the Unaffordable," 32–33.

2. Leopold et al., "Housing Affordability Gap."

3. Quoted in Rivlin, "Cold, Hard Lessons."

4. U.S. Census Bureau, "Structural and Occupancy Characteristics of Housing: 2000," Census Brief, 2003; "American Community Survey 3-Year Summary File, 2005–2007." Because the US Census does not ask whether the nation's mobile homes are located in a park or on a scattered site, we have only the MHI's estimate of fifty thousand land-lease parks for how many parks exist nationally. http://www.manufacturedhousing.org/. Lance George, HAC, believes that upwards of sixty thousand parks (urban and rural) exist nationally. Personal communication to Salamon, March 18, 2017.

5. Foremost Insurance Group, "Manufactured Homes," a relatively recent ten thousand-household survey, by the nation's leading insurer of mobile homes.

6. Rivlin, "Cold, Hard Lessons." The numbers of trailer parks declined nationally, though demand rose during the 2008 housing recession, when many in the middle class lost conventional homes,

7. Grissim, "Home Buyer's Outlook." Grissim is a retired investigative reporter and a manufactured home owner who has spent a decade analyzing and reporting to create a guide for buying these homes, financing, land-lease trailer parks, and other advice.

8. The Housing Assistance Council (HAC) is an important source for rural mobile homes and mobile home parks data. Housing Assistance Council, *Taking Stock,* 39,

estimates that in 2012, 2.3 million households resided in rural mobile home parks. But after 2011 fewer homes were sited in actual parks.

9. Hurley, *Diners, Bowling Alleys, and Trailer Parks*, 219–22, and Wallis, *Wheel Estate*, 207, both detail how parks transformed from the 1920s transient "trailer camps" to more permanent places of residence by the 1950s.

10. Hart, Rhodes, and Morgan, *Unknown World of the Mobile Home*; Hurley, *Diners, Bowling Alleys, and Trailer Parks*; Thornburg, *Galloping Bungalows*; and Wallis, *Wheel Estate*.

11. For the industry's views see http://www.manufacturedhousing.org/understanding_today/index.htm.

12. Wallis, *Wheel Estate*, 214–15.

13. *Consumer Reports*, "Dream Home," 33; Zuckman, "New Fight Likely." We found no more current assessment of manufactured homes, based on owners' assessments. Grissim, "Home Buyer's Outlook," reviews quality issues from a critic's perspective.

14. Grissim, "Home Buyer's Outlook."

15. Ibid.

16. Hurley, *Diners, Bowling Alleys, and Trailer Parks*, and Wallis, *Wheel Estate*, describe single home size in 1956 as "10 wide" with a length that grew from forty-eight feet to a modern ninety feet over time. Firestone, "Governor's Mansion," reported that in 2000 while the Arkansas governor's mansion was being remodeled, Mike Huckabee and his family lived behind it in a new triplewide of 1,200 square feet that was the size of a modest urban apartment.

17. Wapner, M. "Double Wide Mobile Homes."

18. Huss-Ashmore and Behrman, "Transitional Environments"; Liu et al., "Irritant Effects of Formaldehyde"; Brunker, "Are FEMA Trailers 'Toxic Tin Cans'?," reported that the small RVs used to house Hurricane Katrina victims in 2005 had high levels of formaldehyde that sickened people.

19. Healton and Nelson, "Reversal of Misfortune."

20. Runyan et al., "Risk Factors"; Parker et al., "Fire Fatalities"; Mobley et al., "Prevalence of Risk Factors."

21. Shanklin, "Old Mobile Homes."

22. *Consumer Reports*, "Dream Home," 34; Ballard, Koepsell, and Rivera, "Association of Smoking and Alcohol"; Howland and Hingson, "Alcohol as a Risk Factor."

23. National Weather Service, Weather Forecast Office, Milwaukee/Sullivan, WI: http://www.crh.noaa.gov/mkx/?n=taw-part2-tornado_myths (answers myths about tornadoes); http://spc.noaa.gov/faq/tornado/index.htm (answers frequently asked questions about tornadoes).

24. Housing Assistance Council, "Manufactured Housing in Rural America" 19. The issue of manufactured home life and use has evoked a debate that has resulted in anything but a clear consensus. A 1998 report sponsored by the Manufactured Housing Institute estimated the life expectancy of a manufactured home to be 57.5 years. Meeks, *Manufactured Home Life*. However, Consumers Union (publisher of *Consumer Reports*) questioned the methodology of this report, demonstrating that the same data indicated a median life span of 22 years if the methodology used alternative, but reasonable, assumptions. Jewell, *Can We Trust Information?* In reality, longevity for this type of housing is highly variable. An array of factors, such as date of construction, producer, geographic location, and owner upkeep all greatly affect a home's life span.

25. MacTavish, Eley, and Salamon, "Housing Vulnerability."

26. Housing Assistance Council, *Moving Home*; Lance George, Director of Research and Information, Housing Assistance Council, personal communication to MacTavish, 2015; Collins, "Rural America's Housing"; Long, "Manufacturing Affordability."

27. Clayton Homes website, http://claytonhomes.com, describes its one-stop shopping: "Clayton manufactures, sells, finances, leases and insures homes for people throughout the United States." Jennifer Reingold, "The Ballad of Clayton Homes," describes the process of Warren Buffet's purchase of Clayton Homes. See Wagner and Baker, "Minorities Exploited," for an investigative journalism account of Buffet and Clayton Homes' predatory lending and exploitation of poor manufactured home buyers.

28. U.S. Census Bureau, "American Housing Survey for the United States: 2011."

29. Housing Assistance Council, *Taking Stock,* 25; American Housing Survey, "Introductory Housing Characteristics"; Collins, "Rural America's Housing."

30. Berenson, "Boom Built upon Sand." Although thirty-year loans were Berenson's major focus, he says the loan form is relatively new. A thirty-year loan, according to economists, shows how the market goes to whatever it must to get monthly payments to where a low-income family will or can buy. A thirty-year loan also adds to profits for a lender. It is important to note that few of our study families are borrowing the $50,000 loan amount used in table 1.2. We found three families in North Carolina with these loans, which were newer loans for doublewides. But most study families have shorter loans (for fifteen or twenty years) and for less money.

31. Berenson, "Boom Built upon Sand"; Jewell, *Can We Trust Information?*

32. Housing Assistance Council, *Taking Stock,* 32.

33. Housing Assistance Council, *Moving Home*; Morgenson, "Inside the Country-wide Spree."

34. Berenson, "Boom Built upon Sand."

35. Williams, *Debt for Sale,* 22, views predatory lenders as institutions that "extend expensive credit for excessive profits." Such lending practices "ensnare the poor and cultivate a new form of debt peonage, because, like sharecroppers before them, poor people would never be able to pay off their debt."

36. Berenson, "Boom Built upon Sand"; Fuquay, "Lending Perspectives," is a publication of the industry's Manufactured Housing Institute.

37. Berenson, Boom Built upon Sand"; *Consumer Reports,* "Dream Home"; Wallis, *Wheel Estate,* 215–18.

38. Williams, *Debt for Sale,* 6, 22.

39. Myslajek, "Risks and Realities."

40. Ibid.

41. Stevenson and Goldstein, "Wall St. Veterans." Financial firms like Goldman Sachs are now essentially industrializing contract-for-deed loans by buying up "packages" of foreclosed stick homes that are then sold to buyers who no longer qualify for conventional mortgages. Financers like this loan form because they can easily repossess the home and resell it.

42. Housing Assistance Council, *Taking Stock.*

43. Hurley, *Diners, Bowling Alleys, and Trailer Parks*; Wallis, *Wheel Estate.*

44. *Consumer Reports,* "Dream Home"; Knox, "Why Mobile Homeowners"; MacTavish, Eley, and Salamon, "Housing Vulnerability"; Williams, "Precipice of Debt."

45. Salamon and MacTavish, "Quasi-Homelessness."

46. Wallis, *Wheel Estate,* 227–31; Strauss, "Credit and Capital," 12.

47. MacTavish, "Going Mobile in Rural America"; Eley, "Ties That Bind"; U.S. Census Bureau, "Structural and Occupational Characteristics of Housing: 2000."

48. Levere, "Going Mobile."

49. Long, "Manufacturing Affordability"; personal communication with Lance George, Housing Assistance Council, January 17, 2017, regarding the Duty to Serve final ruling in December 2016. In particular the following part of the ruling pertains to manufactured housing.

> Under the final rule, Fannie Mae and Freddie Mac will each submit to FHFA a three-year Underserved Markets Plan that describes the activities and objectives

they will undertake to meet their Duty to Serve requirements. The Plans will become effective January 2018.

For the manufactured housing market, the final rule provides eligibility for Duty to Serve credit for Enterprise activity supporting manufactured homes titled as real property, manufactured homes titled as personal property (also known as chattel), and blanket loans for certain categories of manufactured housing communities.

https://www.fhfa.gov/Media/PublicAffairs/Pages/FHFA-Issues-Final-Rule-on-Fannie-Mae-and-Freddie-Mac-Duty-to-Serve-Underserved-Markets.aspx.

50. Center for Budget and Policy Priorities, "Policy Basics."

51. Equity Lifestyle Properties is a major player in the area of upscale trailer parks.

52. Charles Becker, personal communication to authors, April 22, 2016.

53. Ibid. Parish Manor parks in North Carolina are a model for a generous and family-supportive trailer park. http://www.parrishmanor.com/

54. Effinger and Burton, "Trailer Parks Lure."

55. Rivlin, "Cold, Hard Lessons."

56. Ibid.

57. Quotations are from Rivlin, "Cold, Hard Lessons."

58. Ruditsky, "New Life for Old Mobile Home Parks," 44–45.

59. Grissim, "Home Buyer's Outlook."

60. Rivlin "Cold Hard Lessons."

61. Ibid.

62. Ibid.

63. Becker and Yea," Value of Manufactured Housing Communities"; Becker, personal communication; Becker, *Trailer Park Economics*.

64. Rivlin, "Cold, Hard Lessons."

65. Ibid. See also Wallis, *Wheel Estate,* 194–95, and Hurley, *Diners, Bowling Alleys, and Trailer Parks,* 256–57, for historical accounts of park management; and Ruditsky, "New Life for Old Mobile Home Parks," an earlier investment guide.

66. Rivlin, "Cold, Hard Lessons"; Desmond, *Evicted,* describes the destructive power evictions have on the urban poor.

67. Quotation from Rivlin, "Cold, Hard Lessons." Also see, for example, Apgar et al., *Examination of Manufactured Housing*; Hummon, *Commonplaces*; Fry, "Community as Commodity"; Stone, *Shelter Poverty,* 18.

68. Rivlin, "Cold, Hard Lessons."

69. Ibid.

70. Ibid.; Salamon, *Newcomers to Old Towns,* chap. 4.

71. Rural areas hold a higher proportion of the nation's trailer parks because urban zoning often excludes parks, rural zoning and housing codes are more lax, and land is more abundant and cheaper relative to urban or suburban places. Salamon, *Newcomers to Old Towns,* chap. 4. See Housing Assistance Council, *Moving Home,* 22, 30.

72. Long, "Manufacturing Affordability." Ordinances exist that limit discriminatory zoning for manufactured housing. But such zoning still is widely found: "Approximately 20 states already have enacted laws that require local jurisdictions to treat manufactured housing no differently than site-built homes, and the number is growing each year," 7.

73. Fogarty, "Manufactured Housing Suffers." "Manufactured housing placements have dropped 85% from their market high." Placement of units on a lot "for prefab homes dropped from a market peak of 374,000 in 1998 to just 52,800 in 2012." Despite a slight rise in 2013, manufactured housing suffered the worst decline of any mortgage niche in this period. Fogarty views manufactured housing as particularly important in rural areas where fewer rental units are available. See also Effinger and Burton, "Trailer Parks Lure."

74. Rivlin, "Cold, Hard Lessons."

75. Aiken, "Race as a Factor"; Lichter et al., "Municipal Underbounding."

76. Lobao, "Sociology of the Periphery"; Tickamyer, "Space Matters!" Both discuss the sociological idea of spatial inequality—that space (e.g., a trailer park) can graphically represent the basic inequalities that exist in rural places.

77. Effinger and Burton, "Trailer Parks Lure."

78. Nesbitt, "American Sprawl"; Consumers Union, "Manufactured Homeowners"; Sheehan and Colton, "Problem of Mass Eviction."

79. Salamon, *Newcomers to Old Towns.*

80. Hurley, *Diners, Bowling Alleys, and Trailer Parks,* 224.

2. MAKING ENDS MEET

1. Housing Assistance Council, *Taking Stock,* 24–27.

2. James Baldwin, *Nobody Knows My Name,* 62.

3. See Bell, *Childerley*; Bell, "Fruit of Difference"; Hummon, *Commonplaces;* and Salamon, *Newcomers to Old Towns,* for the meaning of a rural or small-town identity for people.

4. For financial matters we use a survey sample size of 175, which excludes 51 households who declined to provide financial data.

5. Housing Assistance Council, *Moving Home.*

6. Smith and Tickamyer, introduction to Smith and Tickamyer, *Economic Restructuring*; Nelson, "Job Characteristics"; Nelson and Smith, *Working Hard and Making Do.*

7. Brown and Schafft, *Rural People and Communities,* part 4; Smith and Tickamyer, introduction to *Economic Restructuring.*

8. Brown and Schafft, *Rural People and Communities,* 155–56.

9. Gibbs, Kusmin, and Cromartie, "Low-Skill Employment"; Anderson and Weng, "Regional Variation."

10. Shipler, *The Working Poor,* provides a journalistic view of the working poor. Zuberi, *Differences That Matter,* compares the United States with Canada, where hotel worker immigrants are unionized and have good jobs with health care benefits. Over time the Canadian system creates more upward social mobility for the working poor.

11. Falk, Schulman, and Tickamyer, *Communities of Work,* ix–xxiii.

12. Anderson and Weng, "Regional Variation."

13. Falk, Schulman, and Tickamyer, *Communities of Work,* introduction.

14. Brown and Schafft, *Rural People and Communities,* 11; Zimmerman, Ham, and Frank, "Does It or Doesn't It?"

15. Brown and Schafft, *Rural People and Communities,* 199; Zimmerman, Ham, and Frank, "Does It or Doesn't It?"

16. Brown and Schafft, *Rural People and Communities,* 199.

17. See Kaufman and Lutz, "Competing Forces"; Brown and Schaftt, *Rural People and Communities.*

18. Zimmerman, Ham, and Frank, "Does It or Doesn't It?"; Morton et al., "Solving the Problems of Iowa Food Deserts."

19. Zimmerman, Ham, and Frank, "Does It or Doesn't It?," points out that the costs involved in buying "cheap" food at a grocery store are often discounted by rural people accustomed to traveling far to satisfy household necessities.

20. Nelson and Smith, *Working Hard and Making Do,* 127.

21. Ibid., 70–71.

22. Smith and Gozjolko, "Low Income"; Forry and Walker, "Child Care in Rural America."

23. Forry and Walker, "Child Care in Rural America."

24. Lichter and Roempke Graefe, "Rural Economic Restructuring"; Nelson and Smith, *Working Hard and Making Do*; Slack, "Contours and Correlates."

25. Tickamyer and Wood, "Social and Economic Context."

26. Ibid.

27. Brown and Kulcsar, "Household Economic Behavior."

28. Stack, *All Our Kin*, a classic description of kin exchange systems among poor urban African Americans.

29. Gans, *Urban Villagers,* a classic study of urban Italian American networks.

30. Stack, *All Our Kin*; Sahlins, "Sociology of Primitive Exchange," a classic description of indirect reciprocity and other forms of exchange that characterize a family.

31. Komorovsky, *Blue-Collar Marriage*; Stack and Burton, "Kinscripts."

32. This section draws on Eley, *Ties That Bind.* See also a 2012 online survey of 30,600 people, carried out by the American Payroll Association that found 68 percent reported living paycheck to paycheck: http://www.huffingtonpost.com/2012/09/20/living-paycheck-to-paycheck_n_1899685.html.

33. MacTavish, Eley, and Salamon, "Housing Vulnerability."

34. According to Roberts, Povich, and Mather, "Low-Income Working Families," low-income working families are defined as those earning less than twice the federal poverty line. In 2003 (relevant to when the study was done) the low-income threshold was $37,320. In 2011, the low-income threshold for a family of four including two children was $45,622.

35. Williams, *Debt for Sale,*113; also see Williams, "The Precipice of Debt."

36. See Ritzer, *Explorations in the Sociology of Consumption.*

37. Cell phone and cable charges were high in the early years of the 2000s, especially in rural areas, which explains why several families used beepers to keep track of teenagers.

38. Salamon and MacTavish, "Quasi-Homelessness."

39. Three prominent economists share the view that it is foolhardy for *all* Americans to be homeowners. The trade-offs of risk and indebtedness make rentals, from their strict economic perspective, a better option than homeownership for those of modest income. See Krugman, "Home Not-So-Sweet"; Shlay, "Low-Income Homeownership"; and Surowiecki, "Home Economics." See also Karabell, "End of the Ownership Society," which focuses on the 2008 recession and its particular threat to the American Dream of homeownership. The ownership society idea started with George W. Bush in a speech in October 2004: "If you own something, you have a vital stake in the future of our country. The more ownership there is in America, the more vitality there is in America, and the more people have a vital stake in the future of this country." From archive: https://georgewbush-whitehouse.archives.gov/news/releases/2004/08/20040809-9.html.

3. THE ILLINOIS PARK

1. Salamon, *Newcomers to Old Towns,* chapter 4, details how the former farm town of Prairieview became an upscale suburb of a nearby small city in just twenty years, starting in the 1970s about the same time the trailer park was built.

2. Illinois Manufactured Housing Association, personal communication to Salamon and MacTavish, at a 1998 Springfield, Illinois, presentation.

3. Johnson, *Order upon the Land,* 224. The original rectangular plat of the farmland imposed the same grid plan on the park, a layout that affects residents' daily life, especially the difficulty of maintaining privacy.

4. Salamon, *Newcomers to Old Towns,* chap. 4; Meeks, *Manufactured Home Life.*

5. Grier, *Pets in America,* argues that starting in the nineteenth century, pets emerged as companions as well as objects of beauty, status, or pleasure. Thus, the fact that Illinois trailer-park families use scarce financial resources to keep pets demonstrates how mainstream they are and that they perhaps hold middle-class values. Darlin, "Vet Bills and the Priceless Pet," reports a 2006 veterinarian's estimation that the average lifetime cost of a medium-sized dog is $10,400. A cat will cost an average of about $10,600. Almost 40 percent of the cost of raising a medium-sized dog goes to health care. Veterinarians recommend that owners buy health insurance for animals. Park families, however, may not have health insurance even for themselves.

6. MacTavish and Salamon, "Mobile Home Park on the Prairie," 491, on early rent.

7. MacTavish and Salamon, "Mobile Home Park on the Prairie," discuss temporary versus permanent residence perspectives held by Illinois park families. Huss-Ashmore and Behrman, "Transitional Environments," identified the rootlessness of trailer-park folk who expect to move on and therefore prefer not to develop park-neighborhood roots.

8. Putnam, *Bowling Alone,* 222–25.

9. Salamon, "Rural Household," 335–37.

10. See Elder and Conger, *Children of the Land*; Childress, *Landscapes of Betrayal*; Salamon, *Newcomers to Old Towns*; and Schwartz, *Beyond Conformity,* for descriptions of what is "appropriate" small-town behavior, against which trailer-park families are compared.

11. See Salamon, *Newcomers to Old Towns,* chapter 1, for key descriptors for how midwestern small towns work or cooperate in the interests of the community.

12. See, for example, Hudson, *Plains Country Towns;* and Salamon, *Newcomers to Old Towns,* for descriptions of the physical spaces of small towns and how public spaces (coffee shops, parks, etc.) provide places for people to meet.

13. Salamon, *Newcomers to Old Towns.*

14. See Oldenburg, *Great Good Place,* for a classic description of the importance to community integration of "third places" where residents can meet informally.

15. MacTavish and Salamon, "Mobile Home Park on the Prairie," 498–99.

16. Ibid., 502–3. Also see Huss-Ashmore and Behrman, "Transitional Environments."

17. Gans, *Levittowners,* is a classic description of suburban middle-class versus working-class cultural practices that explain whether people discipline a neighbor's child.

18. See Huss-Ashmore and Behrman, "Transitional Environments," for discussion of how local residents compare themselves to others despite observable differences; Salamon, *Newcomers to Old Towns,* 7.

19. See, for example, Baumgartner, *Moral Order*; Gans, *Levittowners,* for descriptions of class differences in the same community.

20. See Howell, *Hard Living on Clay Street,* which provides details of what hard living entails for families.

21. Wallace and Pruitt, "Judging Parents," surveyed legal cases "that have used rural residence as a strike against a parent in termination proceedings. . . . Place may become a proxy for poverty and may be cited to justify removal of a child or termination of parental rights. . . . Courts sometimes make decisions based on rural stereotypes, and these decisions may disservice rural families. . . . Courts sometimes fail to account for rural realities [transportation issues, for example] when making child welfare decisions about populations and circumstances with which they may be less familiar." Ibid., 95–96.

22. Duncan, *Worlds Apart*; Nelson and Smith, *Working Hard*; Perry-Jenkins and Salamon, "Blue-Collar Kin."

23. Davis-Brown, Salamon, and Surra, "Economic and Social Factors," examines marriage choices shaped by proximity in a small community.

24. Nelson and Smith, *Working Hard*; Ehrenreich, *Nickel and Dimed* are classic descriptions of working-class jobs.

25. Desmond, *Evicted,* casts light on the effects of eviction—a factor in some families' lives prior to their settling into a more stable life in a trailer park.

26. Burton and Tucker, "Romantic Unions."

27. See Cahn and Carbone, *Red Families,* 2, which describes the conservatism of families who vote in Red states, where people tend to be antiabortion. Families in these states do not consider abortion even when the mother is young.

28. See Fiese, *Family Routines*; Fiese and Schwartz, "Reclaiming the Family Table," for the importance of family meals and routines.

29. Blue-collar family life takes place in the context of kin. See, for example, Kefalas, *Working-Class Heroes*; Perry-Jenkins and Salamon, "Blue-Collar Kin."

30. See Salamon, *Newcomers to Old Towns,* chap. 3, app. B, for more details about the Prairieview upscale suburban community

31. Ibid., chap. 4; Palen, *The Suburbs*; and Jackson, *Crabgrass Frontier* describe suburbs in greater detail, allowing a comparison of this rural suburb with others nationally.

32. On stigma see Goffman, *Stigma*; Becker, *Outsiders*; Schwalbe et al., "Generic Processes." Lister, *Poverty,* first delineated the idea of "othering" to highlight how one group defines another as inferior—morally or intellectually—differentiating and demarcating them with stigmatization. The term "trailer trash" is similarly used.

33. See Salamon, *Newcomers to Old Towns,* chap. 8; Hartigan, *Odd Tribes.*

34. See Tilly, *Durable Inequality*; Perry-Jenkins and Salamon, "Blue-Collar Kin."

4. THE NORTH CAROLINA PARKS

1. U.S. Census Bureau, "DP-1 Profile of General Demographic Characteristics."

2. U.S. Census Bureau, "DP-4 Profile of Selected Housing Characteristics"; Beale, "The Negro in American Agriculture," 191.

3. U.S. Census Bureau, "American Housing Survey for the United States"; "DP-1 Profile of General Demographic Characteristics"; "DP-4 Profile of Selected Housing Characteristics."

4 Hardaway and McLoyd, "Escaping Poverty," is a literature review of African American studies that found homeownership specifically associated with their social mobility, along with academic achievement, employment, and economic independence.

5 Crouter et al., "Processes Linking Social Class," describe the prevalence of "racial socialization" among African American families, which, regardless of class, shapes ethnic identity and social relationships.

6. Jarrett, Jefferson, and Kelly, "Finding Community," details how urban African American parents use strategies such as kin monitoring to buffer the challenges of living in an inner-city neighborhood.

7. Eley, personal communication, 2004, reports that a home-based Bible study group is common among African Americans wanting to start a church in rural North Carolina, where she was raised.

8. See Herrmann, "Garage Sales." The trailer-park Bible study group, like park yard sales, brings neighbors together in a positive activity that promotes the park's community identity and solidarity attached to place.

9. See Brown and Schafft, *Rural People and Communities,* 176–79.

10. See Beale, "The Negro in American Agriculture." See Gilbert, Wood, and Sharp, "Who Owns the Land?," for historical African American agricultural landownership in the South.

11. Eley, "Ties That Bind." See for details on the rural extended kin networks of African American trailer-park families.

12. Calvin Beale, demographer with the USDA-ERS, personal communication to Salamon, 2002. Rural African American family size declined rapidly in the present generation. African Americans are the last rural population to make this demographic transition.

13. See Burton and Hardesty, "Low-Income Mothers."

14. Stack, *All Our Kin*; Cramer and Bell-McDonald, "Kin Support."

15. See Stack, *All Our Kin*; Aschenbrenner, *Lifelines*; Chatters, Taylor, and Jayakody, "Fictive Kinship." These studies all focus on the strong tradition among African Americans for forming fictive-kin relationships, which operate to extend kin networks and thereby optimize household support.

16. See Burton and Hardesty, "Low-Income Mothers"; Shapiro, *Hidden Costs*.

17. Crouter et al., "Processes Linking Social Class."

18. See Hill, *Strengths of African-American Families*; Taylor and Chatters, "Church Members"; Taylor, Chatters, and Levin, *Religion in the Lives*; Billingsley and Caldwell, "The Church"; *Mack-Jackson, Black Children*; Wiley, Warren, and Montanelli, "Shelter in a Time of Storm."

19. Elder and Conger, *Children of the Land*.

20. Eley, "Ties That Bind"; Jarrett, Jefferson, and Kelly, "Finding Community."

21. See Falk, *Rooted in Place*.

22. Salamon is indebted to a personal communication (August 2016) with Robin Jarrett, who shared her insights about the African American park couples' uniform marriage pattern as related to church membership. Also see Jarrett, Jefferson, and Kelley, "Finding Community."

23. MacTavish, "Going Mobile," provides more detail for why some youth do better than others growing up in a trailer park.

5. THE NEW MEXICO PARKS

1. See Jackson, *A Sense of Place*.

2. "Majority-minority" is a term used to describe a population whose racial composition is less than 50 percent non-Hispanic white.

3. United States Department of Agriculture, Economic Research Service (USDA-ERS), "Report on Rural Poverty," designates a county as persistently poor when it maintains a poverty rate of 20 percent or higher across at least three consecutive decades.

4. Ethnicity is a "self-identification data item" on the US Census. We determined the ethnicity of a household by asking about the primary language spoken in the home, through interview items tracing family history, and through visual observation of families in their homes. Most often families self-identified their ethnic heritage during interviews.

5. An official poverty threshold is established by the US Census annually. The threshold takes into account both family size and household income.

6. Data from the American Housing Survey provided in U.S. Census Bureau, "DP-4 Profile of Selected Housing Characteristics," Census 2000 Summary File 3 (SF3) Sample Data, https://factfinder.census.gov/faces/tableservices/jsf/pages/productview.xhtml?src=bkmk, were used to determine median rent and mortgage costs for Mesa Vista. These figures were then converted to 2000 dollars, reflecting our study year, using conversion tables developed by Robert Sarh, personal communication to MacTavish 2016, "Inflation Conversion Factors." See http://liberalarts.oregonstate.edu/spp/polisci/research/inflation-conversion-factors.

7. The USDA-ERS, "Description and Maps," defines "low employment places" as those with fewer than 65 percent of adults twenty-one to sixty-four years of age employed in 2008–12.

8. Calvin Beale, personal communication to Salamon, 2002.

9. For teen pregnancy rates in New Mexico see Kost and Henshaw, "U.S. Teenage Pregnancies." See Mathews and Hamilton, "Delayed Childbearing," for the average age of US women at birth of their first child. Our figures in all likelihood underestimate early

and unwed parenthood because we did not purposefully ask about either in our park survey interviews.

10. Fischer, "Ever-More Rooted Americans," explains that while residential mobility actually declined in the latter half of the twentieth century, a higher rate of mobility endured for young people in their twenties, representing the pattern of leaving their parents' home and moving toward forming an independent household. Goldscheider and Goldscheider, "Whose Nest?"; and Goldscheider, Thornton, and Young-DeMarco, "A Portrait of the Nest-Leaving Process," describe patterns of leaving the natal home among early adults in the 1980s—the era during which many of our study parents would have been moving out on their own for the first time. The authors indicate that residential independence is often a gradual process in which intermediate steps include moves back into and out of the family home.

11. Stack, *All Our Kin,* documents the same circular support among urban African American families as "what goes round comes round," 32.

12. See Lareau, *Unequal Childhoods*, 81.

13. "Doubling up" refers to the practice of often temporarily moving in with kin or friends in times of housing need. Cohabitation refers to a more permanent coresidential situation. While doubling up has long been documented as a self-help strategy used by lower-income households, the intergenerational trend we note is perhaps evidence of the persistence of working-poor status across generations, with each generation seemingly "just making it."

6. YOUTH AND TRAILER-PARK LIFE

1. Settersten, "Becoming an Adult," lists the "Big Five" traditional markers of a successful transition to adulthood as leaving home, finishing school, getting a job, getting married, and having children. Our study families defined success in adulthood as aligned with these markers.

2. The Housing Assistance Council in its 2012 report *Taking Stock* states that nationally, more than 2.3 million households reside in rural mobile home parks. The number 5 million represents our best approximation of the total number of children under the age of eighteen living in rural mobile home parks.

3. Eccles et al., "Motivational and Achievement Pathways."

4. Bryant, "The Neighborhood Walk."

5. Elder and Conger, *Children of the Land.*

6. Rubin, Bukowski, and Parker, "Peer Interactions"; Brown and Klute, "Friends, Cliques and Crowds"; Horn, "Adolescents' Reasoning about Exclusion."

7. Benson, *Parent, Teacher, Mentor, Friend.*

8. Burton and Jarrett, "In the Mix Yet in the Margins," argue for the importance of including the perspectives of children and adolescents in neighborhood research. We found this guidance invaluable and carefully developed strategies to engage the voices of young people.

9. See Bryant, *The Neighborhood Walk.*

10. Furstenberg et al., *Managing to Make It,* used a framework that considers developmental outcomes across social, academic, and behavioral domains. Elder and Conger, *Children of the Land,* use social and academic competence as well positive self-appraisal and the avoidance of problem behaviors as indicative of successful development among rural youth in the Iowa Project.

11. See Howell, *Hard Living on Clay Street.*

12. We employ a categorical analysis approach often used in sociology. Our categories, like sociological "ideal types," allow us to classify youth as flourishing, steady, or

floundering according to the presence of distinct characteristics. This approach then allowed us to identify developmental experiences associated with each classification or category.

13. Williams and Kornblum, *Growing up Poor,* refer to successful children in the urban ghetto as "Superkids," 15. These young achievers stand out among their urban peers as successful despite having endured hardship such as the loss of a parent due to a drug conviction and early death or divorce.

14. *New York Times, Class Matters,* estimates that only one in four young people experiences social mobility. Our distribution estimates that one in five trailer-park children and only one in six trailer-park youth are headed toward social mobility.

15. See Malchiodi, *Understanding Children's Art.*

16. See Bryant, *The Neighborhood Walk.*

17. See Malchiodi, *Understanding Children's Art.*

18. Masten, "Ordinary Magic," includes the development of competence or the accomplishment of age-salient developmental tasks as central to the conceptualization of positive adaptation and resilience. In middle childhood successful adaptation to the neighborhood is expected for successful development. Eccles et al., "Motivational and Achievement Pathways," assert that a sense of competence stems from positive experiences in both school and the neighborhood at this age. Negative experiences or the failure to develop a sense of competence has long-term implications for development.

19. This pattern of limiting exposure to risks and linking children to resources parallels that documented by urban neighborhood-effects researchers. Jarrett, "Worlds of Development," for example, noted how African American mothers in a low-income area of Chicago restricted children's exposure to neighborhood risks while simultaneously bridging connections to resources outside the immediate neighborhood.

20. Brodksy, "Resilient Single Mothers," shows how resilient single mothers in neighborhoods with more risks than resources define the neighborhood in negative ways to essentially protect their children. Our findings show how in the context of these rural trailer parks, where perhaps the level of risk is diminished, such protective strategies actually inhibit children's positive development in middle childhood.

21. See Bateson, *The Double Bind.*

22. Our findings about the importance of individual characteristics match well the findings of resilience researchers. Shiner and Masten, "Childhood Personality as a Harbinger," for example, assert that personality traits such as childhood conscientiousness, agreeableness, openness, and lower neuroticism are characteristics shared by children who display resilience. See also Werner and Smith, *Overcoming the Odds.*

23. See MacTavish and Salamon, "Pathways of Youth Development."

24. Community-effects researchers—including Elder and Conger, *Children of the Land,* and Furstenberg et al., *Managing to Make It*—emphasize how conventional peers and adult role models serve to buffer children from risks while engagement in activities like meaningful work, community service, and organized sports works to promote positive aspects of development.

25. Elder and Conger, *Children of the Land,* in particular emphasize the value of small-town resources for promoting positive youth development among rural Iowa farm youth. Carr and Kefalas, *Hollowing Out the Middle,* also describe the rich, collective investment offered small-town youth. Both show how these youth, when incorporated into the social networks of town, are essentially cultivated for success by the community at large.

26. Elder and Conger, *Children of the Land.*

27. Furstenberg et al. in *Managing to Make It* include a similar assessment of problem behaviors tied to narrowed life chances.

28. This perspective is in keeping with the rich body of community effects research, namely, in urban contexts beginning with Wilson, *The Truly Disadvantaged*. Also see Leventhal and Brooks-Gunn, "The Neighborhoods They Live In," and Sampson, *Great American City*.

7. REFORMING THE MOBILE HOME INDUSTRIAL COMPLEX

1. See Environmental and Energy Study Institute, *High-Performance Manufactured Housing*, 3, for a discussion of operating costs.

2. See Centers for Disease Control and Prevention and U.S. Department of Housing and Urban Development, *Safety and Health in Manufactured Structures*.

3. Environmental and Energy Study Institute, "High-Performance Manufactured Housing," 7.

4. Ibid.

5. Ibid, 6.

6. Ibid.

7. Polito, "Upwardly Mobile Homes."

8. Environmental and Energy Study Institute, "High-Performance Manufactured Housing," 6.

9. Govtrack.us, "H.R. 1749 (111th): Energy Efficient Manufactured Housing Act of 2009." https://www.govtrack.us/congress/bills/111/hr1749.

10. National Consumer Law Center, "Manufactured Housing Resource Guide."

11. Next Steps, "About Next Steps."

12. Environmental and Energy Study Institute, "High-Performance Manufactured Housing," 8.

13. Jewell, "Raising the Floor, Raising the Roof," 12.

14. Ibid.

15. Information about the implementation of the Manufactured Housing Institute Act is found at http://www.mtgprofessor.com/A%2020Purchasing%20a%20House/implementation_of_mhi_act_of_2000.htm.

16. See Wagner and Baker, "Minorities Exploited," for a definition of predatory lending.

17. Ibid.; also see Baker and Wagner, "The Mobile Home Trap."

18. MacTavish, Ziebarth, and George, "Housing in Rural America."

19. Housing Assistance Council, "Rural Mortgage Activity."

20. Ibid.

21. Ibid.

22. Federal Housing Finance Agency, "News Release: FHFA Issues Final Rule on Fannie Mae and Freddie Mac Duty to Serve Underserved Markets."

23. Ibid.

24. Rivlin, "How Wall Street Defanged Dodd-Frank."

25. Manufactured Housing Institute, "MHI Action Alert."

26. Ibid.

27. For example, the Florida Department of Motor Vehicles and Highway Safety provides the following online mobile home buyer guide: http://www.hsmv.state.fl.us/mobilehome/mobile1.html#2.

28. Public Policy Institute of the American Association of Retired Persons and National Consumer Law Center, *Shifting the Balance of Power*.

29. See, for example, Tremblay and Collins, *Buying Your First Home*.

30. National Consumer Law Center, "Manufactured Housing Resource Guide."

31. Ibid.

32. Ibid.

33. Ibid.

34. Ibid.

35. Rivlin, *Broke.*

36. Bradley, "Manufactured Housing Park Cooperatives."

37. Manufactured Housing Institute, "MHI Action Alert."

38. For more on Oregon's licensing of park owners/managers see http://www.oregon laws.org/ors/90.734.

39. Vermont Law Help, "Mobile Home Park Lot Rent Increases."

40. Sessions, "Manufactured Housing Comes of Age."

41. Wiener and Thompson, "The Role of Nonprofit Organizations."

42. Bradley, "Manufactured Housing Park Cooperatives."

43. Ward, French, and Giraud, "Resident Ownership."

44. Gorenstein, "Home Sweet Mobile Home."

45. Bradley, "Manufactured Housing Park Cooperatives."

46. Sessions, "Manufactured Housing Comes of Age."

47. Ibid.; Minard and Normandin, *Home Loans Matter.*

48. Bradley, "Manufactured Housing Park Cooperatives."

49. Ibid.

50. Ibid.

51. Bradley, "Gaining Ground."

52. Bradley, "Manufactured Housing Park Cooperatives"; Public Policy Institute of the American Associate of Retired Persons (AARP) and National Consumer Law Center, *Shifting the Balance of Power;* Housing Assistance Council, *Moving Home.*

53. MacTavish, Eley, and Salamon, "Housing Vulnerability"; MacTavish, "Wrong Side of the Tracks."

54. Gass, "Frontier Housing."

55. Charles Becker, personal communication to authors, April 22, 2016.

56. MacTavish, "Wrong Side of the Tracks."

57. MacTavish and Salamon, "Pathways of Youth Development."

58. MacTavish, "Creating Inclusive Classrooms"; Benson, *Parent, Teacher, Mentor.*

CONCLUSION

1. See Stack, *All Our Kin.*

2. See Burton et al., "The Role of Trust."

3. See Stack and Burton, "Kinscripts."

4. See Stack, *All Our Kin.*

5. Baldwin, *Nobody Knows My Name,* 62.

6 See Cullen, *The American Dream.* Regardless of their ethnicity, the trailer-park families share with families nationwide a housing dream central to their identity. It is how they envision family success.

7. Streitfeld and Thee-Brenan, "Despite Fears," 2011.

8. Salamon, *Newcomers to Old Towns.*

9. Hartigan, *Odd Tribes,* 1–3, 60, chap. 2.

10. Ibid., chap. 3.

11. Said, *Orientalism,* provides the classic description of "the other" concept.

12. Salamon, *Newcomers to Old Towns,* chap. 4.

13. See Goad, *Redneck Manifesto;* Wray, *Not Quite White;* Isenberg, *White Trash.*

14. Wray and Newitz, *White Trash,* John Waters quoted in first line of introduction.

15. See Goffman, *Stigma;* Link and Phelan, "Conceptualizing Stigma."

16. Mitchell, "In over Our Heads," describes fraud and misrepresentation in sales of manufactured homes.

17. Ibid. Housing Assistance Council, *Moving Home*, 30, describes "discriminatory barriers" to development of trailer parks.

18. Putnam, *Bowling Alone*.

19. See Falk, *Rooted in Place*.

20. See Duncan, *Worlds Apart*; Pew Charitable Trusts, *Pursuing the American Dream*.

21. See Isenberg, *White Trash*, for a historical discussion of class and issues of inferiority from the perspective of poor whites. Reed, *Black Girl*, a biography of a black woman in her seventies raised in Tennessee, provides several derogatory terms used by blacks to express their looking down on poor whites in the late 1930s (e.g., "hunky cracker," 19, and "hillbillies," 65).

22. Duncan, *Worlds Apart*; Sampson, *Great American City*.

23. Pew Charitable Trusts, *Pursuing the American Dream*, 2: "Forty-three percent of Americans raised in the bottom quintile remain stuck in the bottom as adults [thus 53% do not], and 70 percent remain below the middle [thus 30% or fewer than one in three do not]." "Only 4 percent of those raised in the bottom quintile make it all the way to the top as adults, confirming that the 'rags-to-riches' story is more often found in Hollywood than in reality."

24. Stiglitz, "Equal Opportunity, Our National Myth." See also Dadush et al., *Inequality in America*, for a thorough discussion about the growing concentration of income in the United States that inhibits equal opportunity. Reich, *Saving Capitalism*, 115–42, documents how the numbers of working poor have increased and social mobility has declined.

25. A 2012 online survey of 30,600 people, carried out by the American Payroll Association, found that 68 percent reported living paycheck to paycheck, which is explained somewhat by their considering as essential expenses what used to be luxuries—for example, cable TV and a mobile phone. http://www.huffingtonpost.com/2012/09/20/living-paycheck-to-paycheck_n_1899685.html.

APPENDIX A

1. Basic qualitative methodology texts provide the rationale for a controlled comparison study: Patton, *Qualitative Evaluation*; Denzin, *The Research Act*; and Berg, *Qualitative Research Methods*.

2. For the ranking of states like New Mexico and North Carolina, which are in the top ten of states with the proportion of housing in mobile homes, see U.S. Census Bureau, "Structural and Occupancy Characteristics." Also see Geoghegan, "Why Do So Many Americans Live in Mobile Homes?"

3. See MacTavish, "Wrong Side of the Tracks," for a discussion about rental trailer parks in rural Oregon.

4. Patton, *Qualitative Evaluation*, describes how participant observation is a mainstay of anthropological fieldwork methods. Mitchell Duneier's *Slim's Table* provides an accessible explanation for conducting participant observation.

5. See Emerson, Fretz, and Shaw, *Writing Ethnographic Fieldnotes*. For the senior author's approach to qualitative methods, see Salamon, "Farming and Community"; *Prairie Patrimony*, 257–64; *Newcomers to Old Towns*, app. B; and "Describing the Community."

6. Denzin, *The Research Act*, thoroughly examines triangulation as a process for obtaining research validity.

7. Oscar Lewis in the introduction to his 1965 book *La Vida* described interviewing poor families in Puerto Rico by asking about how they acquired every possession in their homes. It is a useful technique we employed for mobile home families. For example, large-screen television sets were typically Christmas gifts.

8. Patton, *Qualitative Evaluation*, provides details for conducting focus groups as a method for evaluation of findings and testing them with informants. Duneier, *Slim's Table*, suggests strategies for checking the validity of findings.

9. See Burton, "One Step Forward and Two Steps Back," and Leventhal and Brookes-Gunn, "The Neighborhoods They Live In."

10. Leventhal and Brookes-Gunn, "The Neighborhoods They Live In," discuss the divergence among child development scholars regarding just when one stage begins and another ends.

11. See Antonucci, Sherman, and Vandewater, "Measures of Social Support."

12. See Fiese, *Family Routines and Rituals*; Salamon, "Farming and Community."

13. Bryant, "The Neighborhood Walk," is the source for the technique of using a neighborhood walk with children to understand their unique world.

14. The anthropological concept of rich, thick data is drawn from the classic Clifford Geertz essay "Thick Description." Other useful qualitative data sources are Denzin, *The Research Act*; Agar, "Toward an Ethnographic Language"; Patton, *Qualitative Evaluation*; and Salamon, "Describing the Community."

15. For good sources of approaches to detailing the social environments of children and youth see Burton and Jarrett, "In the Mix Yet in the Margins"; Leventhal and Brookes-Gunn, "The Neighborhoods They Live In"; Denzin, *The Research Act*; Larson, "Toward a Psychology of Positive Youth Development"; Larson and Richards, "Daily Companionship"; and Antonucci, Sherman, and Vandewater, "Measures of Social Support."

16. Denzin, *The Research Act*, discusses the concept of meaning for objects, which is a central idea in symbolic interaction theory.

Bibliography

Adam, Emma K., and P. Lindsay Chase-Lansdale. "Home Sweet Home(s): Parental Separations, Residential Moves, and Adjustment Problems in Low-Income Adolescent Girls." *Developmental Psychology* 38 (2002): 792–805.

Adams, James Truslow. *The American Dream.* Garden City, NJ: Garden City Books, 1933.

Agar, Michael H. "Toward an Ethnographic Language." *American Anthropologist* 84, no. 3 (1982): 779–95.

Aiken, Charles S. "Race as a Factor in Municipal Underbounding." *Annals of the Association of American Geographers* 77 (1987): 564–79.

Allen, George. "Community Tips." *The Journal,* February 1998.

Aman, Destiny D., and Brent Yarnal. "Home Sweet Mobile Home? Benefits and Challenges of Mobile Home Ownership in Rural Pennsylvania." *Applied Geography* 30, no.1 (2009): 84–95.

American Automobile Association. Digest of Motor Laws, "Titles for Mobile Homes." 2012. http://drivinglaws.aaa.com/laws/titles-for-mobile-homes/.

American Community Survey Office, U.S. Census Bureau. "2005-2007 American Community Survey 3-Year Summary File: Technical Documentation." http://demographics.texas.gov/Resources/ACS/2007/SF/TechDoc/ACS_2005-2007_3-Year_SF_Tech_Doc.pdf.

American Housing Survey. *The American Community Survey Challenges and Opportunities for HUD.* Final report. Department of Housing and Urban Development, 2002. http://www.huduser.org/Publications/pdf/ACS%5F FINAL%5FREPORT.pdf.

———. *Introductory Housing Characteristics—All Housing Units.* Current Housing Reports, Series H150/0, Table 1A-1, 2001. www.census.gov/hhes/www/housing/ahs/ahs01_2000wts/tab1a1.html.

Anderson, Cynthia D., and Chir-Yuan Weng. "Regional Variation of Women in Low-Wage Work across Rural Communities." In *Economic Restructuring and Family Well-Being in Rural America,* edited by Kristin E. Smith and Ann R. Tickamyer, 215–30. University Park: Penn State University Press, 2011. Also available at http://www.ers.usda.gov/topics/rural-economy-population/rural-poverty-well-being/geography-of-poverty.aspx.

Antonucci, Toni, Aurora Sherman, and Elizabeth Vandewater. "Measures of Social Support and Caregiver Burden." *Generations* 21 (1997): 48–51.

Apgar, William, Allegra Calder, Michael Collins, and Mark Duda. *An Examination of Manufactured Housing as a Community—An Asset-Building Strategy.* Joint Center for Housing Studies of Harvard University, 2002. http://www.jchs.harvard.edu/research/publications/examination-manufactured-housing-community-and-asset-building-strategy.

Argonne National Laboratory. Ask a Scientist General Science Archive, "Tornadoes and Mobile Homes." 2010. http://www.newton.dep.anl.gov/askasci/gen99/gen99010.htm.

Aschenbrenner, Joyce. *Lifelines: Black Families in Chicago.* New York: Holt, Rinehart & Winston, 1975.

Ayto, John. *Twentieth Century Words: The Story of New Words in English over the Last 100 Years.* New York: Oxford University Press, 1999.

Baldwin, James A. *Nobody Knows My Name.* New York: Dial Press, 1961.

Ballard, Jane E., Thomas Koepsell, and Fredrick Rivera. "Association of Smoking and Alcohol Drinking with Residential Fire Injuries." *American Journal of Epidemiology* 135, no. 1 (1992): 26–34.

Bateson, Gregory. *The Double Bind.* Chicago: University of Chicago Press, 1972.

Baumgartner, Mary P. *The Moral Order of a Suburb.* New York: Oxford University Press, 1988.

Beale, Calvin L. "The Negro in American Agriculture." In *The American Negro Reference Book,* edited by John P. Davis, 161–204. Englewood Cliffs, NJ: Prentice-Hall, 1966.

Becker, Charles, and Ashley Yea. "The Value of Manufactured Housing Communities: A Dual-Ownership Model." Working Paper No. 196, Economic Research Initiatives at Duke University, 2015. http://ssrn.com/abstract=2681222.

Becker, Charles M., with Caitlin Gorback. *Trailer Park Economics.* Philadelphia: University of Pennsylvania Press, forthcoming.

Becker, Howard C. *Outsiders: Studies in the Sociology of Deviance.* New York: Free Press, 1963.

Belden, Joseph N., and Robert J. Wiener, eds. *Housing in Rural America: Building Affordable and Inclusive Communities.* Thousand Oaks, CA: Sage, 1999.

Bell, Michael. *Childerley: Nature and Morality in a Country Village.* Chicago: University of Chicago Press, 1994.

——. "The Fruit of Difference: The Rural-Urban Continuum as a System of Identity." *Rural Sociology* 57, no.1 (1992): 65–82.

Benson, Janet E. "Good Neighbors: Ethnic Relations in Garden City Trailer Courts." *Urban Anthropology* 19 (1990): 361–86.

Benson, Peter, L. *All Kids Are Our Kids: What Communities Must Do to Raise Caring and Responsible Children and Adolescents.* 2nd ed. San Francisco: Jossey-Bass, 2006.

——. *Parent, Teacher, Mentor, Friend: How Every Adult Can Change Kids' Lives.* Minneapolis: Search Institute Press, 2010.

Berenson, Alex. "A Boom Built upon Sand, Gone Bust: Trailer Owners and Conseco are Haunted by Risky Loans." *New York Times,* November 25, 2001.

Berg, Bruce. *Qualitative Research Methods for the Social Sciences.* 6th ed. New York: Pearson Education, 2007.

Berger, Kathleen Stassen. *The Developing Person through the Life Span.* New York: Worth, 1998.

Berubé, Allan, and Florence Berubé. "Sunset Trailer Park." In *White Trash: Race and Class in America,* edited by Jim Goad, 15–41. New York: Routledge, 1998.

Billingsley, Andrew, and Cleopatra Howard Caldwell. "The Church, the Family, and the School in the African American Community." *Journal of Negro Education* 60, no. 3 (1991): 427–40.

Black, Laurel Johnson. "Stupid Rich Bastards." In *Critical White Studies: Looking behind the Mirror,* edited by Richard Delgado and Jean Stefanic, 387–94. Philadelphia: Temple University Press, 1997.

Boehm, Thomas P., and Alan Schlottmann. "Is Manufactured Housing a Good Alternative for Low-Income Households? Evidence from the American Housing Survey." *Cityscape: A Journal of Policy Development and Research* 10, no. 2 (2008): 159–224.

Booth, Alan, and Ann C. Crouter, eds. *Does It Take a Village? Community Effects on Children, Adolescents, and Families.* Mahwah, NJ: Lawrence Erlbaum, 2001.

Bradley, Paul. "Gaining Ground." *ShelterforceOnline*, no. 149 (2007). National Housing Institute. http://www.nhi.org/online/issues/149/gainingground.html.

——. "Manufactured Housing Park Cooperatives in New Hampshire: An Enterprising Solution to the Complex Problems of Owning a Home on Rented Land." *Cooperative Housing Journal*, 2000, 22–32.

——. "No Longer a Secret: The Manufactured Housing Sector Can Create Long Term Value for Homeowners." *Rural Voices* 8, no. 2 (2003): 16–18.

Brady, David, Andrew Fullerton, and Jennifer Moren Cross. "More Than Just Nickels and Dimes: A Cross-National Analysis of Working Poverty in Affluent Democracies." *Social Problems* 57, no.4 (2010): 559–85.

Brodsky, Ann E. "Resilient Single Mothers in Risky Neighborhoods: Negative Psychological Sense of Community." *Journal of Community Psychology* 24, no. 3 (1996): 347–63.

Brooks-Gunn, Jeanne, Greg J. Duncan, and J. Lawrence Aber, eds. *Neighborhood Poverty.* Vol. 2, *Policy Implications in Studying Neighborhoods.* New York: Russell Sage Foundation, 1997.

Brown, B. Bradford, and Christa Klute, "Friends, Cliques and Crowds." In *Handbook of Adolescence,* edited by Gerald R. Adams and Michael D. Berzonsky, 330–48. Malden, MA: Blackwell, 2006.

Brown, David L., and Laslo Kulcsar. "Household Economic Behavior in Post-Socialist Hungary." *Rural Sociology* 66, no. 2 (2001): 157–80.

Brown, David L., and Marlene Lee. "Persisting Inequality between Metropolitan and Nonmetropolitan America: Implications for Theory and Policy." In *A Nation Divided: Diversity, Inequality and Community in America,* edited by Phyllis Moen, Henry Walker, and Donna Dempster-McClain, 187–207. Ithaca, NY: Cornell University Press, 1999.

Brown, David L., and Kai A. Schafft. *Rural People and Communities in the 21st Century: Resilience and Transformation.* Cambridge: Polity Press, 2011.

Brunker, Mike. "Are FEMA Trailers 'Toxic Tin Cans'?" 2006. MSNBC. http://www.msnbc.com/id/14011193/from/ET.

Bryant, Brenda. "The Neighborhood Walk: Sources of Support in Middle Childhood." *Monographs of the Society for Research in Child Development* 50, no. 3 (1986), serial no. 210.

Burton, Linda M. "Childhood Adultification in Economically Disadvantaged Families: A Conceptual Model." *Family Relations* 56 (2007): 329–45.

——. "One Step Forward and Two Steps Back: Neighborhoods and Adolescent Development." In *Does It Take a Village? Community Effects on Children, Adolescents, and Families,* edited by Alan Booth and Ann C. Crouter, 149–60. Mahwah, NJ: Lawrence Erlbaum, 2001.

Burton, Linda M., Eduardo Bonilla-Silva, Victor Ray, Rose Buckelew, and Elizabeth Hordge Freeman. "Critical Race Theories, Colorism, and the Decade's Research on Families of Color." *Journal of Marriage and Family* 72, no. 3 (2010): 440–59.

Burton, Linda M., Andrew Cherlin, Donna-Marie Winn, Angela Estacion, and Clara Holder-Taylor. "The Role of Trust in Low-Income Mothers' Intimate Unions." *Journal of Marriage and Family* 71 (December 2009): 1107–27.

Burton, Linda M., Raymond Garrett-Peters, and John Major Eason. "Morality, Identity, and Mental Health in Rural Ghettos." In *Communities, Neighborhoods, and Health: Social Disparities in Health and Health Care.* Vol. 1, edited by

Linda M. Burton, Susan P. Kemp, Man Chui Leung, Stephen A. Matthews, and David T. Takeuchi, 91–110. New York: Springer, 2011.

——. *Morality, Identity, and Mental Health in Rural Ghettos.* NY: Springer, 2011.

Burton, Linda M., and Cecily R. Hardesty. "Low-Income Mothers as 'Othermothers' to Their Romantic Partners' Children: Women's Coparenting in Multiple Partner Fertility Relationships." *Family Process* 51, no. 3 (2012): 343–59.

Burton, Linda M., and Robin Jarrett. "In the Mix Yet in the Margins: The Place of Families in Urban Neighborhood and Child Development Research." *Journal of Family Relations* 62, no. 4 (2000):1114–35.

Burton, Linda M., and M. Belinda Tucker. "Romantic Unions in an Era of Uncertainty: A Post-Moynihan Perspective on African American Women and Marriage." *Annals of the American Academy of Political and Social Science* 62 (2009): 132–48.

Cahn, Naomi, and June Carbone. *Red Families v. Blue Families: Legal Polarization and the Creation of Culture.* New York: Oxford University Press, 2010.

Carr, Patrick, and Maria J. Kefalas. *Hollowing Out the Middle: The Rural Brain Drain and What It Means for America.* Boston: Beacon Press, 2009.

Carter, Anne O., Margaret E. Millson, and David E. Allan. "Epidemiologic Study of Deaths and Injuries Due to Tornadoes." *American Journal of Epidemiology* 130, no. 1 (1989).

Caughy Margaret, and P. J. O'Campo. "Neighborhood Poverty, Social Capital, and the Cognitive Development of African American Preschoolers." *American Journal of Community Psychology* 237, no. 1–2 (2006): 141–54.

Center on Budget and Policy Priorities. "Policy Basics: Introduction to Public Housing." January 25, 2013. http://www.cbpp.org/cms/index.cfm?fa=view&id=2528.

Centers for Disease Control and Prevention and U.S. Department of Housing and Urban Development. *Safety and Health in Manufactured Structures.* Atlanta: U.S. Department of Health and Human Services, 2011. https://www.cdc.gov/healthyhomes/manufactured_structures.pdf.

Chatters, Linda, Robert Taylor, and Rukmalie Jayakody. "Fictive Kinship Relations in Black Extended Families." *Journal of Comparative Family Studies* 25 (1994): 297–312.

Childress, Herb. *Landscapes of Betrayal, Landscapes of Joy.* Albany: State University of New York Press, 2000.

Coleman, James S. *Foundations of Social Capital Theory.* Cambridge, MA: Belknap Press of Harvard University Press, 1990.

——. "The Rational Reconstruction of Society." *American Sociological Review* 58 (1993): 1–15.

——. "Social Capital in the Creation of Human Capital." *American Journal of Sociology* 94 (1988): S95–S121.

Coleman, James S., and Thomas Hoffer. *Public and Private High Schools: The Impact of Community.* New York: Basic Books, 1987.

Collins, Michael. "Rural America's Housing of Choice? Exploring Manufactured Housing's Growth Role." *Rural Voices* 8, no. 2 (2003): 2–5.

Consumer Reports. "Dream Home . . . or Nightmare?" February 1998, 30–35. http://www.consumersunion.org/mh/docs/01tips/000799.html.

Consumers Union. "Manufactured Homeowners Who Rent Lots Lack Security of Basic Tenants Rights." Southwest Regional Office Report. February 2001. http://www.consumersuntion.org/other/home/manuf2.htm.

———. "Manufactured Home Warranty Tips." 2013. https://consumersunion.org/wp-content/uploads/2013/04/warrantytips1.pdf.

Countrywide Homes. "We House America Initiative." 2001. PR Newswire. http://www.prnewswire.com/news-releases/countrywide-expands-commitment-to-1-trillion-in-home-loans-to-minority-and-lower-income-borrowers-54027497.html.

Cramer, James C., and Katrina Bell-McDonald. "Kin Support and Family Stress: Two Sides to Early, Childbearing and Support Networks." *Human Organization* 55, no. 2 (1996): 160–69.

Cromartie, John, and Shawn Bucholtz, "Defining the 'Rural' in Rural America." Amber Waves. June 1, 2008. USDA Economic Research Service.http://ers.usda.gov/amber-waves/2008-june/defining-the-"rural"-in-rural-america.aspx#.V9FkrDuc9YM.

Crouter, Ann C., Megan E. Baril, Kelly D. Davis, and Susan M. McHale. "Processes Linking Social Class and Racial Socialization in African American Dual-Earner Families." *Journal of Marriage and Family 70,* no. 5 (2008): 1311–25.

Cullen, Jim. *The American Dream: A Short History of an Idea That Shaped a Nation.* New York: Oxford University Press, 2003.

Dadush, Uri, Kemal Derviş, Sarah P. Milsom, and Bennett Stancil. *Inequality in America Facts, Trends, and International Perspectives.* Washington, DC: Brookings Institution Press, 2012.

Darlin, Damon. "Vet Bills and the Priceless Pet: What's a Practical Owner to Do?" Your Money. *New York Times*, May 13, 2006.

Davis-Brown, Karen, Sonya Salamon, and Catherine A. Surra. "Economic and Social Factors in Mate Selection: An Ethnographic Analysis of an Agricultural Community." *Journal of Marriage and Family* 49, no. 1 (1987): 41–55.

Dean, Eddie. "Paradise, Yeah." *Talk,* September 1999, 133–38.

Denzin, Norman K. *The Research Act.* New York: Basic Books, 1978.

Desmond, Matthew. *Evicted: Poverty and Profit in the American City.* New York: Crown, 2016.

Devine, Jennifer. "Hardworking Newcomers and Generations of Poverty: Discourse in Central Washington State." *Antipode,* 2006, 953–76.

Dickstein, Carla, Lance George, Theresa Singleton, and Hannah Jones. "Subprime and Predatory Lending in Rural America: Mortgage Lending Practices That Can Trap Low-Income Rural People." *Carsey Institute Policy Brief* 4 (2006): 1–10.

Dougherty, Molly C. *Becoming a Woman in Rural Black Culture.* New York: Holt, Rinehart, and Winston, 1978.

Drury, Margaret. *Mobile Homes: The Unrecognized Revolution in American Housing.* New York: Praeger, 1972.

Duda, Mark, and Eric S. Belsky. "Anatomy of the Low-Income Homeownership Boom in the 1990's." In *Low-Income Homeownership: Examining the Unexamined Goal,* edited by Nicolas Retsinas and Eric S. Belsky, 15–63. Washington, DC: Brookings Institution Press, 2002.

Duncan, Cynthia M., ed. *Rural Poverty in America.* New York: Auburn House, 1992.

———. *Worlds Apart: Why Poverty Persists in Rural America.* New Haven, CT: Yale University Press, 1999.

Duneier, Mitchell. *Slim's Table: Race, Respectability and Masculinity.* Chicago: University of Chicago Press, 1992.

Eccles, Jacquelynne, Robert Roeser, Mina Vida, Jennifer Fredricks, and Allan Wigfield. "Motivational and Achievement Pathways through Middle Childhood." In *Child Psychology: A Handbook of Contemporary Issues.* 2nd ed., edited by Lawrence Balter and Catherine S. Tamis-LeMonda, 325–55. New York: Psychology Press, 2006.

Edelstein, Michael. *Contaminated Communities*. Boulder, CO: Westview Press, 2003.

Edwards, Margie. "We're Decent People: Constructing and Managing Family Identity in Rural Working-Class Communities." *Journal of Marriage and Family* 66 (2004): 515–25.

Effinger, Anthony, and Katherine Burton. "Trailer Parks Lure Wall Street Investors Looking for Double-Wide Returns." *Bloomberg News*, April 9, 2014. http://www.bloomberg.com/news/2014-04-10/trailer-parks-lure-investors-pursuing-double-wide-returns.html.

Ehrenreich, Barbara. *Nickel and Dimed: On (Not) Getting By in America*. New York: Henry Holt, 2001.

Elder, Glen Jr., and Rand Conger. *Children of the Land*. Chicago: University of Chicago Press, 2000.

Eley, Michelle. "Ties That Bind: The Informal Social Networks of African-American Mobile-Home Park Families." PhD diss., University of Illinois at Urbana-Champaign, 2005.

Emerson, Robert, Rachel Fretz, and Linda Shaw. *Writing Ethnographic Fieldnotes*. Chicago: University of Chicago Press, 1995.

Environmental and Energy Study Institute. Issue Brief, June 26, 2011. "High-Performance Manufactured Housing." http://www.eesi.org/files/manufactured_housing_072611.pdf.

Erikson, Kai T. *Everything in Its Path: Destruction of Community in the Buffalo Creek Flood*. New York: Simon and Schuster, 1976.

Equity LifeStyle Properties. http://www.equitylifestyle.com.

Eschbach, Karl, Glenn V. Ostir, Kushang V. Patel, Kyriakos S. Markides, and James S. Goodwin. "Neighborhood Context and Mortality among Older Mexican Americans: Is There a Barrio Advantage?" *American Journal of Public Health* 94, no. 10 (2004): 1807–12.

Eskow, Richard. "The Middle Class and Working Poor's Lifelong Losing Game—In 10 Slides." *Huffington Post*, September 16, 2014.

Evans, Gary W., Edith Chen, Gregory Miller, and Teresa Seeman. "How Poverty Gets under the Skin: A Life Course Perspective." In *The Oxford Handbook of Poverty and Child Development*, edited by Valarie Maholmes and Rosalind King, 13–36. New York: Oxford University Press, 2012.

Falk, William W. *Rooted in Place: Family and Belonging in a Southern Black Community*. New Brunswick, NJ: Rutgers University Press, 2004.

Falk, William W., Michael D. Schulman, and Ann R. Tickamyer, eds. *Communities of Work: Rural Restructuring in Local and Global Contexts*. Athens: Ohio University Press, 2003.

Federal Housing Finance Administration. "News Release: FHFA Final Rule on Fannie Mae and Freddy Mac Duty to Serve Underserved Markets." December 13, 2016. https://www.fhfa.gov/Media/PublicAffairs/Pages/FHFA-Issues-Final-Rule-on-Fannie-Mae-and-Freddie-Mac-Duty-to-Serve-Underserved-Markets.aspx.

Fiese, Barbara H. *Family Routines and Rituals*. New Haven: Yale University Press, 2006.

Fiese, Barbara H., and Marlene Schwartz. "Reclaiming the Family Table: Mealtimes and Child Health and Wellbeing." *Society for Research in Child Development Social Policy Report* 33, no. 4 (2008): 3–9.

Firestone, David. "Governor's Mansion Is a Triple-Wide." *Little Rock Journal*, July 19, 2000.

Fischer, Claude. "Ever-More Rooted Americans." *City and Community* 1, no. 2 (2002): 177–98.

Fitchen, Janet M. *Endangered Spaces, Enduring Places: Change, Identity, and Survival in Rural America*. Boulder, CO: Westview Press, 1991.

——. *Poverty in Rural America: A Case Study.* Boulder, CO: Westview Press, 1981.

——. "Why Rural Poverty Is Growing Worse: Similar Causes in Diverse Settings." In *The Changing American Countryside: Rural People and Places,* edited by Emery Castle, 247–67. Lawrence: University Press of Kansas, 1995.

Fogarty, Mark. "Manufactured Housing Suffers Worst Decline of any Mortgage Niche." *National Mortgage News,* 2014. http://www.nationalmortgagenews.com/news/origination/manufactured-housing-suffers-worst-decline-of-any-mortgage-niche-1042023-1.html.

Foremost Insurance Group. "Manufactured Homes: The Market Facts 2008." 2008. http://cp.foremost.com/market-facts-2008/9001479_MH_NFO_08_lores.pdf.

Forry, Nicole D., and Susan K. Walker. "Child Care in Rural America." In *Economic Restructuring and Family Well-Being in Rural America,* edited by Kristin E. Smith and Ann R. Tickamyer, 256–72. University Park: Penn State University Press, 2011.

Fortune. "Countryside Homes Mines the Subprime Mortgage Market." September 15, 2003. http://archive.fortune.com/magazines/fortune/fortune_archive/2003/09/15/349151/index.htm.

Fowler, Robert Booth. *The Dance with Community: The Contemporary Debate in American Political Thought.* Lawrence: University Press of Kansas, 1990.

Friedland, Roger, and Diedre Boden, eds. *NowHere: Space, Time and Modernity.* Berkeley: University of California Press, 1994.

Fry, Christine L. "The Community as a Commodity: The Age Graded Case." *Human Organization* 36, no. 2 (1977): 115–23.

Fuquay, Don. "Lending Perspectives: Doing It the Right Way." Manufactured Housing Institute. 2001. http://www.manufacturedhousing.org/lending_news/default.asp?id=1&article=16.

Furstenberg, Frank. "The Intersections of Social Class and the Transition to Adulthood." *New Direction in Child and Adolescent Development* 119 (April 2008): 1–10.

Furstenberg, Frank, Thomas D. Cook, Glen Elder, and Arnold Samaroff. *Managing to Make It.* Chicago: University of Chicago Press, 1999.

Galinksy, Ellen. *Ask the Children: What America's Children Really Think about Working Parents.* New York: William Morrow, 1999.

Gallagher, Charles A. "White Racial Formation: Into the Twenty-First Century." In *Critical White Studies: Looking behind the Mirror,* edited by Richard Delgado and Jean Stefanic, 6–11. Philadelphia: Temple University Press, 1997.

Gans, Herbert J. *The Levittowners: Ways of Life and Politics in a New Suburban Community.* New York: Vintage Books, 1967.

——. *The Urban Villagers: Group and Class in the Life of Italian-Americans.* New York: Free Press, 1962.

Garbarino, James. *Children and Families in the Social Environment.* New York: Aldine, 1982.

Garbarino, James, and Kathleen Kostelney. "Neighborhood and Community Influences on Parenting." In *Parenting: An Ecological Perspective,* edited by Tom Luster and Lynn Okagaki, 203–26. Hillsdale, NJ: Erlbaum, 1993.

Gass, Anne. "Frontier Housing: Replacement Housing with 'Manufactured Housing Done Right.'" Neighborworks America. 2009. http://neighborworks.issuelab.org/resource/frontier_housing_replacement_housing_with_manufactured_housing_done_right.

Geertz, Clifford. "Thick Description: Toward an Interpretive Theory of Culture." In *Contemporary Field Research: A Collection of Readings,* edited by Robert M. Emerson, 37–59. Prospect Park, IL: Waveland Press, 1983.

Geisler, Charles C., and Hisayoshi Mitsuda. "Mobile-Home Growth, Regulation, and Discrimination in Upstate New York." *Rural Sociology* 52, no. 4 (1987): 532–43.

Geoghegan, Tom. "Why Do So Many Americans Live in Mobile Homes?" *BBC News Magazine,* September 24, 2013. http://www.bbc.com/news/magazine-24135022.

George, Lance. "The Hidden High Costs of Mobile Homes." *Daily Yonder, Rural News,* 2015. http://www.dailyyonder.com/manufactured-housing-sales-bounce-back/2015/01/26/7695.

Gibbs, Robert, Lorin Kusmin, and John Cromartie. "Low-Skill Employment and the Changing Economy of Rural America." Economic Research Report no. 10. USDA Economic Research Service, Washington, DC, 2005.

Gibson, D. W. "America, the Unaffordable: There's a Housing Crisis Everywhere." *Nation,* April 11–18, 2016, 32–33.

Gilbert, Jess, Spencer D. Wood, and Gwen Sharp. "Who Owns the Land? Agricultural Land Ownership by Race/Ethnicity." *Rural America* 17, no. 4 (2002): 55–62. USDA Economic Research Service. http://www.ers.usda.gov/publications/ruralamerica/ra174/ra174h.pdf.

Gilroy, Paul. "Driving While Black." In *Car Cultures,* edited by Daniel Miller, 81–104. New York: Berg, 2001.

Gladwell, Malcom. "Many Katrina Victims Left New Orleans for Good: What Can We Learn from Them?" *New Yorker,* August 24, 2015. http://www.newyorker.com/magazine/2015/08/24/starting-over-dept-of-social-studies-malcolm-gladwell.

Goad, Jim. *Redneck Manifesto: How Hillbillies, Hicks and White Trash Became America's Scapegoats.* New York: Simon and Schuster, 1998.

Goffman, Erving. *Stigma: Notes on the Management of Spoiled Identity.* New York: Simon and Schuster, 1963.

Goldscheider, Claire Weiss, and Frances Goldscheider. "Whose Nest? A Two-Generational View of Leaving Home during the 1980s." *Journal of Marriage and Family,* 55, no. 4 (1993): 851–62.

Goldscheider, Frances, Arland Thornton, and Linda Young-DeMarco. "A Portrait of the Nest-Leaving Process in Early Adulthood." *Demography* 30, no. 4 (1993): 683–99.

Gorenstein, Dan. "Home Sweet Mobile Home: Co-ops Deliver on Ownership." National Public Radio, May 2, 2012. http://www.npr.org/2012/05/02/151863518/home-sweet-mobile-home-co-ops-deliver-ownership.

Greeley, Andrew. "Coleman Revisited: Religious Structures as a Source of Social Capital." *American Behavioral Scientist* 40, no. 5 (1997): 587–94.

Grier Katherine C. *Pets in America: A History.* Chapel Hill: University of North Carolina Press, 2006.

Grissim, John. *The Grissim Ratings Guide to Manufactured Homes.* Sequim, WA: Rainshadow Publications.

——. "Home Buyer's Outlook." *The Grissim Guide to Manufactured Homes and Land.* 2015. http://grissimguides.com.

Govtrack. US. "H.R. 1749 (111th): Energy Efficient Manufactured Housing Act of 2009." https://www.govtrack.us/congress/bills/111/hr1749.

Hardaway, Cecily R., and V. C. McLoyd. "Escaping Poverty and Securing Middle Class Status: How Race and Socioeconomic Status Shape Mobility Prospects for African Americans during the Transition to Adulthood." *Journal of Youth and Adolescence* 38, no. 2 (2009): 242–56.

Hart, John Fraser, Michelle J. Rhodes, and John T. Morgan. *The Unknown World of the Mobile Home.* Baltimore: Johns Hopkins University Press, 2003.

Hartigan, John Jr. *Odd Tribes: Toward a Cultural Analysis of White People.* Durham, NC: Duke University Press, 2005.

Hartup, Willard W. "The Company They Keep: Friendships and Their Developmental Significance." *Child Development* 67 (1996): 1–13.

Hartup, Willard W., and Nan Stevens. "Friendship and Adaptation in the Life Course." *Psychological Bulletin* 121 (1997): 355–70.

Healton, Cheryl, and Kathleen Nelson. "Reversal of Misfortune: Viewing Tobacco as a Social Justice Issue." *American Journal of Public Health* 186 (2004): 187–88.

Herrmann, Gretchen M. "Garage Sales Make Good Neighbors: Building Community through Neighborhood Sales." *Human Organization* 65, no. 2 (2006): 181–91.

Heskin, Allan D. *Tenants and the American Dream: Ideology and the Tenant Movement.* New York: Praeger, 1983.

Hill, Robert B. *The Strengths of African-American Families: Twenty-Five Years Later.* Lanham, MD: University Press of America, 1999.

Hochschild, Jennifer. *Facing Up to the American Dream.* Princeton, NJ: Princeton University Press, 1996.

Horn, Stacey. "Adolescents Reasoning about Exclusion from Social Groups." *Developmental Psychology* 39 (2003): 11–84.

Housing Assistance Council. "Manufactured Housing in Nonmetropolitan Areas: A Data Review." 1996. http://www.ruralhome.org/pubs/hsganalysis/manufactured/toc.htm.

———. "Manufactured Housing in Rural America" *Rural Voices* 8, no. 2 (2003): 1–18.

———. *Moving Home: Manufactured Housing in Rural America.* Report by Lance George and Milana Ball. Washington, DC: Housing Assistance Council, 2005. http://www.ruralhome.org/storage/documents/movinghome.pdf.

———. "Rural Mortgage Activity Declines. Home Purchases are Up but So Are High Cost Loans." Rural Research Note. October 2014. http://www.ruralhome.org/storage/documents/publications/rrnotes/rrn-rural-mortgages.pdf.

———. *Taking Stock: Rural People, Poverty, and Housing at the Turn of the 21st Century.* Washington, DC: Housing Assistance Council, 2002.

———. *Taking Stock: Rural People, Poverty, and Housing in the 21st Century.* Washington, DC: Housing Assistance Council, 2012.

Howell, Joseph T. *Hard Living on Clay Street: Portraits of Blue Collar Families.* 2nd ed. Garden City, NY: Anchor Press, 1991.

Howland, Jonathan, and Ralph Hingson. "Alcohol as a Risk Factor for Injuries or Death Due to Fires and Burns: Review of the Literature." *Public Health Reports* 102 (1987): 475.

Hudson, John. C. *Plains Country Towns.* Minneapolis: University of Minnesota Press, 1985.

Hummon, David M. *Commonplaces.* Albany: State University of New York Press, 1990.

Hurley, Andrew. *Diners, Bowling Alleys, and Trailer Parks: Chasing the American Dream in Postwar Consumer Culture.* New York: Basic Books, 2001.

Huss-Ashmore, Rebecca, and Carolyn Behrman. "Transitional Environments: Health and the Perception of Permanence in Urban Micro-Environments." In *Urbanism, Health and Human Biology in Industrialised Countries,* edited by Lawrence M. Schell and Stanley. J. Ulijaszek, 67–84. Cambridge: Cambridge University Press, 1999.

Hymel, Shelly, Kenneth Rubin, Lynda Rowden, and Lucy LeMare. "Children's Peer Relationships: Longitudinal Prediction of Internalizing and Externalizing Problems from Middle to Late Childhood." *Child Development* 61, no. 6 (1990): 2004–21.

Illinois General Assembly. Illinois Tie Down Act. 1991. http://www.ilga.gov/legislation/ilcs/ilcs3.asp?ActID=1243&ChapterID=21.

Isenberg, Nancy. *White Trash: The 400-Year Untold History of Class in America*. New York: Viking, 2016.

Jackson, John Brinckerhoff. *A Sense of Place: A Sense of Time*. New Haven, CT: Yale University Press. 1996.

Jackson, Kenneth T. *Crabgrass Frontier: The Suburbanization of the United States*. New York: Oxford University Press, 1985.

Jacobs, Harvey M. "Conclusion: Who Owns America?" In *Who Owns America? Social Conflict over Property Rights*, edited by Harvey M. Jacobs, 245–250. Madison: University of Wisconsin Press, 1998.

Jarrett, Robin L. "Growing Up Poor: The Family Experiences of Socially Mobile Youth in Low -Income African American Neighborhoods." *Journal of Adolescent Research* 10 (1995):111–35.

——. "Neighborhood Effects Models: A View from the Neighborhood." *Research in Community Sociology* 10 (2000): 307–25.

——. "Worlds of Development: The Experience of Low-Income, African American Youth." *Journal of Children and Poverty* 9, no. 2 (2003): 157–88.

Jarrett, Robin L., Stephanie R. Jefferson, and Jenelle N. Kelly. "Finding Community in Family: Neighborhood Effects and African-American Extended Kin Networks." *Journal of Comparative Family Studies* 41, no. 3 (2010): 299–328.

Jarosz, Lucy, and Victoria Lawson. "'Sophisticated People Versus 'Rednecks': Economic Restructuring and Class Difference in America's West." *Antipode* 34 (2002): 8–27.

Jensen, Leif, and Eric B. Jensen. "Poverty." In *Encyclopedia of Rural America: The Land and People*, edited by Gary Goreham, 774–79. Millerton, NY: Grey House Publishing, 2008.

Jewell, Kevin. *Can We Trust Information from the Manufactured Housing Association? Expected Life-Span of Manufactured Homes*. Austin, TX: Manufactured Housing Project, Consumers Union, 2001.

——. *Raising the Floor, Raising the Roof: Raising our Expectations for Manufactured Housing*. Austin, TX: Consumers Union, 2003.

Johnson, Hildegard Binder. *Order upon the Land: The U.S. Rectangular Land Survey and the Upper Mississippi Country*. New York: Oxford University Press, 1976.

Johnson, Sheila K. *Idle Haven, Community Building among the Working-Class Retired*. Berkeley: University of California Press, 1971.

Jollife, Dean. "Poverty, Process, and Place: How Sensitive is the Spatial Distribution of Poverty to Cost of Living Adjustments?" *Economic Inquiry* 44, no. 2 (2006): 296–310.

Karabell, Zachary. "End of the 'Ownership Society.'" *Newsweek*, October 20, 2008, 39.

Kasarda, John D., and Maurice Janowitz. "Community Attachment in Mass Society." *American Sociological Review* 39 (1974): 328–39.

Kaufman, Phillip and Steve M. Lutz. "Competing Forces Affect Food Prices for Low-Income Households." *Food Review*, 1997, 8–12.

Kefalas, Maria. *Working-Class Heroes: Protecting Home, Community, and Nation in a Chicago Neighborhood*. Berkeley: University of California Press, 2003.

Kemmis, Daniel. *The Good City and the Good Life: Renewing the Sense of Community*. Boston: Houghton Mifflin, 1995.

Kenny, Lorraine Delia. *Daughters of Suburbia: Growing Up White, Middle Class, and Female.* New Brunswick, NJ: Rutgers University Press, 2000.

Kilgannon, Corey. "Trailer-Park Sales Leave Residents with Single-Wides and Few Options." *New York Times,* April 18, 2007. http://www.nytimes.com/2007/04/18/nyregion/18trailer.html?pagewanted=all&_r=1&.

Kloppenburg, Jack R., and Charles C. Geisler. "The Agricultural Tenure Ladder: Agrarian Ideology and the Changing Structure of U.S. Agriculture." *Journal of Rural Studies* 1, no. 1 (1985): 59–72.

Knox, Margaret L. "Why Mobile Homeowners Want Landlords to Hit the Road." *Business and Society Review* 85 (Spring 1993): 39–42.

Komorovsky, Mira. *Blue-Collar Marriage.* 2nd ed. New York: Vintage, 1967.

Kost, Kathryn, and Stanley Henshaw. "U.S. Teenage Pregnancies, Births and Abortions, 2008: State Trends by Age, Race and Ethnicity." The Guttmacher Institute. 2013. http://www.guttmacher.org/pubs/USTPtrendsState08.pdf.

Kozol, Jonathon. *Ordinary Resurrections: Children in the Years of Hope.* New York: Crown, 2000.

Krauss, Clifford. "Rural U.S. Takes Worst Hit as Gas Tops $4 Average." *New York Times,* June 9, 2008.

Krugman, Paul. "Home Not-So-Sweet Home." *New York Times,* June 23, 2008.

Kunstler, James Howard. *The Geography of Nowhere: The Rise and Decline of America's Man-Made Landscapes.* New York: Simon and Schuster, 1993.

Lamont, Michèle, and Virág Molnár. "The Study of Boundaries in the Social Sciences." *Annual Review of Sociology* 28 (2002): 167–95.

Lareau, Annette. *Unequal Childhoods: Class, Race and Family Life.* Berkley: University of California Press, 2003.

Larson, Reed. "Positive Development in a Disorderly World." *Journal of Research on Adolescence* 21, no. 2 (2011): 317–34.

———. "Toward a Psychology of Positive Youth Development." *American Psychologist* 55, no. 1 (2000): 170–83.

Larson, Reed, and Maryse Richards. "Daily Companionship in Late Childhood and Early Adolescence: Changing Developmental Contexts." *Child Development* 62, no. 2 (1991): 284–300.

Larson, Reed, Maryse Richards, Giovanni Moneta, Grayson Holmbeck, and Elena Duckett. "Changes in Adolescents' Daily Interactions with Their Families from Ages 10–18: Disengagement and Transformation." *Developmental Psychology* 32, no. 4 (1996): 744–54.

Lavenda, Robert H. *Corn Fests and Water Carnivals: Celebrating Community in Minnesota.* Washington, DC: Smithsonian Institution Press, 1997.

Lawson, Victoria, Lucy Jarosz, and Anne Bonds. "Articulations of Place, Poverty, and Race: Dumping Grounds and Unseen Grounds in the Rural Northwest." *Annals of the Association of American Geographers* 100, no. 3 (2010): 655–77.

Leland, John. "Trying to Stay Put in Florida Mobile Homes." *New York Times,* June 2, 2003.

Leopold, Josh, Liza Getsinger, Pamela Blumenthal, Katya Abazajian, and Reed Jordan. *The Housing Affordability Gap for Extremely Low-Income Renters in 2013.* Washington, DC: Urban Institute Research Report, 2015.

Leventhal, Tama, and Jeanne Brookes-Gunn. "The Neighborhoods They Live In: The Effects of Neighborhood Residence on Child and Adolescent Outcomes." *Psychological Bulletin* 126, no. 2 (2000): 309–37.

Leventhal, Tama, Veronique Dupere, and Jeanne Brooke-Gunn. "Neighborhood Influences on Adolescent Development." In *Handbook of Adolescent Development.* Vol. 2,

Contextual Influences on Adolescent Development. 3rd ed., edited by Richard M. Lerner and Laurence Steinberg, 411–43. Hoboken, NJ: Wiley, 2009.

Levere, Andrea. "Going Mobile" from *The Great Divide,* A Series on Inequality. *New York Times,* May 4, 2014. nytimes.com/opinionator.

Lewis, Oscar. *La Vida: A Puerto Rican Family in the Culture of Poverty: San Juan and New York.* New York: Random House, 1966.

Lichter, Daniel T., and Deborah Roempke Graefe. "Rural Economic Restructuring: Implications for Children, Youth, and Families." In *Economic Restructuring and Family Well-Being in Rural America,* edited by Kristin E. Smith and Ann R. Tickamyer, 25–39. University Park: Penn State University Press, 2011.

Lichter, Daniel T., Domenico Parisi, Steven Michael Grice, and Michael Taquino. "Municipal Underbounding: Annexation and Racial Exclusion in Small Southern Towns." *Rural Sociology* 72, no. 1 (2007): 47–68.

Lin, Nan. "Inequality in Social Capital." *Contemporary Sociology* 29, no. 6 (2000): 785–95.

Link, Bruce G., and Jo C. Phelan. "Conceptualizing Stigma." *Annual Review of Sociology* 27 (2001): 363–85.

Linthicum, Kate. "New Mexico Turns a Corner on Drunk Driving." *Los Angeles Times,* July 7, 2009. http://articles.latimes.com/2009/jul/07/nation/na-new-mexico-dwi7.

Lister, Ruth. *Poverty.* Cambridge: Polity Press, 2004.

Liu, Kai-Shen, Fan-Yen Huang, Steven B. Hayward, Jerome Wesolowski, and Ken Sexton. "Irritant Effects of Formaldehyde Exposure in Mobile Homes." *Health Perspectives* 94 (1991): 91–94.

Lobao, Linda. "Continuity and Change in Place Stratification: Spatial Inequality and Middle-Range Territorial Units." *Rural Sociology* 69, no.1 (2004): 1–30.

——. "A Sociology of the Periphery versus a Peripheral Sociology: Rural Sociology and the Dimension of Space." *Rural Sociology* 61, no. 1 (1996): 77–102.

Logan John R. "Growth, Politics, and the Stratification of Places." *American Journal of Sociology* 84, no. 2 (1978): 404–16.

Long, Thayer. "Manufacturing Affordability." *Rural Voices* 8, no. 2 (2003): 6–8.

Low, Setha M., and Irwin Altman. "Place Attachment: A Conceptual Inquiry." In *Place Attachment: Human Behavior and Environment, Advances in Theory and Research.* Vol. 12, edited by Irwin Altman and Setha M. Low, 1–12. New York: Springer, 1992.

Lowenfeld, Viktor, and W. Lambert Brittain. *Creative and Mental Growth.* 8th ed. New York: Macmillan, 1987.

Luthar, Suniya S., Dante Cicchetti, and Bronwyn Becker. "The Construct of Resilience: A Critical Evaluation and Guidelines for Future Work." *Child Development* 71, no. 3 (2000): 543–62.

Mack-Jackson, Fleda. "Black Children and Their Churches." PhD diss., University of Illinois at Urbana-Champaign, 1991.

MacLeod, Jay. *Ain't No Makin' It.* 3rd ed. Boulder, CO: Westview Press, 2008.

MacTavish, Katherine A. "Creating Inclusive Classrooms and Communities for Rural Poor." In *Classroom Diversity and Academic Success,* an online special edition of Education.com, edited by Adrianna Umana-Taylor. 2009. http://www.education.com/reference/article/creating-class-inclusive-classrooms.

——. "Going Mobile in Rural America: The Community Effect of Rural Trailer Parks on Child and Youth Development." PhD diss., University of Illinois at Urbana-Champaign, 2001.

——. "The Wrong Side of the Tracks: Social Inequality and Mobile Home Park Residence." *Community Development* 38 (2007): 74–91.

MacTavish, Katherine A., Michelle L. Eley, and Sonya Salamon. "Housing Vulnerability among Rural Trailer Park Households." *Georgetown Journal of Poverty Law & Policy* 13, no. 1 (2006): 95–117.

MacTavish, Katherine A., and Sonya Salamon. "Mobile Home Park on the Prairie: A New Rural Community Form." *Rural Sociology* 66, no. 4 (2001): 487–506.

——. "Pathways of Youth Development in a Rural Trailer Park." *Family Relations* 55 (2006): 163–74.

MacTavish, Katherine A., Ann Ziebarth, and Lance George. "Housing in Rural America." In *Rural America in a Globalizing World: Problems and Perspectives for the 2010s,* edited by Conner Bailey, Leif, Jensen, and Elizabeth Ransom, 677–692. Morgantown: West Virginia University Press, 2014.

Malchiodi, Cathy. *Understanding Children's Art.* New York: Guilford Press, 1998.

Manufactured Housing Institute. "MHI Action Alert: Dodd-Frank Wall Street Reform and Consumer Protection Act." 2011. http://www.manufacturedhousing.org/webdocs/NCC%20Alert%20032511.pdf.

Manufactured Housing/Oregon State Tenants Association. http://www.mh-osta.org.

Mariscal, Jorge. "The Poverty Draft: Do Military Recruiters Disproportionately Target Communities of Color and the Poor?" *Sojourners Magazine* 36, no. 6 (2007): 32–35.

Marre, Alexander. "Rural Areas Lag Urban Areas in College Completion." Amber Waves, December 1, 2014. USDA Economic Research Service. http://www.ers.usda.gov/amber-waves/2014-december/rural-areas-lag-urban-areas-in-college-completion.aspx#.V88cCzuc9YM.

Massey, Douglas S., Len Albright, Rebecca Casciano, Elizabeth Derickson, and David N. Kinsey. *Climbing Mount Laurel: The Struggle for Affordable Housing and Social Mobility in an American Suburb.* Princeton, NJ: Princeton University Press, 2013.

Masten, Ann S. "Ordinary Magic: Resilience Processes in Development." *American Psychology* 56 (2001): 227–38.

——. "Resilience in Individual Development: Successful Adaptation despite Risk and Adversity." In *Risk and Resilience in Inner City America: Challenges and Prospects,* edited by Margaret C. Wang and Edmund W. Gordon, 3–25. Hillsdale, NJ: Lawrence Erlbaum, 1994.

Masten, Ann S., J. Douglas Coatsworth, Jennifer Neemann, Scott D. Gest, Auke Tellegen, and Norman Garmezy. "The Structure and Coherence of Competence from Childhood through Adolescence." *Child Development* 66, no. 6 (1995): 1635–59.

Masten, Ann S., J. J. Hubbard, Scott D. Gest, Auke Tellegen, Norman Garmezy, and M. Ramirez. "Adaptation in the Context of Adversity: Pathways to Resilience and Maladaption from Childhood to Late Adolescence." *Development and Psychopathology* 11, no. 1 (1999): 143–69.

Mathews, T. J., and Brady E. Hamilton. "Delayed Childbearing: More Women Are Having Their First Child Later in Life." U.S. Department of Health and Human Services, Centers for Disease Control and Prevention-National Center for Health Statistics. 2009. http://www.cdc.gov/nchs/data/databriefs/db21.pdf.

McAdoo, Harriette Pipes, ed., *Black Families.* 4th ed. Thousand Oaks, CA: Sage, 2007.

McKenzie, Evan. *Privatopia: Homeowners Associations and the Rise of Residential Private Government.* New Haven: Yale University Press, 1994.

McMillan, David. "Sense of Community." *Journal of Community Psychology* 24, no. 4 (1996): 315–25.

Meeks, Carol B. *Manufactured Home Life: Existing Housing Stock through 1997.* Arlington, VA: Manufactured Housing Institute, 1998.

——. "Mobile Homes as a Viable Alternative in Rural America." *Rural Development Perspectives*, February 1988, 29–32.

Miller, Steven I., and Beverly Evko. "An Ethnographic Study of the Influence of a Mobile Home Community on Suburban High School Students." *Human Relations* 38 (1985): 683–705.

Minard, Richard, and Nick Normandin. *Home Loans Matter: Buyers and Sellers of Manufactured Homes Benefit from Access to Financing—A Case Study.* Concord, NH: New Hampshire Community Loan Fund, 2012.

Mitchell, Kathy. "In over Our Heads: Predatory Lending and Fraud in Manufactured Housing." Consumers Union Southwest Regional Office Public Policy Series 5. 2002. http://consumersunion.org/pdf/mh/over/report.pdf.

Mobley, Cynthia, Jonathan R. Sugarman, Charles Deam, and Lisa Giles. "Prevalence of Risk Factors for Residential Fire and Burn Injuries in an American Indian Community." *Public Health Reports* 109, no. 5 (1994): 702–5.

Moffitt, Terrie. "Adolescent-Limited and Life-Course-Persistent Anti-Social Behavior: A Developmental Taxonomy." *Psychological Review* 100, no. 4 (1993): 674–701.

Morgenson, Gretchen. "Inside the Countrywide Spree." *New York Times*, August 26, 2007. http://www.nytimes.com/2007/08/26/business/yourmoney/26country. html?_r=0&hp=&adxnnl=1&pagewanted=all&adxnnlx=1415816778-ZO2Wl881x0tEHYNXumUcuA.

Morton, Lois Wright, Ella Annette Bitto, Mary Jane Oakland, and Mary Sand. "Solving the Problems of Iowa Food Deserts: Food Insecurity and Perceptions of Civic Structure." *Rural Sociology* 70 (2005): 94–112.

Myslajek, Crystal. "Risks and Realities of the Contract for Deed." *Community Dividend,* January 1, 2009. Federal Reserve Bank of Minneapolis. http://www. minneapolisfed.org/publications_papers/pub_display.cfm?id=4098.

National Consumer Law Center. "Manufactured Housing Resource Guide: Titling Homes as Real Property." 2009. http://www.nclc.org/images/pdf/manufactured_ housing/titling-homes2.pdf.

Nelson, Margaret K. "Job Characteristics and Economic Survival Strategies: The Effect of Economic Restructuring and Marital Status in a Rural County." In *Economic Restructuring and Family Well-Being in Rural America,* edited by Kristin E. Smith and Ann R. Tickamyer, 136–57. University Park: Penn State University Press, 2011.

Nelson, Margaret K., and Joan Smith. *Working Hard and Making Do: Surviving in Small Town America.* Berkeley: University of California Press, 1999.

Nesbitt, Jim. "American Sprawl Makes an Endangered Species of the Rural Trailer Park." Newhouse News Service. 2001. http://www.newhouse.com/archive/ story1a022001.html.

Newby, Howard. "The Rural Sociology of Advanced Capitalist Societies." In *The Rural Sociology of Advanced Societies,* edited by Frederick H. Buttel and Howard Newby, 1–30. Montclair, NJ: Allanheld, Osmun, 1980.

New York Times. Class Matters. New York: Times Books, 2005.

Next Steps. "About Next Steps." http://nextstepus.org/aboutusoverview.htm.

Notter, Megan, Katherine MacTavish, and Devora Shamah. "Pathways toward Resilience in a Rural Trailer Park." *Family Relations* 57 (2008): 613–24.

O'Hare, William, and Barbara Clark O'Hare. "Upward Mobility." *American Demographics* 15 (1993): 26–34.

Oldenburg, Ray. *The Great Good Place: Cafes, Coffee Shops, Bookstores, Bars, Hair Salons, and Other Hangouts at the Heart of a Community.* New York: Marlowe, 1989.

Oregon Housing and Communities Services. http://www.oregon.gov/OHCS/pages/index.aspx.

OregonLaws.org. "Landlord Duty to Maintain Rented Spaces, Vacant Spaces, and Common Areas in Habitable Condition." http://www.oregonlaws.org/ors/90.730.

Palen, J. John. *The Suburbs*. New York: McGraw-Hill, 1995.

Parker, D. J., D. P. Sklar, D. Tandberg, M. Hauswald, and R. E. Zumwalt. "Fire Fatalities among New Mexico Children." *Annals of Emergency Medicine* 22 (1993): 517.

Patton, Michael Quinn. *Qualitative Evaluation and Research Methods*. 2nd ed. Newbury Park, CA: Sage, 2001.

Perin, Constance. *Everything in Its Place: Social Order and Land Use in America*. Princeton, NJ: Princeton University Press, 1977.

Perry-Jenkins, Maureen, and Sonya Salamon. "Blue-Collar Kin and Community in Small-Town America." *Journal of Family Issues* 23, no. 8 (2002): 927–49.

Peters, Marie Ferguson. "Racial Socialization of Young Black Children." In *Black Children: Social, Educational and Parental Environments*, edited by Harriet Pipes McAdoo and John L. McAdoo, 159–73. Beverly Hills, CA: Sage, 1985.

Pew Charitable Trusts. *Pursuing the American Dream: Economic Mobility across Generations*. Washington, DC: Pew Charitable Trusts, 2012.

Pew Hispanic Center. "Facts Sheet: Hispanics in the Military." 2003. http://pewhispanic.org/files/reports/17.pdf.

Pogash, Carol. "Poor Students in High School Suffer Stigma from Lunch Aid." *New York Times*, March 1, 2008, A1 and A14.

Polito, Rick. "Upwardly Mobile Homes." *Dwell*, October 2008, 178–80.

Prevost, Lisa. "Affordable Housing via Mobile Homes." *New York Times*, June 25, 2006.

PR Newswire. "Countrywide Expands Commitment to $1 Trillion in Home Loans to Minority and Lower-Income Borrowers." Press release from Countrywide Financial Corporation, January 14, 2005. http://www.prnewswire.com/news-releases/countrywide-expands-commitment-to-1-trillion-in-home-loans-to-minority-and-lower-income-borrowers-54027497.html.

Public Policy Institute of the American Associate of Retired Persons (AARP) and National Consumer Law Center. "Manufactured Housing Community Tenants: Shifting the Balance of Power." 2004. http://assets.aarp.org/rgcenter/consume/d18138_housing.pdf.

Putnam, Robert D. *Bowling Alone: The Collapse and Revival of American Community*. New York: Simon & Schuster, 2000.

——. *Making Democracy Work*. Princeton, NJ: Princeton University Press, 1993.

——. *Our Kids: The American Dream in Crisis*. New York: Simon & Schuster, 2015.

Rampell, Catherine. "Americans Think Owning a Home Is Better for Them Than It Is." *Washington Post*, April 21, 2014. https://www.washingtonpost.com/opinions/catherine-rampell-americans-think-owning-a-home-is-better-for-them-than-it-is /2014/04/21/5e9f4dd2-c979-11e3-93eb-6c0037dde2ad_story.html?utm_term=.47ac7611969c.

Ravitz, Mel. "Talking Houses: 'Dunromin' in the Mobile Home: The Role of the Mobile Home in the Housing System." *Town and Country Planning* 63, no. 9 (1994): 232.

Reed, Thelma V. *Black Girl from Tannery Flats*. Berkeley, CA: Ishmael Reed, 2003.

Reich, Robert B. *Saving Capitalism: For the Many, Not the Few*. New York: Knopf, 2015.

Reingold, Jennifer. "The Ballad of Clayton Homes." *Fast Company* 78 (2004): 76.

Rivlin, Gary. . *Broke, USA from Pawnshop to Poverty, Inc.: How the Poor Became Big Business*. New York: Harper Collins, 2010.

———. "The Cold, Hard Lessons of Mobile Home U." *New York Times Sunday Magazine*, March 16, 2014, MM34 et seq. http://www.nytimes.com/2014/03/16/magazine/the-cold-hard-lessons-of-mobile-home-u.html?_r=0.

———. "How Wall Street Defanged Dodd-Frank." *The Nation*, April 30, 2013. https://www.thenation.com/article/how-wall-street-defanged-dodd-frank.

Ritzer, George. *Explorations in the Sociology of Consumption*. London: Sage, 2001.

Roberts, Brandon, Deborah Povich, and Mark Mather. "Low-Income Working Families: The Growing Economic Gap. The Working Poor Families Project." A policy brief published by the Working Poor Families Project. Winter, 2012–13. http://www.workingpoorfamilies.org/wp-content/uploads/2013/01/Winter-2012_2013-WPFP-Data-Brief.pdf.

Robillard, Kevin. "Poll: '47 Percent' Hurt Mitt Romney." *Politico*, October 2, 2012. http://www.politico.com/news/stories/1012/81899.html.

Rogers, Carolyn C. "Changes in the Older Population and Implications for Rural Areas." 2000. USDA Economic Research Service. https://www.ers.usda.gov/webdocs/publications/rdrr90/54012_rdrr90a.pdf.

Rohe, William M., and Harry L. Watson, eds. *Chasing the American Dream: New Perspectives on Affordable Homeownership*. Ithaca, NY: Cornell University Press, 2007.

Rosenbaum, James, Lisa Reynolds, and Stefanie Deluca. "How Do Places Matter? The Geography of Opportunity, Self-Efficacy and a Look inside the Black Box of Residential Mobility." *Housing Studies* 17, no. 1 (2002): 71–82.

Rubin, Kenneth, William M. Bukowski, and Julie Parker. "Peer Interactions, Relationships, and Groups." In *Handbook of Child Psychology*. Vol. 3, *Social, Emotional and Personality Development* . 6th ed., edited by William Damon and Richard M. Lerner, 571–645. Hoboken, NJ: John Wiley, 2006).

Ruditsky, Howard. "New Life for Old Mobile Home Parks: Investing in Parks through Real Estate Investment Trusts." *Forbes*, November 7, 1994, 44–45.

Runyan, C. W., S. I. Bangdiwala, M. A. Linzer, J. J. Sacks, and J. Butts. "Risk Factors for Fatal Residential Fires." *New England Journal of Medicine* 327, no. 12 (1992): 859–88.

Rural Sociological Society Task Force on Persistent Rural Poverty. *Persistent Poverty in Rural America*. Boulder, CO: Westview Press, 1993.

Sahlins, Marshall D. "On the Sociology of Primitive Exchange." In *The Relevance of Models for Social Anthropology*, edited by Michael Banton. A.S.A Monographs, 139–237. New York: Praeger, 1965.

Said, Edward. *Orientalism*. 25th anniversary ed. New York: Pantheon Books, 1978.

Salamon, Sonya. "Cultural Dimensions of Land Tenure in the United States." In *Who Owns America? Social Conflict over Property Rights*, edited by Harvey M. Jacobs, 159–81. Madison: University of Wisconsin Press, 1998.

———. "Culture and Agricultural Land Tenure." *Rural Sociology*, 58, no. 4 (1993): 580–98.

———. "Describing the Community in Thorough Detail." In *Handbook of Community Movements and Local Organizations*, edited by Carl Milofsky and Ram A. Cnaan, 146–62. New York: Springer, 2007.

———. "Farming and Community from the Everyday Life of Farm Families." *Rural Sociologist* 10, no. 2 (1990): 23–30.

———. "From Hometown to NonTown: Rural Community Effects of Suburbanization." *Rural Sociology* 68, no. 1 (2003): 1–24.

———. "Mobile Home Communities." *Encyclopedia of Community: From the Village to the Virtual World*, edited by Karen Christensen and David Levinson, 925–29. Thousand Oaks, CA: Sage Reference, 2003.

——. *Newcomers to Old Towns: Suburbanization of the Heartland.* Chicago: University of Chicago Press, 2003.

——. *Prairie Patrimony: Family, Farming, and Community in the Midwest.* Chapel Hill: University of North Carolina Press, 1992.

——. "The Rural Household as a Consumption Site" In *Handbook of Rural Studies,* edited by Paul Cloke, Terry Marsden, and Patrick Mooney, 330–43. London: Sage, 2006.

Salamon, Sonya, and Katherine MacTavish. "Quasi-Homelessness among Rural Trailer-Park Households in the United States." In *International Perspectives on Rural Homelessness,* edited by Paul Cloke and Paul Milbourne, 45–62. London: Routledge, 2006.

——. "Rural Communities." In *International Encyclopedia of Human Geography.* Vol. 9, edited by Rob Kitchin and Nigel Thrift, 423–28. Oxford: Elsevier, 2009.

Sonya, Salamon, and Jane B. Tornatore. "Territory Contested through Property in a Midwestern Post-Agricultural Community." *Rural Sociology* 59, no. 4 (1994): 636–54.

Sampson, Robert J. *Great American City: Chicago and the Enduring Neighborhood Effect.* Chicago: University of Chicago Press, 2012.

Sampson, Robert J., and John Laub. "Urban Poverty and the Family Context of Significance." *Child Development,* 67 (1994): 1–13.

Sampson, Robert J., Jeffrey D. Morenoff, and Thomas Gannon-Rowley. "Assessing Neighborhood Effect: Social Processes and New Directions in Research." *Annual Review of Sociology* 28 (2002): 443–78.

Save the Children. "America's Forgotten Children: Child Poverty in Rural America." 2002. http://www.savethechildren.org/afc/afc_pdf_02.shtml.

Schafft, Kai A. "Poverty, Residential Mobility and Student Transiency within a Rural New York School District." *Rural Sociology* 71 (2006): 212–31.

Schwalbe, Michael, Sandra Godwin, Daphne Holden, Douglas Schrock, Shealy Thompson, and Michele Wolkomir. "Generic Processes in the Reproduction of Inequality: An Interactionist Analysis." *Social Forces* 79, no. 2 (2000): 419–52.

Schwartz, Gary. *Beyond Conformity or Rebellion.* Chicago: University of Chicago Press, 1987.

Sessions, Cheryl. "Manufactured Housing Comes of Age: A Support Network for Resident-Owned Communities." *Communities and Banking* (Summer 2007): 21–23.

Settersten, Richard. "Becoming an Adult: Meanings and Markers for Young Americans." In *Coming of Age in America,* edited by Mary Waters, Maria Kefalas, and Patrick Carr, 169–90. Berkeley: University of California Press, 2011.

Settersten, Richard, and Barbara E. Ray. *Not Quite Adults: Why 20-Somethings Are Choosing a Slower Path to Adulthood, and Why It's Good for Everyone.* New York: Bantam, 2010.

Shanklin, Mary. "Old Mobile Homes Have Gained Reputation as 'Firetraps.'" *Orlando Sentinel,* June 10, 2003, A7.

Shapiro, Thomas M. *The Hidden Costs of Being African American: How Wealth Perpetuates Inequality.* New York: Oxford University Press, 2004.

Sheehan, Michael F., and Roger Colton. "The Problem of Mass Eviction in Mobile Home Parks Subject to Conversion." 1994. http://www.fsconline.com/downloads/Papers/1994%2012%20massEVIC.pdf.

Sheehy, Colleen J. *The Flamingo in the Garden: American Yard Art and the Vernacular Landscape.* New York: Garland, 1998.

Sherman, Jennifer. *Those Who Work and Those Who Don't: Poverty, Morality and Family in Rural America.* Minneapolis: University of Minnesota Press, 2009.

Shiner, R., and Ann Masten. "Childhood Personality as a Harbinger of Competence and Resilience in Adulthood." *Developmental Psychopathology* 24, no. 2 (2012): 507–28.

Shipler, David K. *The Working Poor: Invisible in America.* New York: Knopf, 2004.

Shlay, Anne B. "Low-Income Homeownership: American Dream or Delusion?" *Urban Studies,* 43, no. 3 (2006): 511–31.

Slack, Tim. "The Contours and Correlates of Informal Work in Rural Pennsylvania." *Rural Sociology* 72, no. 1 (2007): 69–89.

Smith, Kristin E., and Kristi Gozjolko. "Low Income and Impoverished Families Pay More Disproportionately for Child Care." Carsey Institute Policy Brief No. 16, Carsey Institute, Durham, NH, 2010.

Smith, Kristin E., and Ann R. Tickamyer. Introduction to *Economic Restructuring and Family Well-Being in Rural America,* edited by Kristin E. Smith and Ann R. Tickamyer, 1–21. University Park: Penn State University Press, 2011.

Spillman, William J. "The Agricultural Ladder." Supplement, *American Economic Review* 9, no. 1 (1919): 170–79.

Stack, Carol. *All Our Kin: Strategies for Survival in a Black Community.* New York: Harper and Row, 1974.

——. *Call to Home: African Americans Reclaim the Rural South.* New York: Basic Books, 1996.

Stack, Carol, and Linda Burton. "Kinscripts." *Journal of Comparative Family Studies* 24, no. 2 (1993): 157–70.

Stevenson, Alexandra, and Matthew Goldstein. "Wall St. Veterans Are Betting on Low-Income Homebuyers." *New York Times,* April 18, 2015.

Stone, Michael E. *Shelter Poverty: New Ideas on Housing Affordability.* Philadelphia: Temple University Press, 1993.

Strauss, Leslie R. "Credit and Capital Needs for Affordable Rural Housing." In *Housing in Rural America: Building Affordable and Inclusive Communities,* edited by Joseph N. Belden and Robert J. Wiener, 125–36. Thousand Oaks, CA: Sage, 1999.

Streitfeld, David, and Megan Thee-Brenan. "Despite Fears, Owning a Home Retains Its Allure, Poll Shows." *New York Times,* June 30, 2011. http://www.nytimes.com/2011/06/30/business/30poll.html.

Sullivan Teresa A., Elizabeth Warren, and Jay Lawrence Westbrook. *The Fragile Middle Class: Americans in Debt.* New Haven, CT: Yale University Press, 2000.

Surowiecki, James. "Home Economics." *New Yorker,* March 10, 2008, 62.

Taylor, Robert Joseph, and Linda Chatters. "Church Members as a Source of Informal Social Support." *Review of Religious Research* 30 (1988): 193–203.

Taylor, Robert Joseph, Linda Chatters, and Jeff Levin. *Religion in the Lives of African-Americans: Social, Psychological, and Health Perspectives.* Thousand Oaks, CA: Sage, 2004.

Thornburg, David A. *Galloping Bungalows: The Rise and Demise of the American House Trailer.* Hamden, CT: Archon Books, 1991.

Tickamyer, Ann R. "Space Matters! Spatial Inequality in Future Sociology." *Contemporary Sociology* 29, no. 6 (2000): 805–13.

Tickamyer, Ann R., and Janet Bokemeier. "Alternative Strategies for Labor Market Analyses: Multi-Level Models of Labor Market Inequality." In *Inequalities in Labor Market Areas,* edited by Joachim Singelmann and Forrest A. Deseran, 49–68. Boulder, CO: Westview Press, 1993.

Tickamyer, Ann R., and Cynthia M. Duncan. "Poverty and Opportunity Structure in Rural America." *Annual Review of Sociology* 16 (1990): 67–86.

Tickamyer, Ann R., and Teresa A. Wood. "The Social and Economic Context of Informal Work." In *Communities of Work: Rural Restructuring in Local and Global Contexts,* edited by William W. Falk, Michael D. Schulman, and Ann R. Tickamyer, 394–418. Athens: Ohio University Press, 2003.

Tilly, Charles. "Do Communities Act?" *Sociological Inquiry* 43, nos. 3–4 (1973): 209–40.

———. *Durable Inequality*. Berkeley: University of California Press, 1998.

———. "Durable Inequality." In *A Nation Divided: Diversity, Inequality and Community in American Society,* edited by Phyllis Moen, Donna Dempster-McClain, and Henra Walker, 15–33. Ithaca, NY: Cornell University Press, 1999.

Tremblay, Kenneth R. Jr., and R. C. Collins. *Buying Your First Home*. Fort Collins, CO: Colorado State University Extension, 2005.

Tully, Shawn. "Meet the 23,000% Stock. For 20 Years, Countrywide Financial Has Been on a Tear. With the Housing Boom Winding Down, Can This Mortgage Star Keep from Falling?" *Fortune*, September 15, 2003. http://archive. fortune.com/magazines/fortune/fortune_archive/2003/09/15/349151/index. htm.

U.S. Census Bureau. "American Housing Survey for the United States: 1999." Current Housing Reports, Series H150/01. Washington, DC: U.S. Government Printing Office, 2000.

———. "American Housing Survey for the United States: 2001." Current Housing Reports, Series H150/01. Washington, DC: U.S. Government Printing Office, 2002. http://www.census.gov/prod/2002pubs/h150-01.pdf.

———. "American Housing Survey for the United States: 2009." Current Housing Reports, Series H150/09. Washington, DC: U.S. Government Printing Office, 2011. https://www.census.gov/prod/2011pubs/h150-09.pdf.

———. "American Housing Survey for the United States: 2011." Current Housing Reports, Series H150/11. Washington, D.C.: U.S. Government Printing Office, 2013.

———. "DP-1 Profile of General Demographic Characteristics: 2000." Census 2000 Summary File 1 (SF1) 100 Percent Data.

———. "DP-2 Profile of Selected Social Characteristics: 2000." Census 2000 Summary File 3 (SF3) Sample Data.

———. "DP-3 Profile of Selected Economic Characteristics: 2000." Census 2000 Summary File 3 (SF3) Sample Data.

———. "DP-4 Profile of Selected Housing Characteristics." Census 2000 Summary File 3 (SF3) Sample Data.

———. "QT-P20 Educational Attainment by Sex: 2000." Census 2000 Summary File 3 (SF3) Sample Data.

———. "Structural and Occupancy Characteristics of Housing: 2000." Census Brief by Robert Bennefield, and Robert Bonnette. 2003. https://www.census.gov/ prod/2003pubs/c2kbr-32.pdf.

U.S. Department of Agriculture, Economic Research Service. "Description and Maps: County Policy Types." 2015. https://www.ers.usda.gov/data-products/county-typology-codes/descriptions-and-maps.aspx.

———. "Report on Rural Poverty and Well Being." 2015. http://www.ers.usda.gov/topics/ rural-economy-population/rural-poverty-well-being/geography-of-poverty. aspx.

———. "Rural Education at a Glance." 2003. https://www.ers.usda.gov/webdocs/ publications/rdrr98/30685_rdrr98full_002.pdf

U.S. Department of Housing and Urban Development (HUD). Standardized Mobile Home Tie Down Statutes. 2008. http://portal.hud.gov/hudportal/HUD?src=/program_offices/housing/rmra/mhs/ipfaqs.

U.S. Equal Opportunity Commission. EEO-1 Job Classification Guide. http://www.eeoc.gov/employers/eeo1survey/jobclassguide.cfm.

Vermont Law Help. "Mobile Home Lot Rent Increases." http://www.vtlawhelp.org/lot-rent-increases.

Wagner, Daniel, and Mike Baker. "Minorities Exploited by Warren Buffett's Mobile Home Empire." Center for Public Integrity. December 26, 2015. http://www.seattletimes.com/seattle-news/times-watchdog/minorities-exploited-by-warren-buffetts-mobile-home-empire-clayton-homes.

———. "Warren Buffett's Mobile Home Empire Preys on the Poor: Billionaire Profits at Every Step, from Building to Selling to High Cost Lending." Center for Public Integrity. April 3, 2015. https://www.publicintegrity.org/2015/04/03/17024/warren-buffetts-mobile-home-empire-preys-poor.

Wallace, Janet L., and Lisa R. Pruitt. "Judging Parents, Judging Place: Poverty, Rurality, and Termination of Parental Rights." Missouri Law Review 77, no. 1 (2012): 95–147.

Wallis, Allan D. Wheel Estate: The Rise and Decline of Mobile Homes. New York: Oxford University Press, 1991.

Wapner, Milt. "Double Wide Mobile Homes vs Single Wide Mobile Homes." 2016. Ask-What.com. http://www.ask-what.com/double-wide-mobile-homes-vs-single-wide-mobile-homes.

Ward, Sally, Charlie French, and Kelly Giraud. Resident Ownership in New Hampshire's "Mobile Home Parks": A Report on Economic Outcomes. Carsey Institute, September, 2006 (updated March 2010). https://carsey.unh.edu; http://www.rocusa.org/uploads/Carsey%20Institute%20Reprint%202010.pdf.

Waters, Mary C. Ethnic Options: Choosing Identities in America. Berkeley: University of California Press, 1990.

Werner, Emmy E., and Ruth S. Smith. Overcoming the Odds: High Risk Children: From Birth to Adulthood. Ithaca, NY: Cornell University Press, 1992.

Whitener, Leslie. "Housing Poverty in Rural Areas Greater for Racial and Ethnic Minorities." Rural America 15, no. 2 (2000): 2–8.

Wiener, Robert, and Char Thompson. "The Role of Nonprofit Organizations in Affecting Rural Housing Change." In Rural Housing, Exurbanization and Amenity Development, edited by David Marcuolier, Mark Lapping, and Owen Furuseth. Farnham, UK: Ashgate, 2011.

Wiley, Angela L., Henriette Burr Warren, and Dale S. Montanelli. "Shelter in a Time of Storm: Parenting in Poor Rural African American Communities." Family Relations 51, no. 3 (2002): 265–73.

Williams, Brett. Debt for Sale: A Social History of the Credit Trap. Philadelphia: University of Pennsylvania Press, 2004.

———. "The Precipice of Debt." In New Landscapes of Inequality: Neoliberalism and the Erosion of Democracy in America, edited by Jane L. Collins, Micaela di Leonardo, and Brett Willams, 65–90. Santa Fe, NM: School for Advanced Research Press, 2008.

———. Upscaling Downtown: Stalled Gentrification in Washington, DC. Ithaca, NY: Cornell University Press, 1988.

Williams, Bruce B., and Bonnie Thornton Dill. "African-Americans in the Rural South: The Persistence of Racism and Poverty." In The Changing American Countryside: Rural People and Places, edited by Emery Castle, 339–51. Lawrence: University Press of Kansas, 1995.

Williams, Florence. "Living Out the Trailer Dream." *High Country News* 30 (1998): 15. http://www.hcn.org/article_id=4363.

Williams, Terry M., and William Kornblum. *Growing Up Poor*. Lexington, KY: Lexington Books, 1985.

———. *The Uptown Kids: Struggle and Hope in the Projects*. New York: Putnam, 1994.

Wilson, William Julius. *The Declining Significance of Race*. Chicago: University of Chicago Press, 1978.

———. *The Truly Disadvantaged: The Inner City, the Underclass and Public Policy*. Chicago: University of Chicago Press, 1987.

———. *When Work Disappears: The World of the New Urban Poor*. New York: Knopf, 1996.

Wray, Matt. *Not Quite White: White Trash and the Boundaries of Whiteness*. Durham, NC: Duke University Press, 2006.

Wray, Matt, and Annalee Newitz, eds. *White Trash: Race and Class in America*. New York: Routledge, 1997.

Wrobel, Paul. *Our Way: Family, Parish, and Neighborhood in a Polish American Community*. Notre Dame, IN: University of Notre Dame Press, 1979.

Wu, Frank. "Tornadoes and Trailer Parks: A Statistical Correlation." *Annals of Improbable Research* 1, no. 4 (1995): 26–27. http://www.frankwu.com/tornado.html.

Zimmerman, Julie N., Sunny (Seonok) Ham, and Sarah Michelle Frank. "Does It or Doesn't It? Geographic Differences and the Costs of Living." *Rural Sociology* 73, no. 3 (2008): 463–86.

Zuberi, Dan. *Differences That Matter: Social Policy and the Working Poor in the United States and Canada*. Ithaca, NY: ILR Press, 2006.

Zuckman, Jill. "New Fight Likely over Change in Mobile Home Standards." *Congressional Quarterly* 1732, June 2, 1990.

Index